Consumerism an

Consumerism and Prestige

The Materiality of Literature in the Modern Age

Edited by Anthony Enns and
Bernhard Metz

ANTHEM PRESS

Anthem Press
An imprint of Wimbledon Publishing Company
www.anthempress.com

This edition first published in UK and USA 2024
by ANTHEM PRESS
75–76 Blackfriars Road, London SE1 8HA, UK
or PO Box 9779, London SW19 7ZG, UK
and
244 Madison Ave #116, New York, NY 10016, USA

First published in the UK and USA by Anthem Press in 2022

British Library Cataloguing-in-Publication Data
A catalogue record for this book is available from the British Library.

Library of Congress Control Number: 2024935139

ISBN-13: 978-1-83999-254-4 (Pbk)
ISBN-10: 1-83999-254-9 (Pbk)

Cover credit: kerttu / pixabay.com

This title is also available as an e-book.

CONTENTS

ACKNOWLEDGMENTS

The following chapters originally appeared in a special issue of *Belphégor: Littérature populaire et culture médiatique* (journals.openedition.org/belphegor /533), and they have been included here with permission:

Chapter 4.   Only the "Outward Appearance" of a Harem? Reading *Memoirs of an Arabian Princess* as a Material Text
Kate Roy

Chapter 5.   Hidden Codes of Love: The Materiality of the Category Romance Novel
An Goris

Chapter 6.   Stephen King's *The Girl Who Loved Tom Gordon:* A Rhetorical Reading of the Schneekluth Edition Dust Jackets
Thorsten Bothe

Chapter 7.   The Printing of Phantasms: The Illustrations of Nineteenth-Century Serialized Novels and their Appropriation in Max Ernst's Collage Novel *Une semaine de bonté*
Philipp Venghaus

Chapter 8.   From Penny Dreadful to Graphic Novel: Alan Moore and Kevin O'Neill's Genealogy of Comics in *The League of Extraordinary Gentlemen*
Jeff Thoss

CONTRIBUTORS

Thorsten Bothe teaches comparative literature at Chemnitz University in Germany. He is the author of *MemoryEx: Gedächtnis und Beispiel in der Rhetorik* (2017) and coeditor of anthologies such as *Stehende Gewässer: Medien der Stagnation* (2007), *Prekäre Bilder* (2010), and *Bildung und Hochschule: Impulse für Studium und Lehre am Beispiel des Leuphana College* (2016). His work has also appeared in anthologies such as *Am Rande bemerkt: Anmerkungspraktiken in literarischen Texten* (2008), *Satzzeichen: Szenen der Schrift* (2017), and *Der Liebesroman im 21. Jahrhundert* (2017).

Anthony Enns is Associate Professor of Contemporary Culture at Dalhousie University in Halifax, Canada. His work on popular culture has appeared in anthologies such as *Comics and the City* (2010) and *The Oxford Handbook of Science Fiction* (2014) as well as in journals such as *Culture, Theory and Critique*, *Journal of Popular Film and Television*, *Quarterly Review of Film and Video*, *Popular Culture Review*, *Science Fiction Studies*, *Screen*, and *Studies in Popular Culture*.

Laura Rivas Gagliardi holds a PhD in Romance Philology from the Free University of Berlin and is the author of *Literaturgeschichte und Ideologie: Ferdinand Wolfs literaturpolitisches Projekt «Le Brésil littéraire»* (2020). She is currently a research associate at the Portuguese-Brazilian Institute at the University of Cologne, where she is developing the project "New Perspectives on Postcolonial Theory: On History and Knowledge in Brazilian Literary Studies," which is funded by the German Research Foundation.

An Goris completed her dissertation on modern romance fiction at the Catholic University of Leuven, and she also served as managing editor of the *Journal of Popular Romance Studies*. Her work has appeared in journals such as *Poetics Today*, *Journal of Popular Romance Studies*, and *Americana: The Journal of American Popular Culture* as well as anthologies such as *Global Cultures* (2009) and *New Approaches to Popular Romance Fiction* (2012).

Laura Hatry received her PhD in Hispanic Studies from the Autonomous University in Madrid, Spain. Her research focuses on cinematographic adaptations of Latin American literature, and her work has been published in specialized journals as well as academic research monographs. She has also translated books and essays from and to Spanish, English, and German. Her work as a visual artist has also been shown in exhibitions in the United States, Spain, France, Germany, Canada, Austria, and the United Arab Emirates.

Jacob Haubenreich is Assistant Professor of German at Johns Hopkins University. His scholarship focuses on the materiality and visuality of literary texts, particularly in the works of Rainer Maria Rilke, Peter Handke, and Thomas Bernhard, and it has been funded by the Fulbright Program, the German Literature Archive (Marbach), and the Austrian Academy of Sciences. His work has also appeared in journals such as *Word & Image*, *Seminar*, *Monatshefte*, *The German Quarterly*, and *German Studies Review*.

Bernhard Metz is an associate director of the SNF-funded project "Online-Edition der Rezensionen und Briefe Albrecht von Hallers" at the University of Bern. His co-editions include *Literature to Go* (2008), *Am Rande bemerkt* (2008), *Den Rahmen sprengen* (2012), a special issue of *Belphegor: Popular Literature and Media Culture* (2015), and one volume of Alexander von Humboldt's *Sämtliche Schriften: Berner Ausgabe* (2019). His work in book studies, textual criticism, and typography has also appeared in the journals *Zeitschrift für Germanistik*, *Musil-Forum*, *Variations*, *Arcadia*, and *Comparative Critical Studies* as well as the collections *Book Practices and Textual Itineraries* (2014), *Literatur und Typographie* (2016), *Literary Visualities* (2017), *Christian Kracht revisited* (2018), *Literatur JETZT* (2020), *Ambulante Poesie* (2020), and *Refresh the Book* (2021).

Christoph Rauen completed his dissertation on modern German literature at Ludwig Maximilian University in Munich and currently teaches at the University of Kiel in Germany. He is the author of *Pop und Ironie: Popdiskurs und Popliteratur um 1980 und 2000* (2010) and coeditor of *Empirie in der Literaturwissenschaft* (2013) and *Pornographie in der deutschen Literatur: Texte, Themen, Institutionen* (2016). His latest project focuses on the interconnections between fiction and religious faith in the works of Ludwig Tieck.

Kate Roy teaches literature and culture at Franklin University Switzerland. She was also a Visiting Fellow at the University of Liverpool, where she worked on a postdoctoral project on the many retellings of Emily Ruete's life story, and she was a Lecturer in the School of Languages, Cultures, and Societies at the University of Leeds, where she is still an Honorary Research Fellow. Her work has appeared in journals such as *Zeitschrift für deutsche Philologie* and *International Journal of the Humanities* as well as in anthologies such as *Encounters with Islam in German Literature and Culture* (2009), *Alienation and Alterity: Otherness in Modern* *and Contemporary Francophone Contexts* (2009), *Cultural Transformations: Perspectives on Translocation in a Global Age* (2010), *Emerging German-Language Novelists of the Twenty-First Century* (2011), *Metropolen als Ort der Begegnung und Isolation* (2011), *The Poetics of the Margins: Mapping Europe from the Interstices* (2011), and *Zwischen Ritual und Tabu: Interaktionsschemata interkultureller Kommunikation in Sprache und Literatur* (2013).

Massimo Salgaro is Associate Professor of German Studies at the University of Verona and coordinator of the Horizon 2020 project ELIT. Among others, he has been a Visiting Fellow at Columbia University, University of Göttingen, Tongij University of Shanghai, Max Planck Institute for Empirical Aesthetics, and Institute for Advanced Study in Paris. His research areas include German authors of the twentieth and twenty-first century, empirical aesthetics, and digital humanities, and he is coeditor of the anthology *Robert Musil in der Klagenfurter Ausgabe: Bedingungen und Möglichkeiten einer digitalen Edition* (2014) and two special issues of the journal *Scientific Study of Literature* (2015 and 2016).

Pasqualina Sorrentino is a doctoral candidate at the University of Göttingen and an Italian teacher at Leibnitz University in Hannover. She is also treasurer of the International Society for the Empirical Study of Literature. Her main research interests are literary reading in the era of digitalization, vocabulary acquisition, and L2 language learner strategies.

Jeff Thoss Jeff Thoss is an independent scholar based in Graz, Austria. He is the author of *When Storyworlds Collide: Metalepsis in Popular Fiction, Film and Comics* (2015). His work has also appeared in journals such as *Word & Image*, *ImageText*, and *Arbeiten aus Anglistik und Amerikanistik* as well as in anthologies such as *Unnatural Narratives—Unnatural Narratology* (2011), *Metalepsis in Popular Culture* (2011), *The Metareferential Turn in Contemporary Arts and Media* (2011), *Placing America: American Culture and Its Spaces* (2013), *Storyworlds across Media: Toward a Media-Conscious Narratology* (2014), *Fiktion im Vergleich der Künste und Medien* (2016), and *Perturbatory Narration in Film* (2017).

Philipp Venghaus studied cultural studies and literature in Tübingen, Berlin, and Paris. He worked as a cultural mediator in Eastern and Southeastern Europe and was lecturer for the German Academic Exchange Service in Siberia and St. Petersburg for five years. Most recently he curated a touring exhibition on Soviet feminism for the Leibniz Institute for the History and Culture of Eastern Europe, and he is now responsible for the program at the Häselburg Cultural Center in Gera.

INTRODUCTION: CONSUMERISM AND PRESTIGE

Anthony Enns and Bernhard Metz

For many years scholars in the field of book studies have sought to expand the study of literary history by considering how the production, distribution, and reception of literary texts influence their meaning. For example, William Charvat famously urged scholars to examine the "reciprocal influences" between writers, publishers, and readers,[1] and Robert Darnton similarly argued that printers, publishers, and booksellers have "molded the meaning of texts."[2] This foundational work has been expanded in recent years to include a growing interest in literary prestige and materiality. On the one hand, scholars have argued that the identification of certain texts and authors as culturally significant and worthy of artistic status is dependent on both institutional forms of patronage, which are removed from commercial interests, and systems of economic exchange, which are directly tied to consumer capitalism. In his study on literary celebrities, for example, Joe Moran argues that writers are "both cultural capital and marketable commodity" as "they often contain elements of the idea of the charismatic, uniquely inspired creative artist [...] but they also gain legitimacy from the notion of celebrity as supported by broad popularity and success in the marketplace."[3] In his study of literary prizes, James F. English similarly argues that prestige "is woven together with, and cannot be understood apart from, the money economy," and it is therefore necessary to expand the concept of economics "to include systems of nonmonetary, cultural, and symbolic transaction."[4] While consumerism and prestige would seem to represent opposing forces, in other words, they are actually interdependent, as the circulation of cultural capital cannot be entirely removed from the circulation of economic capital. In recent years scholars have also emphasized the importance of understanding how the material properties of literary texts contribute to their meaning. David Pearson argues, for example, that "understanding the history of books, and of the communication of ideas through books, needs to take into account the impact of their physical forms."[5] This work has been largely inspired by the rise of e-books,[6] and it mainly focuses on recent examples of experimental literature that use print technologies in innovative ways.[7] In order to understand the reciprocal influences between writers, publishers, and readers, therefore, it is important to consider the social forces that determine the cultural status of literary texts as well as the technologies that shape their material form.

This anthology explores the intersection between these two recent trends by examining how the material aspects of literary texts, such as the cover, binding, typography, and paper stock, also reflect and potentially even determine their cultural status. Following the industrialization of printing, for example, the use of cheaper materials allowed books to be produced in larger quantities and marketed to a broader readership, which decreased costs and increased profits, yet mass-produced books were often perceived as disposable and therefore inconsequential. The use of more expensive materials could serve to elevate a text's cultural status, yet this often limited the circulation of a text and reduced its profitability. Prestige was thus directly proportional to rarity and price, and in many cases the distinction between highbrow and lowbrow books had little to do with their content, as they more often functioned as markers of socioeconomic status, like clothing or home decor. At the risk of being provocative, one might even go so far as to say that the concept of literary taste gradually becomes more closely related to fashion sense than critical judgment, although such a claim clearly challenges the hermeneutic and philosophical tradition on which distinctions of taste rely for their continued relevance.[8] This anthology seeks to address this claim by examining how the tensions between consumerism and prestige reflect fundamental historical changes with regard to the development of technology, literacy, and social power, and the individual chapters explore how the cultural status of literary texts can be understood as an inherent consequence of their material form, which often changes the value of texts that are otherwise experienced as more or less prestigious.

As historians often note, one of the most significant consequences of the Industrial Revolution was that printing became cheaper, faster, and more easily accessible than ever before.[9] This process began with the development of automatic papermaking machines, which were first invented by the Fourdrinier brothers in England in 1803. Their belt-based machine was capable of producing more paper in a single day than workers could produce by hand in a week. In 1816 an American papermaker named Thomas Gilpin also developed a cylindrical machine that allowed paper to be produced in large widths on a continuous roll, and by 1830 machine-made paper was being used for the majority of all print material, including books.[10] The invention of non-rag-based paper and the introduction of "esparto" grass and later wood pulp further reduced printing costs. In the United States, for example, the price of paper fell dramatically from roughly 17 cents per pound in 1870 to 7 cents per pound in 1889,[11] while in the United Kingdom the price fell from 10 pence per pound in 1836 to 2 pence per pound in 1902.[12]

In 1800 British scientist Charles Mahon, Third Earl of Stanhope, introduced a lever-powered iron printing press that had several advantages over the wooden press, as the lever mechanism required less effort and delivered greater pressure, more evenly, with a larger platen.[13] It was also possible to operate it with a single printer, thus reducing labor costs. Soon after the Stanhope press was introduced, Friedrich Koenig, a German engineer living in the UK, invented a steam-driven press that printed roughly 1,000 pages per hour, which was considerably faster than the 300 pages per hour produced by the lever-powered press. In 1848 English inventor Augustus Applegarth also developed a vertical rotary press, in which the printing surface was attached to the cylindrical surface and rotated against the platen. Paper could be fed into the Applegarth press from 4 different angles to produce 4,000 pages per hour, and by 1850 paper could be fed into this press from 8 different angles to produce 10,000 pages per hour. In 1858 American inventor Richard M. Hoe also introduced a horizontal rotary press, which had up to 10 feeding stations and was capable of producing up to 20,000 pages per hour. Hoe's press soon became the standard technology for printing newspapers.

The nineteenth century also saw several innovations in bookbinding, such as the development of a stabbing machine in 1820; a rolling press in 1840; a folding machine in 1843; a rounder and backer in 1854; and various gilding, marbling, cutting, and trimming machines.[14] By the end of the nineteenth century, the processes of cutting, gathering, stitching, stapling, and gluing pages were entirely mechanized. The industrialization of printing transformed not only the look of books but also labor practices, as more and more uneducated workers, including women and children, entered a status-conscious profession that was traditionally well-paid and organized in guilds.

The techniques of illustration and pictorial reproduction also went through enormous changes. While older technologies like wood and steel engraving were perfected and economized during the nineteenth century, the invention of lithography by German inventor Johann Alois Senefelder revolutionized the printing business. Lithography also gave way to color printing, which was first introduced by Senefelder as color lithography in 1818 and practically applied in 1826.[15] A patent for "chromolithography" was also granted to Franco-German printer Godefroy Engelmann in 1837, and this technique remained in use until the late twentieth century. The emergence and widespread availability of popular fiction were also connected to these new technologies, as many illustrated journals had high print runs and combined popular content with pictures for a mass reading public. Even though most of the books printed between 1830 and 1914 were not illustrated, historians like Michael Twyman maintain that "the illustrated book was a major factor in defining publishing in the period," as "it changed the concept of the book for good."[16]

The expansion of stereotyping in the 1830s and 1840s also allowed print-ers to reprint a text at a later date without having to pay additional com-position costs or storage costs for unused standing type. The development of mechanical typesetting machines like the Pianotype and the Kastenbein reduced printing costs even more by automating the process of composition, which once again led to innovations in the social structure of typesetters since less-paid women were often employed in machine typesetting.[17] The first successful mechanical hot lead typesetting machine was the Linotype, which was invented by German watchmaker Ottmar Mergenthaler in the 1880s. At roughly the same time American inventor Tolbert Lanston devel-oped the Monotype system, which consisted of a separate keyboard and a caster. These machines were able to compose texts much faster than by hand, and they solved the problem of how to redistribute type after usage by melting it. This remained the standard method of composition until the development of phototypesetting devices and computerized prepress systems in the twenti-eth century. The Linotype and Monotype systems also introduced their own typefaces according to technical restrictions and specifications, which were later adapted for other typesetting devices and word processing software. Some of them are still commonly used today, such as Times New Roman, the most widely used typeface of the twentieth century, which was developed by Stanley Morison for *The Times* of London in 1931.[18]

As a result of this combination of machine-made paper, high-speed presses, publisher's bindings, and composing machines, all of the basic elements of the printing process could be mechanized and eventually automated. As these machines required less human labor (and less well-paid and specialized labor), there was a rapid decrease in printing costs and a tremendous increase in the quantity of print runs, which resulted in a sudden explosion of print mate-rial. In the UK, for example, book production rose to over 5,000 titles per year by the 1850s and 10,000 titles per year by 1910.[19] In the United States, book production went up to 4,500 titles per year by 1890 and 12,000 titles per year by 1914.[20] The increase in book production was even more dramatic in Germany, where it rose steadily from 10,000 titles per year in 1850 to 35,000 titles per year in 1913, making German publishers the leading book producers in the world.[21] Between 1900 and 1913, the publishing industry also became the third-largest business in the world.[22] As Steven Roger Fischer points out, this increase in book production was due to a wide range of social changes, including "accelerated urbanization, a higher standard of living, a more sophisticated educational system and higher technical training."[23] These changes led to a greater demand for print material across Europe and North America, as a decrease in the working day and improved education resulted in a sudden increase in literacy rates, particularly among women and the working class. By the 1890s, more than 95 percent of the population in advanced countries could read and write, which resulted in the emergence of a mass reading public.

The question as to whether technological innovations caused the rise of mass literacy or whether mass literacy was the driving force behind these technological innovations has been a major subject of debate among book historians. While most historians argue that mass literacy was a result of the Industrial Revolution, historians like John Feather argue that technological innovations were designed to meet pressing social needs.[24] Martyn Lyons similarly claims that "the industrialization of the book [...] was a response to the expanding possibilities of the market."[25] Other critics, like Cathy N. Davidson, dismiss this issue as an irrelevant "chicken-or-egg style ontogenetic debate."[26] Nevertheless, it is clear that the increase in both the supply and demand for books led to what is known as a "reading revolution." As Rolf Engelsing famously argued (although criticized in many details), people went from reading a few books intensively to reading a wide range of books only once. As readers went from being engaged participants to passive consumers, books effectively lost much of their ritual and religious function and became, in some cases, nothing more than disposable commodities. Reading also went from being an oral practice performed in groups to a solitary practice conducted in silence, which led to the emergence of a new concept of individual subjectivity.[27] This theory obviously does not encompass all readers and reading practices, and certain books continue to be read intensively or aloud today, as is evident by the continued popularity of Bible study groups and book clubs, yet it is undoubtedly true that there was a far greater demand for print material in the late nineteenth century and that this material was increasingly seen as a mass-produced commodity.

As costs decreased and demand increased, books gradually became cheaper than ever before. In the 1820s, for example, the first edition of a novel in the UK consisted of three volumes, which were priced at 31s 6d (these books were known as "three-deckers"). By the 1830s, single-volume reprint editions were priced at five or six shillings. In 1849 George Routledge began selling smaller reprint editions (known as "yellowbacks" because they were bound in glazed yellow boards) for only one or two shillings, and in 1883 he started a "Universal Library" that was priced at one shilling per volume.

In 1885 Cassell answered with their "National Library" at a price of three pence in paper and six pence in cloth. Routledge's reaction was a "World Library" at the same price, and both publishers "entered into an all-out price war."[28] The "underselling" of books (i.e., selling them below their advertised price) was also a common practice.[29] Simon Eliot and Andrew Nash emphasize the tremendous flexibility in this pricing system: "[W]ithin a matter of a few years a reader could buy a novel, which had originally appeared at 31s 6d, at 1/63rd or less of its original price—a price flexibility that even computer manufacturers today would find hard to match."[30] While each of these editions was designed to appeal to different markets, competition between publishers made this pricing system unsustainable over the long term. By 1900 the "three-decker" had disappeared, and most novels were published in one volume priced at six shillings.

In Germany, cheap paperback editions appeared as early as 1841, when Leipzig publisher Christian Bernhard Tauchnitz began printing one title per week. In 1867 Reclam's "Universal Library" also started as a series of small format paperbacks that sold for 20 pfennig each.[31] As a result, cheap paperback editions flooded the market.[32] In France, Charpentier began producing small, single-volume editions at a reduced price in the 1830s. In 1848 Gustave Havard also published a paperback edition of Abbé Prévost's *Manon Lescaut*, which was priced at only 20 centimes. This strategy proved to be enormously successful, and by 1856 Havard had reportedly published 60 million books.[33] In 1855 Michel Lévy also began publishing contemporary novels priced at one franc, and by 1913 French readers could buy novels for only 10 centimes.[34] Similar price reductions appeared in North America with the rise of dime novels, in Italy with the rise of one-lira novels, and in Spain with the rise of one-peseta novels. As books became smaller and cheaper, they were also sold in venues outside the traditional bookstore, such as railway stations—a practice that began as early as 1848 in London and 1853 in Paris.[35] The expansion of the book market through cheap editions was thus an international phenomenon.

The introduction of new publishing formats was accompanied by the introduction of new content, as Simon Eliot and Andrew Nash point out: "[W]ith the decline of the three-volume form came the rise of identifiable branches of genre fiction, such as romance, spy fiction, detective fiction and science fiction."[36] There was thus a direct connection between the expansion of the book market and the rise of popular genre fiction. The serial (or serialized) novel was also introduced with remarkable success, as novels by such renowned authors as Honoré de Balzac and Charles Dickens were first published in newspapers or journals and then republished in book form.[37] Publishers also began employing new marketing strategies to announce and promote their books, including book jackets,[38] promotional posters, press advertisements, and book reviews, which led to the birth of the "bestseller."

As Joseph McAleer points out, popular reading and publishing expanded even further in the early twentieth century, as lower profit margins forced publishers to "accelerate the movement towards cheap-priced books and to accommodate more closely the tastes of the lower-middle and working class."[39] This trend was largely due to the expansion of the paperback market. In 1928, for example, German publisher Ullstein introduced the "Yellow Series" of crime novels, which sold remarkably well.[40] In 1912, Reclam also began installing paperback vending machines in bookstores, railway stations, and hospitals.[41] In 1931, another German publisher, Albatross Books, developed the mass-market paperback format, which featured a brand logo and color-coded covers for different genres. This format was later adopted by Penguin, which was founded in 1935 with the explicit aim of making books available for a low price.[42] The first Penguin paperbacks cost only 6d, which was roughly the price of a pack of cigarettes, and by 1936 Penguin had sold more than three million books. In 1937, Penguin also introduced the "Penguincubator"—a paperback vending machine that was placed in railway stations and Woolworth department stores. The first American paperback publishers, Pocket Books and Avon Books, adopted a similar format.[43] While most paperbacks featured works of popular genre fiction, many publishers also released paperback editions of classic literary works, although these books "suffered initially from a taint of commercialism caused partly by its humble sales outlets and partly by the lurid covers produced for many of its early titles."[44] While paperbacks were generally dismissed by the literary elite, they were embraced by many readers who could not afford more expensive editions and who were unlikely to purchase books in any other format, as bookseller Sidney Gross points out:

> [N]ew customers who rarely buy regular books will be attracted by paperbacks. Some of these buyers are students, some like the convenience of the smaller format, some do not wish to spend too much money for a book, and some are interested in titles that are available only in paperbacks. This author firmly believes that there is another reason, a psychological one. He feels that the paper cover alone makes the scholarly book less forbidding to the buyer and that if the books were issued solely in cloth at the same price, they would not sell nearly as well.[45]

While the material form of paperbacks clearly reflected their low cultural status as cheap, disposable, and standardized commodities, their content encompassed a wide range of genres, from the lowbrow to the highbrow. The format could thus be used to convert works of serious literature into mass cultural artifacts, which disturbed some readers and appealed to others.

These developments in the book trade fundamentally transformed the role of the publisher, as Michael Winship explains:

> For the first time, the publisher was responsible not only for the typography and appearance of the printed sheets but also for the design and production of the binding, [which] could not only reflect a book's content or genre but in itself influence a customer's decision whether or not to purchase it. As a result, [...] publisher and reader were connected in a new way, not just through the text of the works that the former published but also through the package in which the text appeared.[46]

These new publishing formats thus placed greater emphasis on the material properties of books, as their packaging effectively functioned as a form of commercial advertising. Janice Radway points out that the rise of mass literacy, larger print runs, and popular genres also encouraged publishers to begin "contracting with a large pool of writers who wrote books regularly and respectively according to editorial specifications by drawing on well-known material already circulating in the press."[47] As a result, authorship was increasingly seen as an assembly-line process in which writers churned out standardized products as quickly as possible in order to meet production quotas. Mary Noel similarly notes that "demand [...] created a supply," as a new kind of low-class writer emerged who was willing to produce copy on demand for a minimal wage. In other words, this new species of writers (commonly known as "hack writers") was "as much a product of the Industrial Revolution as was the Hoe printing press."[48] Just as books were seen as industrial products, so too were authors seen as industrial workers, as publishing was understood as nothing more than a vast commercial industry designed to maximize productivity and profitability.

Despite the increased availability of cheap editions, most new books still represented a significant investment, particularly for working-class readers. In 1920, for example, the price of a new novel published in the UK was roughly one-fifth of the average weekly wage for an industrial worker. Libraries became the easiest way to access books, yet librarians "frequently concentrated on 'serious' subjects (theology, philosophy, history, biography, travel, etc.) to the exclusion or underrepresentation of fiction," and they "were never going to satisfy what many would have regarded as a vulgar demand."[49] The distribution of popular genre fiction was subsequently taken up by "circulating libraries," which not only served poorer areas but also catered to the specific demands of working-class readers. These libraries soon became known as "two-penny" or "tuppenny" libraries, as this was the initial cost of borrowing a book.[50] The UK was thus primarily a book-borrowing culture, and the circulating libraries served the needs of most readers. By 1935, for example, Boots' Booklovers' Library alone was purchasing more than one million books per year.[51]

Similar developments took place in France, where librarians often sought to direct the reading habits of working-class readers by limiting their holdings to works of serious literature: "[L]ibrary reformers hoped that by providing suitable literature [...] they could soften social tensions. Working-class readers, it was hoped, could be weaned away from drink and from dangerous literature with tendencies towards socialism, excessive superstition or obscenity."[52] However, working-class readers often rejected the kinds of books they were offered, which led to the rise of "popular libraries."[53] Similar developments also took place in Germany, and some of these popular libraries became huge businesses. In Berlin, for example, the Borstell and Reimarus library reportedly offered the public more than 600,000 different titles in 1891.[54] Working-class readers thus struggled to create their own independent literary culture, which would be free of state and church control.

The rise of a mass reading public that preferred genre fiction instead of serious literature immediately inspired fears of cultural decline and moral corruption. As Cathy N. Davidson explains, the application of "Gresham's Law" to book production was already prevalent in the late nineteenth century:

> [M]any people believed in a Gresham's law of texts or reading. Bad new works would supposedly drive out good old ones, so that a print world dominated by the Bible, *The Day of Doom*, sermons, tracts, and sundry other religious works well might be superseded by a new world of predominantly secular reading, of texts designed merely to amuse, not to instruct. [...] The novel threatened not just to coexist with elite literature, but to replace it.[55]

Such fears were most clearly expressed in Noah Porter's *Books and Reading* (1871), which was published shortly after Porter became the president of Yale College and was seen as a kind of mission statement for American institutions of higher education:

> [B]ad books and inferior books are far more common than they once were. Their poison is also more subtle and less easily detected, for as the taste of readers becomes omnivorous, it becomes less discriminating. Besides, the readiness with which good men, and men sturdy in their principles too, read books which they despise and abhor, has introduced a freedom of practice on this

subject, at which other generations would have stood aghast. In many cases too, if the principles are not corrupted by reading, the taste is vitiated. Or if nothing worse happens, delicacy of appreciation suffers from the amount of intellectual food which is forced upon us, and the satisfaction is far less keen and exquisite than was enjoyed by readers of a few books of superior merit.[56]

Porter thus argued that the industrialization of printing had resulted in a tremendous increase in the number of bad books being published and that these books would inevitably lead to a decline in public taste, as they made it more difficult for readers to appreciate good ones.

Other critics argued that this cultural decline was a result of not only the quantity of books being published but also the price and quality of the books themselves, which made it increasingly difficult to distinguish bad books from good ones. As a commentator wrote in the *New York Evening Mail* in 1880:

When a book cost money, it was something to be preserved with care, and guarded and cherished as a thing of value. Hence, the possession of handsome editions of good books was a matter of pride to their owners. At present, books [...] are read and thrown away. [...] The publication which may be bought for a few pence, however worthy its contents, is likely to be regarded like a newspaper, as something to be skimmed over and forgotten.[57]

Critics thus argued that the superior quality of serious literature was directly related to the quality and expense of the books themselves and that good books should appeal to an exclusive readership through smaller print runs, limited distribution, and higher cover prices. Radway describes this as a "discourse of protectionism" that "saw the traditional book as an endangered species and reading as an art in danger of extinction."[58]

In the early twentieth century, publishers often blamed circulating libraries for the poor quality of popular genre fiction and the low standards of popular taste. As publisher Stanley Unwin wrote in *The Truth about Publishing* (1926), "The present system tends to assist the circulation of indifferent and bad books, and to retard the circulation of really good books." Unwin also related an anecdote about a circulating library that "makes a boast of the extent to which it can force its subscribers to take what is given them, which means, in that particular case, what the library can buy cheapest."[59] Publishers thus accused circulating libraries of corrupting the minds of working-class readers by encouraging them to read low-quality material simply because it could be acquired at a low cost. Andrew Nash notes that these concerns were not entirely without reason, as "tuppenny libraries [...] increased the market for popular fiction by promoting shorter books and a greater quantity of titles" and "fiction came to be marketed more and more in the form of branded goods."[60]

The most famous critique of circulating libraries was undoubtedly Q. D. Leavis's *Fiction and the Reading Public* (1932), which similarly argued that the distribution of popular genre fiction represented a threat to serious literature: "When Railway Libraries and 'Yellow Backs' offered a kind of reading that needed little exertion, it was not likely that any other would stand a chance."[61] Leavis's description of popular reading as a "drug habit"[62] that made readers incapable of intellectual exertion clearly echoed American poet James Russell Lowell's earlier claim that printing "supplanted a strenuous habit of thinking with a loose indolence of reading which relaxes the muscular fiber of the mind."[63] Like Unwin, Leavis also saw circulating libraries as the primary cause of this cultural decline, as the reading public "buys its literature in accordance with tastes acquired from its circulating library reading."[64] Circulating libraries directed the tastes of readers toward best-selling novels because it allowed publishers to maximize profits, yet this discouraged the public from reading "anything which by the widest stretch could be included in the classification 'literature.'"[65] As a result, "the general public [...] has now not even a glimpse of the living interests of modern literature, is ignorant of its growth and so prevented from developing with it."[66] According to Leavis, therefore, circulating libraries did not promote literacy by providing greater access to print material; rather, they actively discouraged literacy by threatening the literary establishment: "[T]he critical minority to whose sole charge modern literature has now fallen is isolated, disowned by the general public and threatened with extinction."[67]

Pierre Bourdieu provided a sociological explanation for these fears by describing how serious literature and popular genre fiction were gradually seen as two competing modes of production that obeyed "inverse logics":

> At one pole, there is the anti-"economic" economy of pure art. Founded on the obligatory recognition of the values of disinterestedness and on the denegation of the "economy" (of the "commercial") and of "economic" profit (in the short term), it privileges production [...] oriented to the accumulation of symbolic capital. [...] At the other pole, there is the "economic" logic of the literary and artistic industries which, since they make the trade in cultural goods just another trade, confer priority on distribution, on immediate and temporary success, measured for example by the print run, and which are content to adjust themselves to the pre-existing demand of a clientele. [...] An enterprise moves closer to the "commercial" pole the more directly or completely the products it offers on the market respond to a *pre-existing demand*, and in *pre-established forms* [emphasis in original].[68]

Bourdieu thus argued that publishers saw popular genre fiction as nothing more than a commodity that could be standardized and mass-produced in order to maximize profits, while the literary elite saw serious literature as a higher form of cultural expression that could accumulate cultural value by rejecting these commercial imperatives. The small press publication of Modernist literature offers perhaps the most vivid example of how the rejection of commercial imperatives could enhance the cultural status of literary texts as works of art. Lawrence Rainey notes, for example, that "modernist literature was an experiment in adopting exchange and market structures typical of the visual arts, a realm in which patronage and collecting can thrive because its artisanal mode of production is compatible with a limited submarket for luxury goods."[69] John Guillory also emphasizes the important role played by academic institutions in establishing and maintaining the cultural status of Modernist literature as "the distinction between High Cultural artifacts and mass cultural artifacts" became "the cultural capital of the university."[70]

The tension between these two competing forms of capital helps to explain why works of popular fiction and serious literature were often promoted in different ways, as Ellen Gruber Garvey points out: "Prestige differentiated the products of old-line publishers from the cheap editions [...] of publishers who advertised in posters, eye-catching window displays, and newspaper ads."[71] In other words, books that were heavily promoted would be perceived as popular, which prevented them from accumulating "symbolic capital," while books that received no promotion would be perceived as serious and, therefore, prestigious, which limited their marketability. Unlike Unwin and Leavis, however, Bourdieu argued that popular fiction did not necessarily represent a threat to serious literature, as serious literature could only accumulate "symbolic capital" by differentiating itself from popular fiction. The rise of a mass readership also posed no threat to the literary establishment, as the divide between working-class readers and the literary elite was the very source of the latter's privileged status as the defenders of cultural standards and traditions, and it allowed the literary establishment to consolidate its social power through the founding of nonprofit institutions dedicated to the conservation, interpretation, and celebration of serious literature.[72]

By noting that commercial publishing only focuses on economic profit "in the short term," Bourdieu was also implying that the accumulation of "symbolic capital" could still serve economic interests in the long term, and this idea informs much of the recent work on literary prestige. James F. English points out, for example, that it is impossible wholly to separate these two forms of capital: "There is no question of perfect autonomy or segregation of the various sorts of capital, such that one might occupy a zone or margin of 'pure' culture [...], or such that one might acquire economic capital that is free of all implication in the social, symbolic, or political economics."[73] Instead of simply maximizing short-term profits, for example, many publishers seek to enhance the symbolic value of books through the production of deluxe editions. Already at the end of the eighteenth century, Cotta published the collected works of the German poet Christoph Martin Wieland in four different formats, thus offering an enormous range of options for the acquisition of the always identical text.[74] In 1854 George Putnam similarly offered an edition of Washington Irving's works in seven different types of prestige bindings: cloth ($19); sheep ($20); half calf ($30); half morocco, gilt tops ($33); calf, extra ($37.50); calf, antique ($40); and morocco, super extra ($48). For many readers, therefore, the appearance of a book mattered as much, if not more, than its content. As Ronald Zboray points out, "The conspicuous consumption of books during the era meant that some readers preferred owning books over reading them."[75] David McKitterick makes a similar point concerning the use of gold blocking: "The discovery that [cloth] could be gold-blocked led to some of the greatest changes in the appearance of bindings—and, hence, in the ways that books could be publicised and presented to potential readers. [...] Books could be sold almost as much by their outside as by their contents."[76]

The market for deluxe books expanded dramatically in the early twentieth century, particularly in North America, where there was "a seemingly insatiable demand for fine books."[77] As bookseller J. Ainslie Thin wrote in 1935,

> The last decade saw a mad period of rising prices in rare and pseudo-rare books. [...] The private presses, taking advantage of this extraordinary period, increased in numbers, and increased not only the number of books they published but also the number of copies printed of each book. [...] Editions de luxe of quite ordinary books appeared, some of them of extraordinary large numbers.[78]

These deluxe editions were thus designed to have the appearance of rarity in order to maximize profits, as their material properties were perceived as indicators of their cultural and economic value; however, their method of production directly contradicted the connotations of their material form, as they were actually mass-produced. Andrew Nash notes that some ordinary trade publishers in the UK, like Chatto & Windus, also produced expensive editions of unremarkable titles in order to "break even—and in some cases make a profit—on books that were likely to make a loss if published in the ordinary way."[79] In this case, smaller print runs were used to justify higher prices, and genuine scarcity was used to promote increased sales. Jim Collins also notes that the differences between economic and symbolic capital have become even more blurred today, as "the delivery systems for literary experiences become increasingly large-scale, but the mechanisms of taste distinction appear to grow ever more intimate as reading taste becomes more personalized."[80]

This emphasis on the appearance of books clearly reflects the idea of literature as a commodity, as the symbolic value of a book's content was gradually seen as equivalent to the economic value of its material form. As Radway points out, "The book was conceived of [...] as a permanent and precious possession," and "[s]ince its intrinsic value was understood to increase with age [...] it required a design that would promote longevity; hence the need for high-quality paper, secure bindings, and hard covers."[81] The symbolic value of a book also enhanced the cultural status of its owner:

> Potentially, then, every book sale could generate two forms of profit. On one hand it could generate cash for its publishers. On the other hand it could also produce perceived changes in the status of the individual who bought it because the more traditional discourse about the book had managed to associate the social prestige of learning with the particular technology for producing that learning in the first place, that is, with the leather- or cloth-covered book itself.[82]

A nineteenth-century guide to home decoration notes, for example, that "there is nothing which does so much to furnish a room [...] as shelves of prettily-bound, neatly-kept, and well-arranged books," as "their rows are the tree-avenues which mark the residence of the aristocracy of mental culture."[83] Mary Benton employs the term "bookaflage" to describe this practice of purchasing and exhibiting certain editions for the purpose of constructing a "cultural persona": "Books played a prominent, often featured role in the widespread preoccupation with fashioning one's domestic environment, which in turn suggested—and presumably shaped—one's very persona. [...] One's books could be selected and arranged to present whatever impression one wished to make, be it literary delicacy, friendly charm, or erudite intellect."[84] This practice also explains why books appeared in nearly 30 percent of magazine advertisements, where they were used as "props or part of the background scene to telegraph implicit messages about the intelligence, social class, and personal values of the depicted subject," and these values were conveyed not through titles or authors but rather through "heft, dimensions, and often a subdued, elegant binding."[85]

Certain bindings also became associated with certain publishers, as Jeffrey D. Groves points out:

[A] house style [...] communicated a message of literary quality: if some of the books brought out by a publisher achieved canonical status, and the external design of most of the publisher's books looked identical, then the intended message from producer to consumer seems to have been that, like their appearance, the quality of the publisher's book was consistent. Moreover, the development of house styles as texts for communicating such value judgments was historically concurrent with publishers' increasing sophistication in literary promotion, and the synthesis of book design and promotion encouraged consumers to read bindings as guarantors that literary quality awaited within.[86]

These house styles thus "presented a prestigious spine to the world and so could function as status statements on a bookshelf."[87] The brown cover of Ticknor and Fields' books, for example, "came to suggest gravity, elegance, and good taste."[88] Instead of promoting the idea of books as disposable commodities, these covers effectively served as markers of socioeconomic status—regardless of whether or not the books they adorned were actually read. By signaling distinctions of class as well as taste, deluxe editions can thus be understood as reified forms of social relations—or, in Bourdieu's words, as a "social relationship made flesh."[89]

The material properties of a book can also be understood as part of its "paratext"—a term introduced by Gérard Genette to refer to the extratextual features of a literary work. Genette famously defined the paratext rather metaphorically as a "threshold" that "enables a text to become a book and to be offered as such to its readers and, more generally, to the public."[90] He also described it as "an 'undefined zone' between the inside and the outside, a zone without any hard and fast boundary on either the inward side (turned toward the text) or the outward side (turned toward the world's discourse about the text), [...] a zone between text and off-text, a zone not only of transition but also of *transaction*: a privileged place of a pragmatics and a strategy, of an influence on the public" [emphasis in original].[91] Genette's approach was deeply anchored in the French literary tradition, and he offered plenty of striking explanations, examples, and thought-provoking contradictions, but his definition was never more than an invitation, and its openness and boundlessness helped the concept to become very successful in literary studies. While Genette's approach has been criticized for many reasons, especially for its obscurity, it is indeed interesting to classify and taxonomize aspects of textual meaning that are so far out of the range and perspective of more traditional literary studies, such as formats, series, covers, title pages, dedications, and pre- or postfaces. Genette's distinction between text and paratext thus provided a conceptual framework regarding textual effects that lay outside the narrow notions of textuality as linguistically encoded meaning, and his definition of textual meaning beyond linguistic or referential uses has since led to more elaborated distinctions, including material approaches—an area where Genette himself was rather blind, having a concept of text that was restricted to linguistic or at least symbolic sign systems while almost entirely neglecting aspects like paper, typography, binding, and so on. The concept of paratext is also used in some of the chapters of this volume—not as a precise and well-defined term but as a term that is helpful for heuristic reasons.

Jerome McGann offered another taxonomy concerning the material aspects of books that distinguished between the "bibliographic code," which refers to the material layer or physical realization of a book, and the "linguistic code," which refers to its symbolic layer or communicative realization. According to McGann, it is important that both layers or codes signify, as "meaning is transmitted through bibliographical as well as linguistic codes," but these "signifying processes of the work become increasingly collaborative and socialized."[92] McGann also emphasized that this distinction is extremely important for textual criticism: "Without making and implementing the distinction in detailed ways, textual critics cannot fully elucidate—cannot analyze—the lines of materials which descend to them."[93] This distinction is also important for understanding the material aspects of literary texts and their related social meaning and status. The bibliographic code is certainly not all there is to know about a given publication, but the material properties are often all one needs to evaluate its social importance and significance as an object on the market, as its prestige is directly related to bibliographic decisions concerning the cover, binding, typography, paper, and so on.

The chapters included in this anthology all examine how the material properties of literary texts reflect the tensions between consumerism and prestige, and they have been arranged both historically and thematically. On the one hand, they cover a broad historical trajectory, which extends from publishing practices in the Romantic era to the recent emergence of e-books, and they examine the materiality of literature in many different cultural contexts, including Germany, Brazil, France, Spain, the United Kingdom, and the United States. On the other hand, there are also several thematic threads that weave their way through the chapters, such as the relationship between literary value and marketing techniques, the construction of taste distinctions both between and within different literary fields (including highbrow, lowbrow, and liminal domains), and the affordances and constraints of various publishing and reading technologies.

The opening section focuses on "Material Forms and Literary Publishing," and it begins with Christoph Rauen's chapter "Devotion and Consumption: Ludwig Tieck, Literary Pocketbooks, and the Novella Craze," which examines the relationship between the novella genre and the production of literary pocketbooks in nineteenth-century Germany. While pocketbooks effectively democratized literature by making texts more affordable and accessible, Rauen points out that they were also perceived as a threat to the prestige of literature, as they were mass-produced in serial form and the most highly esteemed writers refused to be published in them. Rauen also describes how some publishers sought to secure and sustain the cultural authority of serious literature through the use of leather covers, gold rims, and silk lining. These external, material strategies were closely related to internal, textual strategies that were similarly designed to enhance the status of the pocketbook form, such as the inclusion of highbrow literary works by prestigious authors. Rauen particularly focuses on the pocketbooks that contained the most well-known novellas by German writer Ludwig Tieck, whose work often addressed the material properties of books as well as their economic and social status. More specifically, Rauen argues that Tieck's novellas dramatized the struggle between two competing notions of literary reception: intensive reading, which is described as a form of devotion that involves reading a single work many times, and extensive reading, which involves the consumption of many works that are ready quickly and immediately discarded. Rauen thus concludes that the material properties of Tieck's works reflected the conflicting tensions between art and commerce in the early nineteenth century.

Jacob Haubenreich's chapter "Packaging Process: Peter Handke's Writing for Sale" examines how the material properties of Austrian writer Peter Handke's printed books announced their social status as works of serious literature by replicating the form and style of handmade books and by including facsimiles of the author's own handwritten manuscripts. These features could be dismissed as simply gimmicks of a consumerist economy, but Haubenreich argues that they served to defamiliarize the mass-produced book by evoking the auratic quality of art. In contrast to works of popular genre fiction, which were designed to be read quickly and then discarded, Handke's publications were intended to be read slowly, which was part of his larger project to "resacralize" the act of writing and reading. Haubenreich thus concludes that the material properties of Handke's books were meaningful extensions of his artistic project and that he used the materiality of literature to reinforce traditional distinctions of taste and to challenge the idea of the novel as a mass-produced commodity.

Laura Rivas Gagliardi's chapter "Contrasts in the Brazilian Book Market in the Early Twenty-First Century" examines the emergence of deluxe book publishers in contemporary Brazil. While the rise of deluxe book publishing was made possible by government subventions in education, an increase in literacy rates, and an expansion of the middle class, Gagliardi points out that this development primarily served to reinforce the power of the ruling class, as prestige was associated with the material properties of books, and the consumers of deluxe editions used them to acquire respect and admiration within their social spheres. She illustrates this development by describing the history of two Brazilian publishing companies, Companhia das Letras and Cosac Naify, which sought to enhance their reputation by producing high-quality books that were often sold at a loss. She also describes the recent economic problems in the Brazilian book market, as the target audience for deluxe editions began to decline in the 2010s and these companies were forced to either merge with larger media conglomerates or file for bankruptcy. Gagliardi thus concludes that the reputations of these companies were largely founded on the material properties of their books, yet this strategy proved to be ineffective because the books remained inaccessible to the majority of the population.

The second section focuses on "Material Distinctions in Popular Fiction," and it begins with Kate Roy's chapter "Only the 'Outward Appearance' of a Harem? Reading *Memoirs of an Arabian Princess* as a Material Text," which examines the publication history of the German- and English-language editions of Emily Ruete's famous book. Roy argues that these editions often reflect a tension between the internal or textual elements of the text, which was a serious work of autobiographical nonfiction that sought to introduce Muslim and East African culture to Western readers, and the external or material elements of its various instantiations, which were often marketed as popular works of erotic "harem" fiction that reinforced the exoticization of Eastern cultures. While early editions emphasized the value of the text as one of the first autobiographies ever written by an Arab woman, for example, later editions sought to capitalize on the exotic appeal of Arab women, including a recent Kindle edition published under the title *Dangerous Romance* that includes various soft-core porn images. Roy thus concludes that the packaging of this book has been shaped by genre expectations, even though the content of the text tells a completely different story, and this interaction between material and textual elements reflects a tension between the publishers' desire to satisfy reader expectations and the writer's desire to defy cultural stereotypes—a tension that can still be seen in contemporary novels about the writer and her life.

An Goris's chapter "Hidden Codes of Love: The Materiality of the Category Romance Novel" similarly examines the significance of popular publishing formats by analyzing the material properties of category romance novels. While the romance genre represents perhaps the most iconic example of lowbrow fiction, and the material properties of these novels often encourage simplistic and superficial interpretations, Goris describes them as complex sign systems that generate a multitude of meanings to readers familiar with their cultural codes. She also argues that these features serve as brand markers that signify distinctions readers familiar with the genre can easily understand. While the physical similarities between romance novels have often been ridiculed as a reflection of their inherently formulaic and standardized content—and perhaps even a reflection of their readers' low level of intelligence—Goris argues that the generic transparency of these novels is the result of a material strategy that publishers have successfully used to maximize profits and that the material properties of these books actually reflect a tremendous wealth of variation, which experienced readers have learned to recognize and identify. Goris thus describes romance readers as an interpretive community that has developed its own way of interpreting the material properties of romance novels and the cultural distinctions that these properties represent.

Thorsten Bothe's chapter "Stephen King's *The Girl Who Loved Tom Gordon*: A Rhetorical Reading of the Schneekluth Edition Dust Jackets" employs a similar method to analyze the material properties of a horror novel that was published with two different dust jackets. Bothe argues that readers choosing between these jackets are essentially choosing between two different books and that their purchasing decision reflects their expectations or interpretations of the novel itself, such as whether the ending will be happy or sad. Like Goris, Bothe also argues that this decision is informed by their knowledge of genre conventions as well as their own distinctions of taste. In other words, these jacket variants serve the same function as deluxe editions by implying scarcity and exclusivity, and the purchasing of one or both versions allows readers familiar with the genre to display their taste preferences to other readers within their interpretive community. Bothe thus concludes that dust jackets are not trivial and inconsequential; rather, they are just as important as the content of the books they cover, as they serve a crucial function in shaping and conditioning the reading experience. Like the other chapters in this section, Bothe's chapter also shows how the same cultural distinctions discussed in the first section in relation to the material properties of serious literature also apply to the material properties of popular genre fiction.

The third section, "Cultural Prestige and Graphic Narratives," focuses on how the material properties of visual texts reflect or shape their cultural status, and this section begins with Philipp Venghaus's chapter, "The Printing of Phantasms: The Illustrations of Nineteenth-Century Serialized Novels and their Appropriation in Max Ernst's Collage Novel *Une semaine de bonté*," which examines the significance of the source materials used to produce one of the earliest collage novels. Venghaus argues that the collages created for this book primarily consisted of illustrations from nineteenth-century serialized novels, which mostly featured crime and suspense stories that offered the possibility for exciting visuals that would attract readers. Venghaus notes that these novels were often condemned by critics as a sign of cultural decline and a reflection of the "low" taste of the reading public, although many of them were later recognized as literary classics. He also notes that the protagonists in these novels provided a model for the modern "superhero," as they often possessed special powers that set them above ordinary human beings. While this publishing format had already fallen out of fashion in the early twentieth century, when Ernst created his collage novel, Venghaus argues that his readers would have still recognized the style of these illustrations and that they would have seen them as a reflection of the society in which they were produced and consumed. More specifically, he argues that they often reflected the rise of urbanization and industrialization, and they thus indirectly reflected the conditions of their own industrialized mode of production. This idea also informs Ernst's collages, albeit in an altered form, as he sought to use the material techniques of fragmentation and juxtaposition to defamiliarize the illustrations and critique their latent content, such as their promotion of authoritarianism and industrialized warfare. Ernst's collage novel thus takes the material form of the serialized novel and turns it into a new material form—the artist's book—that represents a merging of "low" and "high" art.

Jeff Thoss's chapter "From Penny Dreadful to Graphic Novel: Alan Moore and Kevin O'Neill's Genealogy of Comics in *The League of Extraordinary Gentlemen*" similarly examines how artists have commented on the history of popular culture by incorporating and transforming older publishing formats. In this case, Thoss focuses on a contemporary comic book series that borrows characters from nineteenth-century texts and that was designed to imitate the form of nineteenth-century publications, such as illustrated newspapers, penny dreadfuls, and boys' weeklies, which helped to pave the way for the emergence of the comic book form. Like Ernst's *Une semaine de bonté*, therefore, Alan Moore and Kevin O'Neill's *The League of Extraordinary Gentlemen* appears to employ a collage aesthetic that takes material elements from the past and alters them to generate new meanings. Like Ernst, these artists also use this material to reflect on the historical development and cultural status of graphic narratives, which are only now being recognized as a legitimate art form due to the rise of new publishing formats like the graphic novel. Thoss thus describes this project as a homage that reflects the artists' appreciation for the somewhat tawdry aspects of these publications, and he also points out that they often juxtapose "low" and "high" art forms in ways that unsettle any easy distinction between childish, sleazy, and cheap comic books and more mature, tasteful, and sophisticated graphic novels. Thoss thus concludes that these artists are not merely celebrating the lowbrow status of graphic narratives or promoting their acceptance as a legitimate art form; rather, they are attempting to show how these cultural distinctions are merely the result of the material forms in which graphic narratives have historically been published, distributed, and consumed.

The third section concludes with Anthony Enns's chapter "Comic Books versus Graphic Novels: Commodity Forms and Cultural Prestige," which similarly examines the relationship between the material forms and cultural prestige of graphic narratives by looking more closely at the history of the graphic novel. While this new publishing format was embraced by critics, publishers, teachers, and librarians because it conveyed a sense of maturity and sophistication that was seen as lacking in comic books, Enns points out that the distinctions between these two formats were often ambiguous, as comic books often include serious content, including autobiographical narratives, literary adaptations, and formally experimental work, and graphic novels often reprint material that was originally published in comic book form. These contradictions have led some critics to conclude that the rise of the graphic novel marked a cultural shift not in terms of content but rather in terms of the packaging and marketing of graphic narratives, which has inspired some artists to reject the format as nothing more than a marketing gimmick. Enns provides a history of these debates by exploring how the cultural prestige of graphic novels was closely linked to their appearance as "real" books, and he concludes that the distinction between comic books and graphic novels is primarily based on their material properties (such as their covers, binding, and paper stock), which serve to reinforce their status as durable works of art that are worthy of being sold in bookstores and preserved in libraries. The fact that the distinction between comic books and graphic novels depends largely on their material properties also illustrates the tenuous nature of the divide between "low" and "high" art, as it allows publishers to repackage previously lowbrow content in a new form that grants the material a certain degree of cultural respectability.

The fourth and final section on "Electronic Publishing and Reading Practices" examines how new forms of electronic display are currently transforming the status of literary texts, and it begins with Bernhard Metz's chapter "The Book and the E-Book: Footnotes, Margins, and Typography in *The Brief Wondrous Life of Oscar Wao*," which focuses on how the celebrated novel *The Brief Wondrous Life of Oscar Wao* was converted from a print book to an e-book. Metz argues that the epigraphs and footnotes in the original novel stage a tension between "low" and "high" culture, as the novel includes numerous references to popular culture (including science fiction, fantasy, and comic books), yet these references are offset by the narrator's editorial annotations, which provide a more serious commentary on the narrative's historical, political, and social context. The book's status as one of the preeminent novels of the early twenty-first century was thus largely dependent on the interplay between the main text and the note text, yet the notes were either omitted or relegated to a different section in all of the available e-book versions. As a result, the main text and the note text cannot be read in concert with one another, and all of the typographic features that visually indicate their relationship have been lost, such as the positioning of the text on the page or the use of different-sized fonts. Metz thus concludes that the cultural prestige of this novel was largely dependent on the material properties of the print editions, which could not be transferred to the e-book editions, and that it is difficult if not impossible to replicate the qualities of "bookishness" using current electronic formats.

Instead of focusing on the problems that arise when converting print books to e-books, Laura Hatry's chapter "E-Book Collections as an Opportunity to Recover Unpublished or Forgotten Texts" focuses on the advantages of publishing literary texts in electronic formats. She primarily argues that electronic publishing enables the recovery of literary texts that have gone out of print due to a lack of commercial interest. Given that the cost of producing e-book editions is lower than the cost of producing print editions, editors now have the unique ability to choose texts based on their cultural rather than commercial value. An example of this new approach is Clásicos Hispánicos, an e-book series created by a scholar from Madrid who realized that there were no serious digital editions of classical works of Hispanic literature. As a result of this project, it became possible to recover material that had been forgotten for cultural, political, or economic reasons. Another important aspect is that these editions are in the care of recognized academics who annotate the texts with footnotes that explain their historical and literary significance. Unlike Metz, who argues that literary prestige is dependent on the qualities of "bookishness" associated with print books, Hatry thus concludes that e-books are potentially more prestigious than print books because they are less dependent on the economic imperatives of the publishing industry. She also argues that innovative editorial projects like Clásicos Hispánicos challenge the stigma that e-book editions are of poor quality and display a lack of scholarly rigor, as they show that e-books also offer advantages for scholars and readers interested in serious literature by reducing the gap between upper-class readers, who can afford to buy expensive out-of-print editions, and lower-class readers, who no longer have to pay such exorbitant prices.

While Metz and Hatry disagree concerning the cultural status of electronic texts, Pasqualina Sorrentino and Massimo Salgaro's chapter "How Much Does the Symbolic Capital of Books Cost? Operationalizing the Prestige of Books in the Digital Age" outlines an empirical study that sought to determine how material substrates influence the perception of literary prestige.

Like many of the contributors to this volume, Sorrentino and Salgaro describe the prestige of literature as the product of a tension between symbolic and economic capital, as works that are heavily promoted, mass-produced, and commercially successful are often perceived as less serious and, therefore, less prestigious, and their study attempted to determine whether the material form of a literary text (as a print book or an e-book) was also seen as an indicator of its quality, appeal, or target audience. Based on the results of their study, Sorrentino and Salgaro argue that print books are still more deeply invested with symbolic capital than e-books, as they are perceived as more serious, rare, and expensive. Like Metz, therefore, they conclude that distinctions of taste are largely dependent on the material properties of literary texts and that print books continue to serve a crucial nonliterary function as markers of cultural status.

The editors hope that these diverse and stimulating contributions will provide valuable insight into the relationships and interdependencies between literary production and distinctions of taste. Through a broad survey of historical and contemporary case studies, the contributors have addressed the impact of materiality in many different cultural and temporal contexts, and this comparative approach clearly shows that prestige is not a fixed and stable entity that reflects a general consensus among the literary elite but rather a complex and ongoing process that reflects the interaction between many different actors, including writers, publishers, designers, printers, distributors, booksellers, reviewers, and readers. By comparing how the material properties of literary texts have reflected and shaped their cultural status in different countries and time periods, these case studies repeatedly demonstrate the malleability of literary prestige, particularly when a literary text is transferred from one material form to another, as many of the chapters show how texts that were originally received as lowbrow could later be received as highbrow through the acquisition of a new material form (and vice versa). The final section also shows how the material distinctions established during earlier historical periods are now being reconfigured through new forms of electronic display, which have the potential to reaffirm traditional distinctions of taste or create entirely new distinctions. While the theoretical concepts used by the contributors are often quite different, they all emphasize that the study of literary history encompasses more than just the study of literary form, as it also requires a consideration of the social, economic, and technological factors that influence literary production, distribution, and reception. A consideration of these factors also reveals that material distinctions are more relevant today than ever before due to the ever-expanding range of publishing formats, and there is still a need for more studies on the complex relationship between consumerism and prestige.

Notes

1 William Charvat, *The Profession of Authorship in America, 1800–1870*, ed. Matthew J. Bruccoli (Columbus: Ohio State University Press, 1968), 284.

2 Robert Darnton, *The Forbidden Best-Sellers of Pre-Revolutionary France* (New York: Norton, 1995), 184.

3 Joe Moran, *Star Authors: Literary Celebrity in America* (London: Pluto Press, 2000), 6–7.

4 James F. English, *The Economy of Prestige: Prizes, Awards, and the Circulation of Cultural Value* (Cambridge, MA: Harvard University Press, 2005), 4.

5 David Pearson, *Books as History: The Importance of Books Beyond Their Texts* (London: British Library; New Castle, DE: Oak Knoll Press, 2008), 38.

6 See Bonnie Mak, *How the Page Matters* (Toronto: University of Toronto Press, 2011); N. Katherine Hayles and Jessica Pressman (eds.), *Comparative Textual Media: Transforming the Humanities in the Postprint Era* (Minneapolis: University of Minnesota Press, 2013).

7 See Alexander Starre, *Metamedia: American Book Fictions and Literary Print Culture after Digitization* (Iowa City: University of Iowa Press, 2015); Kiene Brillenburg Wurth, Kári Driscoll, and Jessica Pressman (eds.), *Book Presence in a Digital Age* (New York: Bloomsbury, 2018); Heike Schaefer and Alexander Starre (eds.), *The Printed Book in Contemporary American Culture: Medium, Object, Metaphor* (Cham, CH: Palgrave Macmillan, 2019).

8 See Jennifer Tsien, *The Bad Taste of Others: Judging Literary Value in Eighteenth-Century France* (Philadelphia: University of Pennsylvania Press, 2012).

9 This development took approximately 20–30 years in all parts of this worldwide business, as David McKitterick writes concerning the UK: "For decades after 1800, books, periodicals, newspapers and all kinds of minor works continued to be set by hand, with type cast by hand, and printed by means of hand-presses. [...] But nevertheless, by about 1830 some of the major changes in manufacture, materials, market demands and economic possibilities had become sufficiently widespread for it to be possible to claim that a revolution of some kind had been effected." David McKitterick, "Introduction," in *The Cambridge History of the Book in Britain*, ed. John Barnard, D. F. McKenzie, David McKitterick, and I. R. Willison, 7 vols. (Cambridge: Cambridge University Press, 1998), 6: 1–74 (3).

10 David McKitterick, "Changes in the Look of the Book," in *The Cambridge History of the Book in Britain*, ed. John Barnard, D. F. McKenzie, David McKitterick, and I. R. Willison, 7 vols. (Cambridge: Cambridge University Press, 1998), 6: 75–116 (93).

11 Megan L. Benton, "Unruly Servants: Machines, Modernity, and the Printed Page," in *A History of the Book in America*, ed. David D. Hall, 5 vols. (Chapel Hill: University of North Carolina Press, 2000–2010), 4: 151–69 (154). The literary text most relevant to these developments is David Séchard's invention of reed-based paper for Honoré de Balzac's *Illusions perdues* (Lost Illusions, 1837–1843). For more on the connections between authorship, copyright, and paper production, see Heinrich Bosse, *Autorschaft ist Werkherrschaft: Über die Entstehung des Urheberrechts aus dem Geist der Goethezeit* (Paderborn: Schöningh, 1981).

12 McKitterick, "Changes in the Look of the Book," 95.

13 For a famous comparison of the traditional wooden press, the Stanhope press, and subsequent changes in the printing business, see the opening pages of Balzac's *Illusions perdues*.

14 Ronald J. Zboray, *A Fictive People: Antebellum Economic Development and the American Reading Public* (Oxford: Oxford University Press, 1993), 11. For more on these developments,

see Peter Neumann, "Herstellungstechnik und Buchgestaltung," in *Geschichte des Deutschen Buchhandels im 19. und 20. Jahrhundert. Bd. 1: Das Kaiserreich 1870–1918*, ed. Georg Jäger (Frankfurt: Buchhändler-Vereinigung and MVB Marketing- und Verlagsservice des Buchhandels, 2001), 170–96.

15 See Alois Senefelder, *Vollständiges Lehrbuch der Steindruckerey enthaltend eine richtige und deutliche Anweisung zu den verschiedenen Manipulations-Arten derselben in allen ihren Zweigen und Manieren belegt mit den nöthigen Musterblättern nebst einer vorangehenden ausführlichen Geschichte dieser Kunst von ihrem Entstehen bis auf gegenwärtige Zeit* (Munich: Thienemann, 1818).

16 Michael Twyman, "The Illustration Revolution," in *The Cambridge History of the Book in Britain*, ed. John Barnard, D. F. McKenzie, David McKitterick, and I. R. Willison, 7 vols. (Cambridge: Cambridge University Press, 1998), 6: 117–43 (143).

17 For more on the rise of women typesetters in the United States, see Zboray, *A Fictive People*, 6–11. For more on the rise of women typesetters in France, see Brigitte Robak, "Schriftsetzerin—Ein Beruf für Frauen. Pariser Projekt aus der Revolutionszeit," *Journal Geschichte* 2/3 (1991): 18–27. For more on the rise of women typesetters in Germany, see Brigitte Robak, *Vom Pianotyp zur Zeilensetzmaschine: Setzmaschinenentwicklung und Geschlechterfrage 1840–1900* (Marburg: Jonas, 1996).

18 Stanley Morison, *Memorandum on a Proposal to Revise the Typography of "The Times"* (London: *The Times*, 1930) and *Supplement to the Memorandum* (London: *The Times*, 1931). See also Claire Hoertz Badaracco, *Trading Words: Poetry, Typography, and Illustrated Books in the Modern Literary Economy* (Baltimore: Johns Hopkins University Press, 1995), 106–11.

19 Martyn Lyons, *A History of Reading and Writing in the Western World* (New York: Palgrave Macmillan, 2010), 139.

20 William J. Sonn, *Paradigms Lost: The Life and Deaths of the Printed Word* (Lanham, MD: Scarecrow Press, 2006), 166.

21 Lyons, *A History of Reading and Writing*, 140. See also Svend Dahl, *History of the Book* (New York: Scarecrow Press, 1958), 220; Reinhard Wittmann, *Geschichte des deutschen Buchhandels: Ein Überblick* (Munich: C. H. Beck, 1991), 271.

22 Badaracco, *Trading Words*, 4. Morison described the printing trade in the UK in 1930 as "ranking as the fourth industry in the country." Morison, *Memorandum*, 296.

23 Steven Roger Fischer, *A History of Reading* (London: Reaktion, 2003), 281.

24 John P. Feather, "The Book in History and the History of the Book," in *The History of Books and Libraries: Two Views*, ed. John P. Feather and David McKitterick (Washington, DC: Library of Congress, 1986), 1–16 (6).

25 Lyons, *A History of Reading and Writing*, 138.

26 Cathy N. Davidson, "Towards a History of Books and Readers," *American Quarterly* 40, no. 1 (1988): 7–17 (12).

27 See Rolf Engelsing, *Analphabetum und Lektüre: Zur Sozialgeschichte des Lesens in Deutschland zwischen feudaler und industrieller Gesellschaft* (Stuttgart: Metzler, 1973); *Rolf Engelsing Der Bürger als Leser: Lesergeschichte in Deutschland 1500–1800* (Stuttgart: Metzler, 1974); Erich Schön, *Der Verlust der Sinnlichkeit oder die Verwandlung des Lesers: Mentalitätswandel um 1800* (Stuttgart: Cotta, 1987).

28 Simon Eliot and Andrew Nash, "Mass Markets: Literature," in *The Cambridge History of the Book in Britain*, ed. John Barnard, D. F. McKenzie, David McKitterick, and I. R. Willison, 7 vols. (Cambridge: Cambridge University Press, 1998), 6: 416–42 (440).

29 Stephen Colclough, "Distribution," in *The Cambridge History of the Book in Britain*, ed. John Barnard, D. F. McKenzie, David McKitterick, and I. R. Willison, 7 vols.

(Cambridge: Cambridge University Press, 1998), 6: 238–80 (239). For more on print runs of best-selling books in nineteenth-century France, see Martyn Lyons, "Les best-sellers," in *Histoire de l'édition française*, ed. Henri-Jean Martin, Roger Chartier, and Jean-Pierre Vivet, 4 vols. (Paris: Promodis, 1985), 3: 369–97.

30 Simon Eliot and Andrew Nash, "Mass Markets," 423.

31 This was related to the so-called Klassikerjahr in 1867, going back to the Prussian Law dating from 1837 for the right of reprinting any text of an author during his lifetime and 30 years after his death. From 1867 on, the entire collection of German classical texts was in the public domain, which led to the formation of new publishing houses like Reclam. See *Reclam: 125 Jahre Universal-Bibliothek 1867–1992*, ed. Dietrich Bode (Stuttgart: Reclam, 1992).

32 Fischer, *A History of Reading*, 282.

33 Ibid., 280.

34 Lyons, *A History of Reading and Writing*, 142.

35 Jean-Yves Mollier and Marie-Françoise Cachin, "A Continent of Texts: Europe 1800–1890," in *A Companion to the History of the Book*, ed. Simon Eliot and Jonathan Rose (Oxford: Blackwell, 2007), 303–14 (308).

36 Eliot and Nash, "Mass Markets," 424.

37 See Graham Law and Robert L. Patten, "The Serial Revolution," in *The Cambridge History of the Book in Britain*, ed. John Barnard, D. F. McKenzie, David McKitterick, and I. R. Willison, 7 vols. (Cambridge: Cambridge University Press, 1998), 6: 144–71; Lise Queffélec, *Le roman-feuilleton français au XIXe siècle* (Paris: Presses Universitaires de France, 1989); Lise Dumasy, *La querelle du roman-feuilleton: Littérature, presse et politique, un débat précurseur* (Grenoble: Éditions littéraires et linguistiques de l'université de Grenoble, 1999).

38 Catherine Turner notes that advertisements began to appear on book jackets in 1829, and pictures began to appear in 1890. This was a common practice by the 1910s, and jackets became increasingly ornate in the 1920s. Catherine Turner, *Marketing Modernism between the Two World Wars* (Amherst: University of Massachusetts Press, 2003), 65.

39 Joseph McAleer, *Popular Reading and Publishing in Britain, 1914–1950* (Oxford: Clarendon Press, 1992), 51.

40 Wittmann, *Geschichte des deutschen Buchhandels*, 314.

41 By 1917 there were roughly 2,000 book-vending machines in operation in Germany, and they "exploited a hunger for self-education and a renewed cultural nationalism." Alistair McCleery, "The Paperback Evolution: Tauchnitz, Albatross and Penguin," in *Judging a Book by Its Cover: Fans, Publishers, Designers, and the Marketing of Fiction*, ed. Nicole Matthews and Nickianne Moody (Aldershot: Ashgate, 2007), 3–17 (4).

42 Director Allen Lane emphasized the importance of Penguin as a brand: "In making what amounted to the first serious attempt at introducing 'branded goods' to the book trade, we realized the cumulative publicity value of, first, a consistent and easily recognizable cover design, and, secondly, a good trade-mark that would be easy to say and easy to remember." Allen Lane, "Penguins and Pelicans," *The Penrose Annual* 40 (1938): 40–42 (42).

43 Pocket Books was founded in 1939, two years before Avon Books, and they sued Avon for plagiarizing their format, even though it was inspired by their European counterparts. McCleery, "The Paperback Evolution," 15.

44 James L. W. West III, "The Expansion of the National Book Trade System," in *A History of the Book in America*, ed. David D. Hall, 5 vols. (Chapel Hill: University of North Carolina Press, 2000–2010), 4: 78–89 (85).

45 Sidney Gross, "How to Stock," in *How to Run a Paperback Bookshop*, ed. Sidney Gross and Phyllis B. Steckler (New York: R. R. Bowker, 1965), 52–64 (58).

46 Michael Winship, "Manufacturing and Book Production," in *A History of the Book in America*, ed. David D. Hall, 5 vols. (Chapel Hill: University of North Carolina Press, 2000–2010), 3: 40–69 (59–60).

47 Janice A. Radway, *A Feeling for Books: The Book-of-the-Month Club, Literary Taste, and Middle-Class Desire* (Chapel Hill: University of North Carolina Press, 1997), 132–33.

48 Mary Noel, *Villains Galore: The Heyday of the Popular Story Weekly* (New York: Macmillan, 1954), 5–6.

49 Simon Eliot, "Circulating Libraries in the Victorian Age and After," in *The Cambridge History of Libraries in Britain and Ireland*, ed. Peter Hoare, 3 vols. (Cambridge: Cambridge University Press, 2006), 3: 125–46 (125).

50 Ibid., 128.

51 Andrew Nash, "Literary Culture and Literary Publishing in Inter-War Britain: A View from Chatto and Windus," in *Literary Cultures and the Material Book*, ed. Simon Eliot, Andrew Nash, and Ian Willison (London: British Library, 2007), 323–42 (326).

52 Martyn Lyons, "New Readers in the Nineteenth Century: Women, Children, Workers," in *A History of Reading in the West*, ed. Guglielmo Cavallo and Roger Chartier, trans. Lydia G. Cochrane (Amherst: University of Massachusetts Press, 1999), 313–44 (334).

53 Ibid., 333.

54 Lyons, *A History of Reading and Writing*, 148. For a more detailed description, see Wittmann, *Geschichte des deutschen Buchhandels*, 253–55.

55 Cathy N. Davidson, *Revolution and the Word: The Rise of the Novel in America* (Oxford: Oxford University Press, 1986), 41.

56 Noah Porter, *Books and Reading; or, What Books Shall I Read and How Shall I Read Them?* (New York: Scribner, 1871), 6.

57 Qtd. in John William Tebbel, *A History of Book Publishing in the United States*, 4 vols. (New York: R. R. Bowker, 1975), 2: 502–03. Complaints about the quantity of books being published actually date back to antiquity. See, for example, Tsien, *The Bad Taste of Others*, 14–38.

58 Radway, *A Feeling for Books*, 139.

59 Stanley Unwin, *The Truth About Publishing* (London: Allen & Unwin, 1926), 191.

60 Nash, "Literary Culture and Literary Publishing in Inter-War Britain," 324–25.

61 Q. D. Leavis, *Fiction and the Reading Public* (London: Chatto & Windus, 1939), 162.

62 Ibid., 7.

63 James Russell Lowell, *The Function of the Poet and Other Essays* (Boston: Houghton Mifflin, 1920), 62.

64 Leavis, *Fiction and the Reading Public*, 19.

65 Ibid., 17.

66 Ibid., 35.

67 Ibid.

68 Pierre Bourdieu, *The Rules of Art: Genesis and Structure of the Literary Field*, trans. Susan Emanuel (Stanford: Stanford University Press, 1995), 142.

69 Lawrence Rainey, *Institutions of Modernism: Literary Elites and Public Culture* (New Haven: Yale University Press, 1998), 75.

70 John Guillory, *Cultural Capital: The Problem of Literary Canon Formation* (Chicago: University of Chicago Press, 1993), 172.

71 Ellen Gruber Garvey, "Ambivalent Advertising: Books, Prestige, and the Circulation of Publicity," in *A History of the Book in America*, ed. David D. Hall, 5 vols. (Chapel Hill: University of North Carolina Press, 2000–2010), 4: 170–89 (171).

72 Bourdieu, *The Rules of Art*, 170.

73 English, *The Economy of Prestige*, 10.

74 Matt Erlin, "How to Think About Luxury Editions in Late Eighteenth- and Early Nineteenth-Century Germany," in *Publishing Culture and the "Reading Nation": German Book History in the Long Nineteenth Century*, ed. Lynne Tatlock (Rochester: Camden House, 2010), 25–54 (33–35). Otto Mazal also argues that decorative luxury in postrevolutionary France (as well as other European countries) influenced the aesthetics of bookbinding. Otto Mazal, *Einbandkunde: Die Geschichte des Bucheinbandes* (Wiesbaden: Reichert, 1997), 289. For more on luxury, taste, and publishing, see Michael Cahn, "*Opera Omnia*: The Production of Cultural Authority," in *History of Science, History of Text*, ed. Karine Chemla (Dordrecht: Springer, 2004), 81–94.

75 Ronald J. Zboray, "Antebellum Reading and the Ironies of Technological Innovation," *American Quarterly* 40, no. 1 (1988): 65–82 (74). For more on the "book fool" or "bibliomaniac" as a detested figure, see Bernhard Metz, "Bibliomania and the Folly of Reading," *Comparative Critical Studies* 5, no. 2 (2008): 249–69.

76 McKitterick, "Changes in the Look of the Book," 99.

77 Megan L. Benton, *Beauty and the Book: Fine Editions and Cultural Distinction in America* (New Haven: Yale University Press, 2000), 3.

78 *The Book World*, ed. Henry Scheurmier (London: Thomas Nelson, 1935), 153–54.

79 Nash, "Literary Culture and Literary Publishing in Inter-War Britain," 334.

80 Jim Collins, *Bring on the Books for Everybody: How Literary Culture Became Popular Culture* (Durham: Duke University Press, 2010), 33.

81 Radway, *A Feeling for Books*, 137.

82 Ibid., 145.

83 "Books in House Decoration," *New York Times*, April 14, 1878, 6.

84 Mary Benton, "'Too Many Books': Book Ownership and Cultural Identity in the 1920s," *American Quarterly* 49, no. 2 (1997): 268–97 (279).

85 Ibid., 280. For an analysis of advertising in German magazines, see Ursula Rautenberg, "Das Buch in der Alltagskultur: Eine Annäherung an zeichenhaften Buchgebrauch und die Medialität des Buches," in *Buchkulturen: Beiträge zur Geschichte der Literaturvermittlung. Festschrift für Reinhard Wittmann*, ed. Monika Estermann, Ernst Fischer, and Ute Schneider (Wiesbaden: Harrassowitz, 2005), 487–516.

86 Jeffrey D. Groves, "Judging Literary Books by Their Covers: House Styles, Ticknor and Fields, and Literary Promotion," in *Reading Books: Essays on the Material Text and Literature in America*, ed. Michele Moylan and Lane Stiles (Amherst: University of Massachusetts Press, 1996), 75–100 (76).

87 Ibid., 93.

88 Ibid., 78.

89 Pierre Bourdieu, *Distinction: A Social Critique of the Judgement of Taste*, trans. Richard Nice (Cambridge: Harvard University Press, 1984), 499–500.

90 Gérard Genette, *Paratexts: Thresholds of Interpretation*, trans. Jane E. Lewin (Cambridge: Cambridge University Press, 1997), 1.

91 Ibid., 2.

92 Jerome McGann, *The Textual Condition* (Princeton: Princeton University Press, 1991), 57–58. This distinction was also used in his later publications.

93 Ibid., 52.

Section One

MATERIAL FORMS AND LITERARY PUBLISHING

Chapter 1

DEVOTION AND CONSUMPTION: LUDWIG TIECK, LITERARY POCKETBOOKS, AND THE NOVELLA CRAZE

Christoph Rauen

Robert Musil once called Egon Erwin Kisch, also known as *der rasende Reporter* (the hurrying reporter), a *Tagesschriftsteller*: "[He was] not a poet who failed the test of eternity but rather one who ran away from it."[1] The term *Tagesschriftsteller*, which essentially means "journalist," stresses that journalistic texts are different compared to highbrow literature in that they are supposed to have an expiry date. It thus refers to the journalistic profession, which is concerned with issues of the day, rather than the "eternal" affairs that some think art deals with.

In this chapter, I want to address the opposition between these two models of writing and publishing and the role it played around 1820 and in the following decades. Roughly speaking, this time saw a shift toward a new kind of literary interest in realism. In 1805, Johann Gottfried Seume wrote: "The time of poetry is over, reality has arrived."[2] This sentence could serve as a motto for the writers associated with the name *Junges Deutschland* (Young Germany), who voted in favor of realism and were convinced that literature should be socially useful and promote political change.

Since the 1770s, however, other writers had promoted an opposite conception of art that was related not so much to the everyday but rather to the imagination. From this point of view, the right way to approach a work of art was considered to be devotion. Immanuel Kant, Friedrich Schiller, and the brothers August Wilhelm and Friedrich Schlegel, for example, regarded art as something that expresses the most noble and prestigious human ideas, such as freedom and happiness—a telos that the artist might never reach but nevertheless had to strive for.[3] This concept tended to isolate the work of art from its empirical context, from the time and place of its production and reception, and most certainly from all economic circumstances. From this perspective, art was considered to be untouchable and sacred.

Obviously, this model of art and literature contrasts with another one that highlights aspects of production and consumption. The latter views art as a kind of communication taking place between specific producers and an anonymous, mixed audience at a specific point in time and space. It conceives of art not as functionless and autonomous but rather as designed to cause specific effects, like empathy, which can be described in psychological terms.[4] According to this view, art is made to be consumed by a particular audience, which may or may not understand it but is willing to pay for it in order to fulfill certain needs and to react to certain wishes.[5] The tensions between the idealized and sacred conception of art and the empirical, pragmatic, and sometimes even cynical approach to writing, theater, and the visual arts can clearly be seen in the works of Ludwig Tieck, who started writing in the transitional period between the late Enlightenment and early Romanticism.

When the young Tieck wrote a psychological essay on poetic strategies and effects in William Shakespeare's plays, especially *A Midsummer Night's Dream* and *The Tempest*, and concentrated on the relationship between the supernatural and the question of plausibility, he was criticized rather harshly by August Wilhelm Schlegel, the most important critic of the *Jenaer Kreis* (Jena Circle) near Weimar, where Johann Wolfgang von Goethe lived. Schlegel claimed that whoever wrote this anonymously published essay was distracted by contingencies, was still reliant on the anachronistic principle of verisimilitude (instead of concentrating on the internal structure of the work of art), and did not have a grasp of the actual meaning of (autonomous) fiction.[6] After several years, in the collaborative collection *Herzensergießungen eines kunstliebenden Klosterbruders* (Outpourings of an Art-Loving Friar, 1796) and his novel *Franz Sternbalds Wanderungen* (Franz Sternbald's Journeying Years, 1798), Tieck became committed to an idea of art that might be called *kunstreligiös* (i.e., conceiving of art as a kind of goddess), as it was quite indifferent to its empirical surroundings, which he now considered to be mundane. An attitude of worship was the only right way to approach the works of Raphael, Michelangelo, and Dürer as well as Shakespeare and Goethe, because the study of these artists focused no longer on the technical and functional aspects of their works but rather on the transcendence that their works were said to provide.

Realism and idealization, autonomy and usefulness—these dichotomies lay at the very heart of early nineteenth-century aesthetics. Where did they stem from? According to Reinhard Wittmann, a "profanation and professionalization of literary production"[7] took place in the late eighteenth century, which stimulated the emergence of an emotional, social, and pseudo-religious concept of art that completely suppressed its economic and materialistic aspects:

> With the emergence of the new reading public and the modernization of the book distribution system, the role of the author became more professional, and the result was the "free writer," who on the one hand insisted on the autonomy of his creativity, but on the other hand had to submit to the laws of anonymous exchange of goods. In the last third of the century, however, this necessity of prostitution drove the author and the reader to an endeavor to intensify the contact with the recipient or producer, to build a community of souls founded by the book whose commodification was suppressed.[8]

In Tieck's early texts, the conflicting perspectives of autonomy and commodification are almost always of great significance, even when, at least on the surface, they might be dealing with only one of them. This has to do with the trajectory of his career as a writer. Having left college without a degree, he began to produce very quickly numerous texts of varying quality for the powerful publisher Friedrich Nicolai in Berlin, whose fame had originated in the heyday of the Enlightenment, when he had been closely associated with Gotthold Ephraim Lessing and Moses Mendelssohn. The tales (and one short play) through which Tieck made his living were called *Straußfedern* (Ostrich Feathers, 1795–1798) and were published anonymously. He also supplied the publishing company of Nicolai's son Carl August with manuscripts, among them such well-known works as *Der gestiefelte Kater* (Puss in Boots, 1797) and *Der blonde Eckbert* (Blond Eckbert, 1797). When he began to correspond with August Wilhelm Schlegel, Tieck seems to have had in mind texts like the *Straußfedern* when he eagerly admitted to having treated art with contempt so far, meaning he had to prostitute himself on the literary market, as Wittmann puts it, and he failed to invest the time and vigilance necessary to reach the lofty heights of high art. In a letter of confession, he displayed a great amount of self-loathing and submissiveness: "I am devoted to art, I even worship it, it is the deity that I believe in, and that is why I would like to produce something of considerable value at some point in time."[9] Please note the way he addresses art as an ideal—something of such tremendous estimation that it has yet to be fully realized—as well as his willingness to completely discard everything he has worked on in the past.

Literary Pocketbooks

If there is one form of publication that is most perfectly suited to illustrate the opposing conceptions of art in the early nineteenth century, as discussed

earlier, then it has to be what was called the *literarisches Taschenbuch* or "literary pocketbook." This is because it can serve as a container and medium of
ideal art, like any other format, but it can barely hide its mundane and even
profane character because its status as a commodity is so obvious. Invented
together with the *Musenalmanach* (Muses' Almanac) in the last third of the
eighteenth century, it is usually defined by its small format, which made it
easy to carry and read wherever you please. This sets it apart from older formats like the folio, which, by contrast, now appeared to be immobile, heavy,
and old-fashioned. As Wittmann explains,

> At the beginning of the bourgeois reading culture of the Age of Enlightenment,
> the handy octave format had prevailed, and over the course of the next decades
> books became ever slimmer and smaller [...]. Often the interior corresponded
> to the delicate appearance—the literary, especially poetic, small forms asserted
> themselves alongside the novel as preferred genres. Their form of presentation
> was the almanac, the poetic pocketbook [...]. The literary pocketbooks were
> soon accompanied by scientific and popular ones as well as political and satiri-
> cal almanacs; in total, more than two thousand of these appealing, indeed
> luxurious little volumes were published.[10]

Tieck's contemporary Jean Paul also recalled "the old, very heavy folios,
bound in wood, leather, brass fittings and brackets, venerable stools of scholarly life with brass tacks," and he claimed that pocketbooks were an improvement, as "pigskin leather turned into Morocco leather, brass points to gold
rims, brackets and metal buckles to silk linings."[11] Jean Paul was thus pleas-
antly surprised about this change in the book market, as he was clearly fond
of the elegant and refined character of these books as artifacts, and he did not
lament the disappearance of traditional formats and, in general, cultural loss.
Please also note that the downsizing of books went hand-in-hand with a process of refinement and dematerialization, which reflected the trend toward
spiritualization in aesthetics, as documented in Georg Hegel's lectures on art
held in Berlin in the 1820s.

The content of this medium was typically selected according to the principle of variety.[12] Unlike a *Musenalmanach*, a pocketbook featured not only poetry
but also prose, scholarly essays, and occasionally even charades, riddles, and
sheet music. Obviously, this mixture was aimed at the needs, expectations,
and wishes of a highly differentiated and at the same time sociable audience.
Furthermore, the same edition could be produced in several different versions
with different bindings, covers, paper stock, ornamentation, and so on, in
order to appeal to different types of buyers. For example, an editorial notice in
Johann Friedrich Gleditsch's *Taschenbuch zum geselligen Vergnügen auf das Jahr 1822*

(Pocketbook for Social Enjoyment for the Year 1822), which contained the first in a series of successful novellas by Tieck, *Die Gemälde* (The Paintings), refers to a "better edition" with colored engravings depicting Cupid and Psyche. One of the most famous texts published in a pocketbook around 1800, Goethe's *Hermann und Dorothea* (Hermann and Dorothea), is said to have been produced in no less than eight different versions.[13] It must also not be forgotten that these texts could later be republished as part of complete editions.

The special status of prose is particularly significant with regard to the novellas that Tieck published in pocketbooks. A shift from poetry to prose took place at the end of the Goethezeit, as the enthusiasm of the *Sturm und Drang* (Storm and Stress) movement and early Romanticism gave way to the more moderate, sober tendencies of the Biedermeier era and the *Vormärz* (Pre-March, referring to the period preceding the 1848 March Revolution). I will return to this topic later, but for now we need to consider whether the form of the pocketbook "as a novelty, a piece of art, precious luxury and as a product of fashion"[14] inspired skepticism regarding the seriousness of its content. Attracting consumer acceptance at least partly by means of its looks, it risked appearing to be superficial, if not vain. Thus, Roger Paulin comments on Tieck's "turn to the pocketbook," which coincided with his move to Dresden in 1819:

> There has been talk about a descent into literary production following fashion, and Friedrich Schlegel certainly expressed not only his own opinion when he stated that he regretted Tieck's turning away from "poetry." The terms "pattern card," "fashion article" or "taste of the public" in the correspondence with Heinrich Brockhaus make it clear that for Tieck high literary quality alone was not indicative.[15]

One of the most important aspects of the production and consumption of pocketbooks was the annual frequency of their publication. As Klussmann observed, "By naming a year, which is usually attached directly to its title, the pocketbook identifies itself as the current annual edition as well as a serialized operation that seeks to recruit readers for future publications."[16] One of the aspects of this serial form is that authors were commonly associated with certain pocketbooks, and contracts ensured that they provided new material for each issue: "Publishers wooed respected authors, who were enticed to produce new works whose delivery was agreed upon in advance."[17] Another aspect is the yearly deadlines, which might be said to have fostered a "standardized" way of writing. This seems to have been the case with Tieck, who employed an occasionally formulaic way of writing in his novellas, especially with respect to characters and plots.

One aspect of periodicals like newspapers, almanacs, and pocketbooks has, up to this point, not yet received the attention it deserves—namely, the fact that current issues will invariably be replaced by new ones. This form of planned obsolescence might very well have contributed to the somewhat dubious reputation of pocketbooks, which "by virtue of their materiality alone [...] evoke the idea of closure and timelessness."[18] This was why Goethe and Tieck took precautions to be entitled to republish texts that first saw the light of day in pocketbooks within complete editions. By this strategy, timelessness and transcendence—the very principles on which the prestige of sacred art was based and which were jeopardized by the pocketbook later—could to some extent be regained.

The trend toward more precious and costly designs was also perhaps meant to counteract the impression of superficiality and transience created by the seriality of their production. As "beautiful and precious objects," pocketbooks were more likely to be kept in "a special or preferred place [...] for valuable and important items, where readers might plan to collect a series of the same or competing pocketbooks as beautiful possessions."[19] Readers of this medium were, of course, not supposed to reread the same issues again and again, thereby perhaps exploring different layers of meaning; rather, they were encouraged to consume the current issue quickly in order to make way for a new one. This permanent renewal surely undermined the devotional quality assigned to literature as art, and it brought the category of "consumption" into play as a description of a certain mode of literary reception that was associated with using, eating, or burning something up.

Reflections within the Text

Let us now examine some references to literary production, extensive reading, and the consumption of books *within* the works that Tieck published in periodicals or pocketbook series. His early play *Die Theegesellschaft* (The Tea Party, 1797) was part of the abovementioned annual collection *Straußfedern*, which young Tieck supervised on behalf of Nicolai. In the beginning of the play, its protagonist Werner is utterly disappointed because he has been dumped by his loved one in favor of a shady aristocrat who later reveals himself to be a crook. At one point he mentions that in need of distraction he found relief in books written by Carl Gottlob Cramer—an infamous but in economic terms highly successful writer of gothic novels and chivalric romances in the late eighteenth century, who can be compared to Christian August Vulpius, Carl Friedrich August Grosse, and Christian Heinrich Spieß. Reading them one after the other seems to soften the effects of Werner's depression, but at the same time it reflects on an important connection between misanthropy, melancholy, and consumption. Werner, who is well aware of the low status of Cramer's works, exhibits the desperate and, at the same time, humorous attitude of somebody who thinks he has been betrayed by life and is no longer obliged to engage with content that expresses self-esteem:

> When I was in love, everything was very dear to my heart; I took my bride to the theatre and watched Kotzebue's plays with great devotion; I discussed the sermons of the local preachers; I read the literary journal to keep up my good taste; I went with silken stockings, even in bad weather, and read Woldemar to her with great emotion;—I, in short, lived as wisely and deliberately as one can ask; but now everything has gone to hell.[20]

Werner is openly embracing profanity because his more passionate, dutiful, and elaborate ambitions have led him nowhere. For him, there is no use anymore in honing his taste, keeping it up to date, and cultivating the sensibility propelled by serious literature. Having become aesthetically careless, he no longer expects books to bring out the best in him but instead regards them as only a means to kill time: "I can sit for half a day and think of nothing, or look out the window and talk with the acquaintances who pass by, or have delivered some of Cramer's novels, which I then read to myself—sometimes I even wish that I could smoke tobacco."[21] Consuming tobacco, the most mundane drug of them all, can be seen as the ultimate habit of profanity. Just like looking out of the window for hours or reading trashy novels, it is a way of almost sinfully wasting time—an obscene inversion of the values of the late Enlightenment, motivated by rejection and ultimately by being forced to acknowledge the worthlessness of it all. Getting things deliberately wrong is Werner's way of surviving a world gone wrong.

The next example I want to briefly examine is Tieck's *Poetisches Journal* (Poetic Journal, 1800), a one-man periodical that was only published once and that already featured, as Roger Paulin put it, "the typical mixture of late Romantic and Biedermeier pocketbooks."[22] It contained, for example, a play, an aesthetic diary, an essay on mythology, and poetry. In the introduction, Tieck addresses the futility and lack of results of all attempts at establishing serious art and art criticism in the German-speaking world. Right at the heyday of Romanticism, an era that Germans typically view as the golden age of German literature, he talks about art as being completely degraded and treated as a kind of luxury good and commodity, which is here today and gone tomorrow. Through habitualization, he claims, art has become a kind of secondary need, similar to physical needs like hunger, which contrasts sharply with the ideal and divine quality it can develop when exercised properly. The most perverted attitude toward art, however, is using it for pedagogical purposes. Here, again, functionality indicates profanity:

> In every country poetry and art have already been treated for a long time as
> manufactured goods, which an increase in luxury also made necessary, and
> those who sought to distinguish themselves by an eminently reasonable way
> of thinking put it this way: poetry and art make people human, and more art
> produces more humanity, so any man who does not want to appear unedu
> cated must in his leisure time not only learn the principles of criticism but even
> proceed to good reading in order to avoid being left behind in the realm of
> refined humanity.[23]

The abovementioned shift to prose and the rise of the pocketbook as one of
the most popular publishing forms, which began in the 1820s, were accompanied by the success of a certain genre of narrative, and Tieck put himself at
the forefront of this development:

> Tieck's second production phase, which began in the 1820s and deals exclu
> sively with prose, represents this historical restructuring of the genre system
> [...] : on the one hand the turning away from other literary genres or styles
> respectively (poetry, drama) in favor of prose and, on the other hand, within
> the production of novellas, the departure from romantic and fantastic narra
> tives in favor of a new, more realistic way of writing, which, although it can
> not yet be described as "realistic" in the historical sense of "Bürgerlicher" or
> "Poetischer Realismus," establish a new type of narrative by representing that
> everyday reality that was considered by the Goethean aesthetics to be of no
> literary value.[24]

Tieck's work from the 1820s, 1830s, and early 1840s consisted almost entirely
of novellas, which were first published in pocketbooks, and these novellas also
incorporated the imagery and semantics of books and periodicals as well as
extensive or consumptive reading. He especially loved to poetically ruminate
on the production and consumption of books and to use this as a springboard
for philosophical and religious reflections. I will give just one example by
citing his novella *Des Lebens Überfluß* (Life's Luxuries, 1839), which was first
published in *Urania: Taschenbuch auf das Jahr 1839*. There is one passage in this
text that perfectly illustrates the dubious image of periodical publication I
mentioned earlier. This assumed inferiority is so striking that it can be used
metaphorically to evoke the protagonist's most dreadful fears of obliteration.
Heinrich Brand, as he is called, has fled together with his lover Clara when
her father denied them permission to get married. No longer able to make

a living as a diplomat, they run out of money and have to start selling their belongings in order to survive. One night Brand experiences a nightmare that clearly reflects his fears of social degradation, as he dreams of being auctioned with nobody willing to bid on him. The auctioneer then includes him in a combined lot: "Since nobody wants to offer anything for this diplomat, we will combine him with these three journalists: a stale editor of a weekly paper, a writer of correspondence articles, and a theater critic. What is now offered for this bunch?"[25] This group of journalists is thus composed of an editor, a critic, and somebody who writes "correspondence articles," which could refer to a journalistic correspondent or an agent and informer, as these were the days of political persecution, which ended with the German revolution of 1848. Eventually "a dirty little Jewish boy" is willing to pay a hilariously small amount of money for the whole package.[26] Obviously, these were also times when anti-Semitism was gaining strength, and Tieck could not resist conforming to common resentments here.

I want to end with another short passage that addresses the topic of consumption. Back in 1798, when the aesthetics of idealism were in bloom, Goethe wrote that "real" art always elevates the recipient's existence: "[The true enthusiast] feels that he must rise to the artist in order to enjoy the work; he feels that he must concentrate and leave all distractions behind, to live with the work of art, to look at it repeatedly, and thereby obtain a higher form of existence."[27] The idea of living with and repeatedly looking at art clearly illustrates the distinction between intensive and extensive reception. More than 30 years later, in *Des Lebens Überfluß*, Tieck plays around with this distinction and finds some entertaining illustrations for it. As winter approaches, Heinrich and Clara finally have to burn their staircase in order to not freeze to death. When their landlord returns from a trip and finds the staircase gone, Heinrich tells him that it has been "consumed" because they did not really need it: "[It belonged to] the superfluities of life, the vain luxury, the useless inventions. If it is noble to limit one's needs, to be content with what is yours, as many philosophers claim, these useless stairs have saved me from freezing to death."[28] Heinrich thus describes a useful element in everyday life, a staircase, as nothing more than a kind of luxury good that merely fulfills what has become a secondary need. To do without it is even regarded as noble-minded, as he considers everything that does not fulfill their primary, vital need as superfluous. In other words, Heinrich and Clara can do without the staircase, which connected them to the social world, because they prefer their isolated, poetic existence on the upper floor. Consumption thus becomes a means of breaking through to what is considered to be of real worth.

In conclusion, Tieck was always very much aware of the distinction between intensive and extensive writing, publishing, and reading, and he often tended to speak in favor of the former, especially during the era of early Romanticism, when he and the *Jenaer Kreis* promoted an esoteric understanding of art. In addition, he had a profound sensibility for the complex cultural and economic realities of literature, including its commodification. He was surely able, though not always willing, to refrain from an elitist judgment about popular culture;[29] yet his acceptance of the more mundane and inclusive aspects of literature seems to have increased after the 1820s, when he became the leading author of novellas published within pocketbooks—a periodical format associated with fashionable but not necessarily lasting works of art. The tension between these two modes of production and reception continued to inform his work, and it served as one of the most important topics and sources of conflict in his novellas. While Tieck did not unambiguously promote one mode in favor of the other or critique the rise of consumptive reading per se, he did address the dissonant and complementary perspectives on literature described in this chapter, and he used them as a platform for developing a witty and aesthetically appealing form of prose.

Notes

1 Robert Musil, "Almanach auf das Jahr 1925 (Ende 1924): Mit den dreihundertfünfundsechzig Geschenkbüchern überreicht von der Hellerschen Buchhandlung (Wien I)," in *Gesammelte Werke*, ed. Adolf Frisé, 9 vols. (Reinbek bei Hamburg: Rowohlt, 1978), 2: 1714–16 (1715).

2 Johann Gottfried Seume, *Mein Sommer 1805* (Leipzig: Steinacker, 1806), 146.

3 Stefan Matuschek, "Literarischer Idealismus. Oder: Eine mittlerweile 200-jährige Gewohnheit, über Literatur zu sprechen," *Deutsche Vierteljahrsschrift für Literaturwissenschaft und Geistesgeschichte* 3 (2012): 397–418.

4 This is important because to stress the effects of art is to underline that it fulfills a function for the reader, which is rarely thematized within the frame of an idealized concept of art. See Frauke Gries on the "Briefe über Shakespeare," in Tieck's *Poetisches Journal* (1800): "Significantly Tieck includes observations on the interconnectedness of writer and audience, as he did in his earlier paper on Shakespeare. But now he is less concerned with the psychological effect of a drama on the spectator; the author's dependence on his audience is stressed. At the same time, the dramatist can educate and shape these people by confronting them with his poetic work." Frauke Gries, "Ludwig Tieck as Critic: Sociological Tendencies in his Criticism," PhD diss. (Stanford University, 1967), 32–33.

5 See the story of the fictitious composer Joseph Berglinger in *Herzensergießungen eines kunstliebenden Klosterbruders*, who has to make a living by composing music for a superficial courtly audience while strongly believing in a metaphysical concept of art.

6 Ludwig Tieck, "Über Shakspeare's Behandlung des Wunderbaren," in *Schriften in zwölf Bänden*, ed. Manfred Frank, Achim Hölter, Ruprecht Wimmer, and Uwe Schweikert, 12 vols. (Frankfurt am Main: Deutscher Klassiker Verlag, 1991), 1: 681–722, 1235–49. For Schlegel's review, first published in March 1797 in the *Allgemeine Literatur-Zeitung*, see Ibid., 1219–24.

7 Reinhard Wittmann, "Der Roman um 1800 auf dem Buchmarkt: Eine Handvoll Digressionen," in *August Lafontaine (1758–1831): Ein Bestsellerautor zwischen Spätaufklärung und Romantik*, ed. Cord-Friedrich Berghahn and Dirk Sangmeister (Bielefeld: Verlag für Regionalgeschichte, 2010), 21–40 (37).

8 Ibid., 34.

9 Ludwig Tieck und die Brüder Schlegel, *Briefe*, ed. Edgar Lohner (Munich: Winkler, 1972), 25.

10 Reinhard Wittmann, *Geschichte des deutschen Buchhandels* (Munich: C. H. Beck, 1999), 220–21.

11 Cited Ibid., 200–01.

12 Paul Gerhard Klussmann, "Das Taschenbuch im literarischen Leben der Romantik und Biedermeierzeit: Begriff, Konzept, Wirkung," in *Literarische Leitmedien: Almanach und Taschenbuch im kulturwissenschaftlichen Kontext*, ed. Paul Gerhard Klussmann and York-Gothart Mix (Wiesbaden: Harrossowitz, 1998), 47–64 (55).

13 Ibid., 56.

14 Ibid., 53–54.

15 Roger Paulin, "Ludwig Tieck und die Musenalmanache und Taschenbücher: Modellfall oder Ausnahme?," in *Literarische Leitmedien: Almanach und Taschenbuch im kulturwissenschaftlichen Kontext*, ed. Paul Gerhard Klussmann, York-Gothart Mix (Wiesbaden: Harrossowitz, 1998), 133–45 (139).

16 Klussmann, "Das Taschenbuch im literarischen Leben der Romantik und Biedermeierzeit," 47.

17 Ibid., 59.

18 Philipp Böttcher, "Tieck und seine Verleger," in *Ludwig Tieck: Leben–Werk–Wirkung*, ed. Claudia Stockinger and Stefan Scherer (Berlin: De Gruyter, 2011), 148–64 (162).

19 Klussmann, "Das Taschenbuch im literarischen Leben der Romantik und Biedermeierzeit," 52–53.

20 Ludwig Tieck, "Die Theegesellschaft," *Straußfedern* 7 (1797): 145–206 (153–54).

21 Ibid., 154.

22 Paulin, "Ludwig Tieck und die Musenalmanache und Taschenbücher," 136.

23 Ludwig Tieck, "Einleitung," *Poetisches Journal* 1, no. 1 (1800): 1–10 (1–2).

24 Wolfgang Lukas and Madleen Podewski, "Novellenpoetik," in *Ludwig Tieck: Leben–Werk–Wirkung*, ed. Claudia Stockinger and Stefan Scherer (Berlin: De Gruyter, 2011), 353–64 (355).

25 Ludwig Tieck, "Des Lebens Überfluß," in *Schriften in zwölf Bänden*, ed. Manfred Frank, Achim Hölter, Ruprecht Wimmer, and Uwe Schweikert, 12 vols. (Frankfurt am Main: Deutscher Klassiker Verlag, 1986), 12: 193–249 (233).

26 Ibid., 223.

27 Johann Wolfgang von Goethe, "Über Wahrheit und Wahrscheinlichkeit der Kunstwerke: Ein Gespräch," in *Werke*, ed. Erich Trunz, 14 vols. (Munich: Deutscher Taschenbuch Verlag, 1998), 12: 67–73 (72).

28 Tieck, "Des Lebens Überfluß," 240–41.

29 See also Ludwig Tieck, introduction to *Die Insel Felsenburg oder wunderliche Fata einiger Seefahrer: Eine Geschichte aus dem Anfange des achtzehnten Jahrhunderts*, ed. Johann Gottfried Schnabel, 6 vols. (Breslau: Josef Max und Komp, 1828), 1: v-liii. See also Stefan Martus, "Der Literaturkritiker," in *Ludwig Tieck: Leben–Werk–Wirkung*, ed. Claudia Stockinger and Stefan Scherer (Berlin: De Gruyter, 2011), 389–407.

Chapter 2

PACKAGING PROCESS: PETER HANDKE'S WRITING FOR SALE

Jacob Haubenreich

The Weight of the World

In 1975, Austrian writer Peter Handke began an experiment in writing that continues to the present: a practice of daily note-taking. A space for "spontaneous recording of aimless perceptions," Handke's notebooks are heterogeneous in both their semantic content and material form: montages of thoughts, impressions, landscape descriptions, and reading notes are inscribed in pencil and colored ink into pocket-sized notebooks of different bindings and paper qualities with a range of inserted ephemera.[1] In describing his process, Handke writes: "I now practiced reacting to everything that befell me immediately with language. [...] It is not the narration of a consciousness, rather an immediate, simultaneously captured reportage of it."[2] The majority of Handke's notebooks from 1975 to 2018 have been acquired by the Deutsches Literaturarchiv in Marbach, which currently houses 229 notebooks containing more than 33,000 pages. Handke's notebooks are neither diaries nor journals in the traditional sense nor merely "pre-text" for to-be-published works. Rather, they are part of a distinct artistic-writerly project that undergirds much of Handke's published work.[3]

In 1977, Handke published *Das Gewicht der Welt: Ein Journal (November 1975–März 1977)* (The Weight of the World: A Journal [November 1975–March 1977]). The book was the first in what would become a series of so-called journal volumes containing selections of notes edited and transformed into typographic text. The journal volumes are essentially abridged versions of Handke's notebooks, indications of the manuscript wholes from which they were drawn. The cover of *Das Gewicht der Welt*, however, offers the reader a literal glimpse of the notebooks from which it was produced: a color facsimile

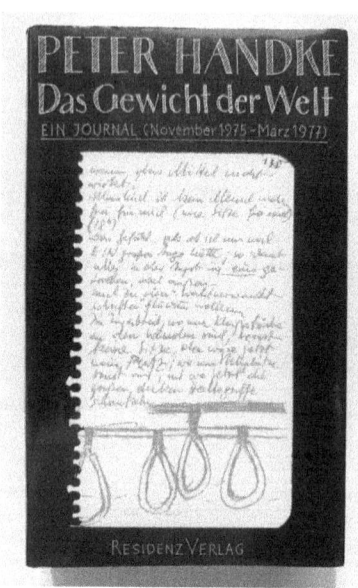

Figure 2.1 Peter Handke, *Das Gewicht der Welt* (1977). *Source*: © Residenz Verlag.

of a torn-out page with both written script and a drawing of tramcar hand-holds (see Figure 2.1). The title, author's name, and publisher's name are also handwritten, rather than in typeface, and printed in orange and white, the visuality and materiality of the notebook page thus expanded through the cover design to envelop the book's printed contents. Semantically, the fac-similed notes capture a feeling of exclusion or isolation ("Gradually no one is free for me"). Seeing and reading ("ONE large eye; wanting to retreat to 'Elective Affinities'"),[4] which would become two central topics for Handke, are evoked, tinged here with feelings of anxiety and withdrawal. The space of the tramcar morphs into a quasi-ontological projection of Handke's "place" in the world: "In the train compartment with only folding seats on the walls, otherwise no seats, that would be my place now; where there is otherwise now only standing room, and where the large, thick hand holds are now swaying." Standing rather than sitting, swaying in the movement of the car, the pas-senger is stabilized by the grasp of the hand—an image that metaphorically grasps Handke's writerly relationship to the world, the ideal place of his writ-ing: not seated at a desk but perpetually in motion, on the go. Preserved in his notebooks, Handke's notes remain as traces of his journeys both physical and writerly.

On page 112 of *Das Gewicht der Welt*, the reader again encounters the man-uscript reproduced on the cover, this time in printed form:

More and more people are "taken" when I want them (like seats at the movies) / Wanting to flee to "Elective Affinities" / The feeling that I have only *one* big eye; in my fear everything seems fused into one and projected outward / In a train compartment with folding seats along the walls, jiggling straps, and no place to sit down—this is where I belong now [emphasis in original].[5]

The reader is thus afforded the opportunity to compare the two versions, to consider a range of transformations that have taken place in moving from manuscript to print: syntactic, lexical, and orthographic changes, as well as reorderings, additions, and eliminations. That is to say, the reader is enabled, for an instant, to engage in the activity of a text philologist. The representation of the scene of writing on the cover of the published book offers a peek into its manuscript origins. The reader thus enters the text through the so-called pre-text, through the invocation, indeed visualization, of its earlier, alternative incarnation.

From their cover designs to their papers and bindings to the inclusion of manuscript facsimiles within their pages, Handke's published books confront the reader with their origins in handwork. The practices of note taking and hand drafting are essential to Handke's poetological project of slowness, careful observation, and re-sacralization of life through literature. This project emerged out of a crisis of writing in the late 1970s that led to a so-called classical turn or turn to nature—a reorientation from the more overtly politicized, experimental avant-garde poetics of his earlier work toward a mode of narration informed by German Romanticism and Classicism.[6] In a rapid-paced, technologically mediated modernity defined by a seemingly hollow proliferation of texts and images, Handke's books are "slow reads" by design.[7]

Part of the slowness results from a range of strategies by which Handke's printed books stop the reader in her tracks and open a vista onto the scenes of their production. In some cases, such as *Das Gewicht der Welt*, excerpted drawings or whole notebook pages are reproduced in facsimile as cover illustrations. The book jackets of Handke's five *Versuche* (essays) are facsimiles of the first manuscript page of each text, wrapping the printed versions in their manuscript origins.[8] In *Abschied des Träumers vom neunten Land* (The Dreamer's Farewell to the Ninth Country, 1991), images of notebook pages are interspersed among printed pages, staging a direct confrontation of manuscript and print.[9] Facsimiles of full-length manuscripts have also been published in limited editions, and in 2015 Insel-Bücherei released an affordable, mass-market facsimile edition of a notebook.[10]

While such facsimiles visualize the scene of (hand)writing, other paratextual elements conjure the materiality of handmade books. *Das Gewicht der Welt*, for example, was bound using a composite binding with visible gatherings of leaves both sewn and glued to the spine. In many of Handke's books published by Suhrkamp Verlag, the use of laid papers and sewn binding techniques render the text a more materially valuable object, in turn conferring a sense of literary value. Though machine-fabricated, these material elements mimic handmade paper and manual bookbinding techniques. These design features are in fact typical of hardbacks by Suhrkamp Verlag; as part of Handke's texts, however, they take on additional layers of significance, becoming meaningful extensions of the writer's broader poetological project in ways that challenge the basic distinction between "text" and "paratext." The material, visual forms of Handke's books are not incidental to the "texts" they contain; rather, they work together in the integrated experience of reading.

Handke often played an active role in the design of his books, as is documented in his published correspondence with Suhrkamp Verlag editor-in-chief Siegfried Unseld. Extensive exchange regarding the design of Handke's second novel *Der Hausierer* (The Peddler, 1967) demonstrates just how much emphasis Handke placed on paratextual features. For example, he makes the following requests:

> The first: to approximate (not precisely mimic) a detective novel in the design of the book. [...] The book should not be finely bound, but rather a paperback like all detective novels. [...] The font size should be maximally larger than in *Die Hornissen* [The Hornets, 1966], so that each sentence will strike a blow. Each sentence should be recognizable as an individual sentence, not as a sentence in a succession of sentences. Each sentence should be readable for itself, so that the reader can stumble after each sentence. (He also should.) That would also ease the experience of reading, since the text demands a change in reading habits, and the attempt to read the text "as a novel" would immediately present resistance, exhausting and frustrating the reader.[11]

Modeled on the cheap paperback detective novel, the design aesthetics of this early work contrast markedly with those that would come to characterize many of Handke's books from the late 1970s onward, after his poetological "turn." But already in his early works, one sees that for Handke typographical form is not incidental to semantic and linguistic textual features; the larger font size, Handke asserts here, is necessary in order to produce a specific effect: namely, a deceleration of the reading pace that will force the reader to "stumble" over every sentence, to experience it as text—written and occupying space on a page—in its own right.

Through various paratextual strategies the readers of Handke's work are frequently confronted with evocations of manual production processes that similarly cause them to "stumble," to pause and notice its material, visual form. These design features could be easily dismissed as gimmicks of today's consumerist economy that capitalize on the nostalgia for and a renewed interest in artisanal methods and analogue practices. Yet, these are not merely market-driven "paratextual" stunts; rather, they participate in defamiliarizing the mass-produced book in ways that extend Handke's project of reauratization into the very materiality of his mass-disseminated books. From glimpses into their manuscript origins to binding and typographical features reminiscent of manual craft, the design of Handke's first editions often conveys qualities of unique artworks in ways that not only endow them with a sense of prestige but can also be understood as part of his project of elevating literature as an art form. This chapter examines several remarkable examples representing a range of strategies by which Handke draws the scene of writing into the published form of his books, making process part of product in ways that challenge and expand, I suggest, our basic notions of what constitutes literature.

Slow Homecoming

In 1978, Handke undertook a trip to Alaska and across the continental United States, writing extensively in his notebooks along the route. His notes served as the basis for *Langsame Heimkehr* (Slow Homecoming, 1979), the first text of a tetralogy by the same name.[12] The semi-autobiographical text describes European geologist Valentin Sorger's "search for forms" in the Alaskan landscape through observing and studying traces of the *longue durée* of geological time visible in layers of the earth's crust.[13] Sorger's experience of the landscape was crucially mediated by processes of careful recording, specifically drawing: "Even in his work, he preferred drawing to photography, because it was only through drawing that he came to understand the landscape in all its forms."[14] Visual and material acts of representation are also key topics of the subsequent text in the tetralogy *Die Lehre der Sainte-Victoire* (The Lesson of Mont Sainte-Victoire, 1980). An extensive engagement with the painting of Paul Cézanne, which began on the heels of his North America trip, led Handke to undertake two trips—in July and December 1979—to Aix-en-Provence to travel the Route Cézanne, a path through the countryside along sites that Cézanne painted repeatedly. Handke's own travels in the painter's footsteps, his retrospective observations of and notes on Cézanne's "*réalisation*" of nature in paint, became the basis for *Die Lehre*. Products of a new aesthetic program that emerged out of a deep crisis of writing, *Langsame Heimkehr* and *Die Lehre* have been understood, both by scholars and by Handke himself, to represent a turning point in his career. Like the protagonist Sorger,

Handke was engaged in a writerly "search for forms" during this period, honing his attunement to inner and outer worlds and searching for a mode of representation adequate to capture and transform his experiences into text.

Handke's "search for forms" included experimentation not only with note taking and narration but also with the material and visual designs of his books as integral components of the writerly *réalisation* of nature and lived experience. The first edition of *Langsame Heimkehr* is hardbound with a linen cover, laid endpapers, and a fake smythe-sewn binding (the pages appear to be gathered but are glued together rather than sewn), all features that simulate manual production techniques. The dust jacket is particularly striking (see Figure 2.2): composed of white laid paper, it features no illustrations; the title, author's name, and publisher's name are printed per Handke's specification in a "type-writer font."[15] These are concentrated in the top third of the surface, leaving two-thirds of the jacket blank. As many sellers' notes on used copies attest, the jacket is particularly prone to wear, tear, and discoloration; indeed, the texture of the laid paper (the grooves in its surface) encourages the accumulation of dirt, which becomes particularly visible on the white paper. While protecting the cover, this *Schutzumschlag* (dust jacket, literally "protective cover") is simultaneously a *Schmutzumschlag* (dust cover) that *accumulates* dust over time. By dint of its resolute blankness, the jacket itself becomes a kind of record-keeper, an inscriptional surface, an index of the *longue durée* of the book's life that registers the passage of time and the history of the object's use.

In the process of drafting *Die Lehre der Sainte-Victoire*, Handke had clear visions of the material form that his to-be-published text would take. In the first letter to Unseld in which he mentions the work (March 22, 1980), Handke writes: "I have been working on a narrative for a couple weeks and often take

Figure 2.2 First-Edition Covers of the *Langsame Heimkehr* Tetralogy: *Langsame Heimkehr* (1979), *Die Lehre der Sainte-Victoire* (1980), *Kindergeschichte* (1981), *Über die Dörfer* (1981). *Source*: © Suhrkamp Verlag.

great joy in it. It is called 'The Lesson of Sainte-Victoire.' [...] If it comes to be a book, I would like to have it in paperback, but not as a Taschenbuch.[16] [...] The cover should be like that of *The Left-Handed Woman*, only with a small mountain contour as signum instead of the bull."[17] With the title, author's name, and publisher's name in "typewriter font," the cover—designed by Willy Fleckhaus, who designed the majority of Handke's Suhrkamp covers during this this period—also features a facsimile of a pencil sketch of the mountain from one of Handke's own notebooks (see Figure 2.2).[18] The cover thus re-presents the multi-mediality of the text's production: the drawing is a reminder of the manuscript notebooks that accompanied Handke along the Route Cézanne, where the typewriter font references Handke's practice—until his shift in the late 1980s to composing prose works entirely by hand—of composing text drafts on the typewriter.

Such evocations of manual production processes—handwriting, drawing, typewriting, papermaking, bookbinding—in Handke's published works function in part to defamiliarize the mass-produced book as the reader crosses the threshold into the printed text. But Handke's published books not only simulate handmade design; several of them are actually made through traditional, manual processes. In 1976, Handke published a collection of 18 poems, based on notes from a notebook dated January 17–February 22, 1976, titled *Das Ende des Flanierens* (The End of Flânerie) in a limited edition of 150 by the Davidpresse in Vienna. Featuring letterpress text and linoleum cuts by Hermann Gail, each copy was signed by Gail and Handke. In 1990, 10 years after the publication of *Die Lehre*, Handke produced a volume of essays titled *Noch einmal für Thukydides* (*Once Again for Thucydides*)—which included an account of yet another journey to Mont Sainte-Victoire—in the Residenz Verlag series Liber: Libertas. Like all the volumes in the series, the book is hand-bound: the cover is made of bare, uncovered book board; page gatherings are sewn with colored threads; and the spine is covered in hand-applied laid paper. An image—a standing leaf casting a shadow, in this case—is also blind embossed onto each book's board cover.

Although these examples of actual manual production techniques are exceptional within Handke's oeuvre, they crystalize an underlying impulse found in many of his books. One tends to handle a handmade book or letterpressed text more carefully, more delicately, than a mass-produced one, for they are crafted more slowly, individually, and carefully. Such a relationship to the book as object is emblematic of the relationship to the world, an ethos of slowness and care, that Handke seeks to cultivate through his writing.

Comparison of the first editions of the *Langsame Heimkehr* tetralogy to later editions highlights the material and visual effects of their published forms. The first editions vary in terms of their format, binding, and cover design:

Langsame Heimkehr is a hardback with a white book jacket and no cover illustration; *Die Lehre, Kindergeschichte* (Child Story, 1981), and *Über die Dörfer* (Across the Villages, 1981) are all paperbacks, in gray, silver and pink paper, respectively, with hand-drawn cover illustrations—by Handke in the case of *Die Lehre* and by his young daughter Amina in the case of the latter two (see Figure 2.2). Each book, in turn, is encountered as a unique object. In the second editions, whose covers were designed by Willy Fleckhaus and Rolf Staudt, format and typography are homogenized to conform to the Suhrkamp Taschenbuch series design scheme: all are paperbacks, bound in blues varying slightly in tone, with the author's name, title, and press name in bolded font (see Figure 2.3). *Die Lehre, Kindergeschichte*, and *Über die Dörfer* retain their cover drawings; notably, however, the second edition of *Langsame Heimkehr* introduces a cover illustration not present in the first: a colored drawing by Handke from a notebook. Reminiscent of the kind one might imagine the protagonist Sorger to draw, this drawing also represents a piece of work's substratum (to use a geological metaphor) that rises to the surface.

If the surfacing of the notebook drawing on the second edition cover of *Langsame Heimkehr* represents a small seismic event, 2015 witnessed an earthquake in both the edition history of *Langsame Heimkehr* and in Handke's published oeuvre broadly. A color, to-scale, partial facsimile edition of the notebook dated August 31, 1978 to October 18, 1978, containing notes from Handke's travels in North America, was published by Insel-Bücherei. The selection includes three full-page colored drawings of sites in Alaska (Fort Yukon and Earthquake Park in Anchorage), one of which was used for the second edition of *Langsame Heimkehr*. Instead of a colorful patterned cover, for which the collectible Insel-Bücherei series is known, the book is bound in facsimiled pages of Handke's notes (see Figure 2.4).

Figure 2.3 Second-Edition Covers of the *Langsame Heimkehr* Tetralogy: *Langsame Heimkehr* (1984), *Die Lehre der Sainte-Victoire* (1984), *Kindergeschichte* (1984), *Über die Dörfer* (1984). *Source*: © Suhrkamp Verlag.

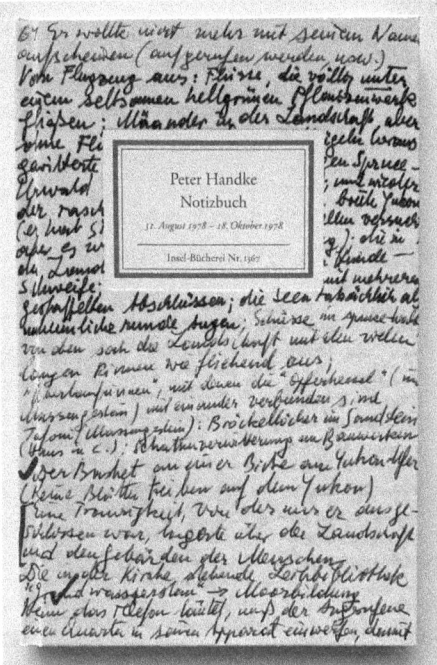

Figure 2.4 Peter Handke, *Notizbuch* (2015). *Source*: © Suhrkamp Verlag.

Whereas *Das Gewicht der Welt* offered the reader a single notebook page, the Insel edition of 14 pages enables a more extensive opportunity to compare notebook passages to the published novel.[19] To invoke prominent motifs from *Langsame Heimkehr* and *Die Lehre*, the reader assumes the position of a textual geologist (i.e., philologist), exploring the "fissures" and "fracture points" in the textual surface, through which buried "layers" of the work's material history are made visible.[20]

In Gérard Genette's typology of paratexts, Handke's notebooks can be categorized as "intimate epitexts"—"epi-" because they are outside of the published book and "intimate" because they are "addressed" to the writer himself.[21] Through the publication of the Insel facsimile edition, an intimate epitext becomes a "public epitext": Handke's notes circulate publicly as part of the texts' context but remain outside the book.[22] Through the facsimile reproduction of notes in and on the covers of Handke's books, an intimate epitext becomes a "peritext," *part* of the book itself.[23] The categorizations, however, are less important than this fact: once we have *seen* these notes, we cannot unsee them; there is no going back.[24] These notebook pages irrevocably alter how we read, indeed see, the text. The strategies Handke employs, I suggest, prompt us to challenge the distinctions between text and paratext and between text and pre-text, to consider them together as constitutive, inextricable parts of Handke's work.

The Essays

The media technology of the notebook allowed Handke to write by hand on the go instead of seated at a desk with a typewriter. As Handke continued to fill notebooks year after year, the pencil—a much slower writing medium than typing—came to take on an increasingly significant role, materially and conceptually, as both instrument and object of reflection. As Handke famously wrote in *Die Geschichte des Bleistifts* (The Story of the Pencil, 1982), "What corresponds to me as tool? Not the camera, also not the typewriter (and not the fountain pen or brush). What corresponds to me as tool? The pencil."[25]

In the late 1980s, Handke shifted from composing text drafts on the typewriter to composing them entirely by hand in pencil. The first pencil manuscript was *Versuch über die Müdigkeit* (Essay on Tiredness, 1989). Two further *Versuche*, also composed entirely in pencil, appeared soon after: *Versuch über die Jukebox* (Essay about the Jukebox, 1990) and *Versuch über den geglückten Tag* (Essay on the Successful Day, 1991). The first editions of these books were bound in hardback, with laid endpaper and relatively large font size, line spacing, and margins. The book jackets of each volume, designed by Hermann Michels, include facsimiles of the first page of each manuscript, onto which Handke's name, work title, and publisher's name are printed (see Figure 2.5). Though they are uniform in their use of manuscript facsimile, there are also notable differences in the designs. The rear flaps of the jackets of *Versuch über die Jukebox* and *Versuch über den geglückten Tag* also feature images: in the first case, a notebook drawing of a jukebox, which was later reproduced again in facsimile in *Abschied des Träumers vom neunten Land*, and in the second, a detail reproduction of a color plate from a 1749 engraving by William Hogarth (at the National Portrait Gallery in London) after his 1745 self-portrait *The Painter and his Pug* (at the Tate Modern), which is referenced in the opening passage of *Versuch über den geglückten Tag*: "A self-portrait of the painter William Hogarth, in London, a moment out of the eighteenth century, with a palate, and on this, dividing it in two, approximately in the middle, a delicately curved line, the so-called 'Line of Beauty and Grace.'"[26]

Displaying strike-throughs, erasures, additions, and interlinear insertions, the manuscript facsimiles present alternative versions of the in-process texts that correspond to the first several pages of each printed text.[27] The book jackets of the *Versuche* thus stage a dual entry into the text, through two versions simultaneously, manuscript and print. These facsimile book covers allow

Figure 2.5 Book Jacket of Peter Handke, *Versuch über die Müdigkeit* (1989). *Source*: © Suhrkamp Verlag.

the reader to observe not only changes between manuscript and printed text but also the evolution of Handke's practice as he began to draft entirely in pencil. Visually, the text of these manuscripts is significantly less dense, with larger letter forms and greater interlinear spacing, than that of *Versuch über die Müdigkeit*. The first page of the *Versuch über die Müdigkeit* manuscript, for example, contains 2,331 characters that cover 4 pages of printed text, while the first pages of the *Versuch über die Jukebox* and *Versuch über den geglückten Tag* manuscripts contain 1,425 and 1,488 characters, respectively, each covering two pages of printed text. The visual density of the *Versuch über die Müdigkeit* manuscript more closely resembles the visuality of Handke's typescript first drafts, single-spaced with text stretching to the very edge of the margins. This mode of filling the page is common for typist-writers, who fill the page maximally to avoid disrupting the flow of writing required to remove one sheet and feed another into the machine. In composing *Versuch über die Jukebox* and *Versuch über den geglückten Tag*, by contrast, Handke began to move away from this principle of efficiency; with fewer characters per page, greater interlinear spacing, and wider margins, the page layout more closely resembles the typographical layout of the printed versions, which display relatively large margins and fairly ample interlinear spacing. Like the sentences of *Der Hausierer*, which are typographically presented so as to *strike* the reader individually, the space around the lines and sentences of Handke's manuscript similarly allows them to arrest the reader—indeed Handke himself, as his own first reader—*as* sentences.

The representation of manuscript versions at the reader's entry into these texts foregrounds the fact that these *Versuche* (essays, literally "attempts," as in the French term *essayer*) are not only intellectual but also material experiments, transpiring through a dynamic of inscription and erasure, formation and deformation in a process of (re)discovering a new mode of writing, a new stage in Handke's writerly evolution and project of slowness. Entering the text through the manuscript highlights the contingency of the printed version, reminding readers that the text they are encountering exists in distinct instantiations—the mass-produced printed text, the unique, singular manuscript—and that this manuscript maintains a connection to the printed work, even if it is not immediately available to view in its entirety. In addition to the representation of handwriting, distinctive typographical features also evoke processes of human making, or at least individual decision making. Whereas the body text of each book is set in Garamond with similarly sized margins, the cover text varies in color (purple, red, and blue) and typeface. Though the *Versuche* are more unified in their design scheme than the first editions of the tetralogy, these typographical distinctions simultaneously evoke a sense of individualized, handcrafted design.

In addition to the first manuscript pages on the jackets, the complete manuscripts of the first three *Versuche* were published in a facsimile edition in 1992—a prestige edition in honor of one of Suhrkamp Verlag's most prestigious authors—on the occasion of Handke's 50th birthday.[28] One might consider the features of this edition as purely market-oriented: limited to 1,000 exempla, each signed by the author and housed in a linen box, the facsimiles are to-scale reproductions on unbound sheets to maximally mimic the material form of the original, loose-leaf manuscripts. Straddling the divide between technological reproduction and unique, individual object, these features also intersect with the thematics and poetics of Handke's writing, as part of a broader project of reauraticizing literature by defamiliarizing the literary object.[29]

The "text" is often understood to mean the printed, published version of a work that is essentially the same across editions and that is distinguished temporally, materially, and ontologically from the so-called pre-text. Yet Handke's notes and production processes are not paratextual with respect to his work; rather they constitute a crucial site of his literary art. In the process of writing, the visuality and materiality of production always have the potential to produce recursive effects on what and how writing proceeds. But in the publication history of Handke's work, the emerging market for his handwriting as part of his published texts produces the circumstances for a particular meta-reflection on the visuality of his manuscripts with respect to his creative project alongside their commercial value. The inclusion of manuscript notes and drawings as part of the packaging of his printed work might be thought to participate in producing a kind of "*Nachlassbewusstsein*," a consciousness of the market both scholarly and commercial for his printed texts as well as his manuscripts: Handke's writing for sale.[30]

The Dreamer's Farewell and Repetition

Approximately two months after the publication of *Versuch über den geglückten Tag*, Handke published a book titled *Abschied des Träumers vom neunten Land*. A shorter version of the essay also appeared on July 26/27 in the *Süddeutsche Zeitung*. *Abschied des Träumers* was the first of several texts in which Handke responded to the disintegration of the former Yugoslavia, which generated a controversy that was reignited in 2019 when Handke won the Nobel Prize in Literature. Criticism of these texts is polarized, ranging from vehement condemnation of the author as a Milošević-regime apologist to defense of his response as primarily a media critique of the exploitative coverage of the Yugoslav wars and International Criminal Tribunal. In the first book edition of *Abschied des Träumers*, Handke reproduced facsimile images of full notebook pages inscribed on wanderings through Slovenia in 1978 and 1980, over 10 years prior to the country's declaration of independence (on June 25, 1991). Unlike the case studies examined above, however, these facsimiled notes do not correspond to the text they accompany, or at least not directly; rather, they serve a particular political function in the context of Handke's disappointment with the failure of the Yugoslav experiment.

In *Abschied des Träumers*, Handke laments Slovenia's declaration of independence and argues against its necessity. As Scott Abbott has written, Handke was aware of Serbian domination but nonetheless maintained a belief in the ideal of a multiethnic state that allowed its inhabitants to live more freely and authentically, as natives and foreigners at once.[31] Slovenia, the mythical "Ninth Land," had represented for Handke a paradisiacal ideal "standing outside history" and outside the problems of Western modernity, a vision articulated several years before in his monumental work *Die Wiederholung* (Repetition, 1986).[32] Slovenia, Handke writes in *Abschied des Träumers*, is pervaded by a more palpable sense of reality, of *Gegenständlichkeit* (objectivity), its things more thingly, as opposed to those of the Western world, which "evade and elude"; and he fears a time when "each flavor of country, region, space, place and reality will have been smothered."[33]

For the publication of the essay as a book, Handke included 14 facsimile images of notebook pages displaying notes and drawings depicting the phenomena—landscapes, rock formations, gardens, plants, animals, and objects—that had "accompanied" him on earlier wanderings in Slovenia. These facsimile images are interspersed among the standard printed pages. In some cases, a notebook page confronts a printed text page across the space of the gutter (see Figure 2.6); in others, a two-page opening is presented, the

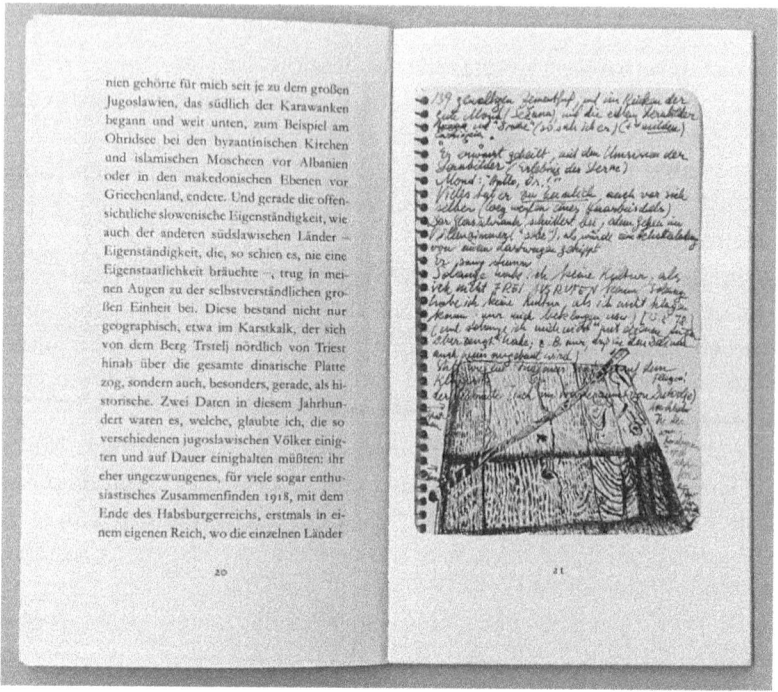

Figure 2.6 Peter Handke, *Abschied des Träumers vom neunten Land* (1991). *Source*: ©
Suhrkamp Verlag.

gutter of the printed text and that of the facsimiled notebook coinciding.
Unlike the facsimile manuscripts included on the cover and jackets of *Das
Gewicht der Welt* and the *Versuche*, which directly correspond to the printed
texts, the facsimiled pages in *Abschied des Träumers* serve another function:
filled with traces, notes, and drawings of places Handke traversed, the notebooks become relics of another time, the "bygone reality" prior to Slovenian
independence that is called forth in the book.

While the manuscript notes reproduced in *Abschied des Träumers* do not correspond to the printed text, a reader familiar with Handke's work may recognize in
them references to *Die Wiederholung*, such as the obvious reference to "the Ninth
Country," which is described in *Die Wiederholung* as "the legendary country [...]
the goal of our collective longings,"[34] and a reference to "the blind window,"
which is a recurrent symbol in *Die Wiederholung* and the title of the first chapter.[35]
The drawing of a hiking stick on a table from the last page of *Die Wiederholung*
reappears as well. But whereas the page is cropped in *Die Wiederholung* to show
only the table and stick, the entire notebook page is reproduced in *Abschied des
Träumers* (see Figure 2.6).[36] Here, however, it serves to evoke not only the connections between walking and writing, hiking stick and pencil, but also a particular

time and place.[37] In the full-page reproduction, one finds a date, "15.8.78," and a handwritten caption, "the sun-lit table in the waiting room of Dutovlje." Recontextualized within the book, the drawing remains crucially rooted in a time and place prior to Slovenian independence, a time and place that no longer exists but is preserved in Handke's notebooks and offered up to the reader.

Handke's return to these notebook pages and their reproduction in *Abschied des Träumers* reflects his conceptions of the power of writing, of *Schreiben* and *Schrift*, as articulated in *Die Wiederholung*. "A time will come," he writes, "when walking, even walking in the heartland, will no longer be possible, or no longer effective. But then the story will be here and reenact the walking."[38] Remembering, narrating, and writing, for Handke, are all practices of *Wiederholung* (repetition), which includes processes of repeating (*Wieder*holung) but also of recapturing (Wieder*holung*).[39] For Handke, writing is not only pervaded by absence but also understood as a process of *Bewahrung* (preserving).[40] In its sensory, bodily materiality, writing "*vergegenwärtigt*" (makes present).[41] In Handke's notebooks, traces of his Slovenia, his "Ninth Country," remain. In turn, the creation and reception of text, writing and reading, become endowed with a sacral quality. Narrating, for Handke, is a process of repetition and recollection that endows the remembered with a presence and meaning beyond that of the original events.[42] In the process of drafting his texts of the late 1970s and 1980s, Handke would extensively reread his notes and incorporate them into his text drafts through a kind of writerly repetition. The journal volumes offer an opportunity to retrace Handke's adventures in note taking in mediated form, edited and transformed into printed text. The facsimiled pages in *Abschied des Träumers* offer the reader an illusion of even closer proximity to his act of note taking, to his journeys both physical and metaphysical through Slovenia.

Notebook suhrkamp taschenbuch: Chronicle of Running Events

In various ways, as this chapter has explored, Handke's books evoke and represent the scene of writing in their published form, destabilizing the seeming fixity of the printed text by highlighting its contingency. Mediating handwriting through facsimile images, at times literally enshrouding his texts in manuscript, evoking their handmade origins: these so-called paratextual strategies make visible the slow, repetitive processes through which his texts were created. In turn, the material and visual forms of Handke's books challenge us to recognize that the generative processes themselves, processes of note taking and composing in pencil, are not simply "pre-" or "para-" with respect to his texts but crucial components of his projects of slowness, re-attunement, and repetition and thus essential to understanding his work.

To be sure, Handke's books are commercial objects: Handke's (hand)writing is for sale. But as we have seen, the packaging of his texts extends the artistic project of slowness into the very form of the published books themselves. If Handke's writing can, to some, feel self-indulgent, it is also designed to reorient readers in today's accelerated, hyper-mediated world, prompting them to follow in Handke's steps, to slow down and re-attune, and perhaps even to pick up their own pencils.

This sentiment is literalized in the publication of a notebook by Suhrkamp Verlag that bears the title of a work by Handke. But the pages it contains bear neither Handke's writing nor his text. Rather, they are blank. Beginning in 2015, Suhrkamp Verlag began publishing blank notebooks designed to mimic visually the standard designs of various book series: a yellow paperback notebook with black lettering in the style of the edition suhrkamp; a white hardback notebook with a book jacket in the style of the Bibliothek Suhrkamp; a black paperback notebook with red and white lettering in the style of the suhrkamp taschenbuch wissenschaft series; and several in the Insel-Taschenbuch series, with their iconic colorful, patterned covers (see Figure 2.7). Replete with ISBN numbers and appearing in WorldCat.org, these notebooks bear the "titles" *Notizen* (notes) or *Notizbuch* (notebook). Several notebooks are also produced

Figure 2.7 Blank Notebooks. *Source*: © Suhrkamp Verlag.

in the style of the Romane des Jahrhunderts (a special subseries of suhrkamp taschenbuch)—black paperback with cover text in raised, metallic lettering—bearing titles, cleverly employed, of famous works published by Suhrkamp: Thomas Bernhard's *Korrektur* (Correction), Marcel Proust's *Auf der Suche nach der verlorenen Zeit* (In Search of Lost Time), Roland Barthes's *Mythen des Alltags* (Mythologies, literally "myths of the everyday"), among others. A quote by the respective author appears on the back cover of each volume.

One notebook in the series bears the title of a work by Handke: *Chronik der laufenden Ereignisse* (Chronicle of Running Events, 1971).[43] Handke composed the screenplay for and directed the 1971 television film by the same name (first aired May 10, 1971); a book based on the screenplay, including film stills, was published on September 21, 1971, in the suhrkamp taschenbuch series. The design of the notebook named after this book, however, mimics that of the Romane des Jahrhunderts series, in which two of Handke's most monumental works—*Die Wiederholung* (1986, 1999) and *Mein Jahr in der Niemandsbucht* (My Year in the No-Man's-Bay, 1994, 2000)—were reissued. The quote on the back cover, from the journal volume *Gestern Unterwegs* (Traveling Yesterday), reads, "Writing: it's impossible without the shine."[44]

In the case of these blank notebooks, what is "for sale" is not merely, or even primarily, paper for note taking. Rather, it is paratext without text: the publisher's binding of the iconic Suhrkamp Verlag series, to which consumers will supply the text, becoming themselves Suhrkamp writers. Publishing, in this case, precedes writing. If paratexts shape how readers encounter a text and its author, these notebooks prompt us to think about the ways in which paratextual forms—the material, visual form of published works—might in turn shape writing itself, constructing the author and constructing us *as* authors. Who is the audience for these notebooks? One might imagine students and scholars, writers, or lovers of literature to be the most likely consumers of such volumes. What scenes of writing might transpire in them, and what texts might be inscribed? Shopping lists? Gas mileage records? Perhaps. But one might imagine these notebooks to solicit texts more intellectual in nature: ideas and outlines, quotes and lecture notes, references and contact information for intellectual interlocutors, and perhaps even notes for articles or other in-progress texts. Writing in a Suhrkamp volume endows the written with a different weight, linking it intertextually—or perhaps, rather, interparatextually—to texts by important Suhrkamp writers.

In the case of the "Handke" notebook *Chronik der laufenden Ereignisse*, something else is also at play. If Handke's published works sometime mediate the scenes of their production, extending the poetological project and process of note taking into the form of his published books, this Suhrkamp notebook might be understood to extend Handke's project of writing, of "chronicling" lived experiences in his notebooks, a step further: encouraging readers to create their own "journal volumes," to pick up their own pens or pencils and join Handke in slowing down, attuning, seeing the world anew, and taking note.

Notes

1 Peter Handke, *Das Gewicht der Welt: Ein Journal (November 1975–März 1977)* (Salzburg: Residenz, 1977), 5.

2 Ibid., 6.

3 For a thorough overview of Handke's project of note taking, see Katharina Pektor, "'Wartet nur—ich bin jemand, der sich organisiert': Peter Handkes Projekt des Notierens," in *"Gedanken reisen, Einfälle kommen an": Die Welt der Notiz*, ed. Marcel Atze and Volker Kaukoreit (Vienna: Praesens, 2016), 300–23.

4 Handke is referring here to Johann Wolfgang von Goethe's *Die Wahlverwandtschaften* (1809).

5 Handke, *Das Gewicht der Welt*, 112.

6 Hans Höller, *Eine ungewöhnliche Klassik nach 1945: Das Werk Peter Handkes* (Berlin: Suhrkamp, 2013), 9; Alexander Huber, *Versuch einer Ankunft: Peter Handkes Ästhetik der Differenz* (Würzburg: Königshausen & Neumann, 2005), 111.

7 Much has been written on this topic. For a recent overview, see Thorsten Carstensen, *Romanisches Erzählen: Peter Handke und die epische Tradition* (Göttingen: Wallstein, 2013).

8 Peter Handke, *Versuch über die Müdigkeit* (Berlin: Suhrkamp, 1989); Peter Handke, *Versuch über die Jukebox* (Berlin: Suhrkamp, 1990); Peter Handke, *Versuch über den geglückten Tag* (Berlin: Suhrkamp, 1991); Peter Handke, *Versuch über den Stillen Ort* (Berlin: Suhrkamp, 2012); Peter Handke, *Versuch über den Pilznarren* (Berlin: Suhrkamp, 2013).

9 Peter Handke, *Abschied des Träumers vom Neunten Land: Eine Wirklichkeit, die vergangen ist: Erinnerungen an Slowenien* (Berlin: Suhrkamp, 1991).

10 Peter Handke, *Versuch über die Müdigkeit; Versuch über die Jukebox; Versuch über den geglückten Tag: Faksimiles der drei Handschriften* (Berlin: Suhrkamp, 1992); Peter Handke, *In einer dunklen Nacht ging ich aus meinem stillen Haus: Faksimile der Handschrift* (Salzburg: Stiftung Salzburger Literaturarchiv, 2002); Peter Handke, *Notizbuch: 31. August 1978–18. Oktober 1978* (Berlin: Insel, 2015).

11 Peter Handke and Siegfried Unseld, *Der Briefwechsel*, ed. Raimund Fellinger (Berlin: Suhrkamp, 2012), 62–63.

12 The other volumes of the tetralogy include *Die Lehre der Sainte-Victoire* (Berlin: Suhrkamp, 1980), *Kindergeschichte* (Berlin: Suhrkamp, 1981), and *Über die Dörfer* (Berlin: Suhrkamp, 1981).

13 Peter Handke, *Langsame Heimkehr* (Berlin: Suhrkamp, 1979), 9.

14 Ibid., 45; Peter Handke, *Slow Homecoming*, trans. Ralph Manheim (London: Methuen, 1985), 28–29.

15 Handke and Unseld, *Der Briefwechsel*, 361.

16 He is referring here to the Suhrkamp Taschenbuch paperback series.

17 Handke and Unseld, *Der Briefwechsel*, 392.

18 Ibid., 409.

19 This can be compared to Donald Reiman's notion of "versioning" or the presentation of "enough different *primary* textual documents and states of major texts [...] so

that readers, teachers, and critics can compare for themselves" [emphasis in orignal]. Donald H. Reiman, *Romantic Texts and Contexts* (Columbia: University of Missouri Press, 1987), 169.

20 Handke, *Langsame Heimkehr*, 111–12; Handke, *Die Lehre der Sainte-Victoire*, 39, 108–09. On Louise DeSalvo's notion of the "submerged" version, see Brenda L. Silver, "Textual Criticism as Feminist Practice: Or, Who's Afraid of Virginia Woolf Part II," *Representing Modernist Texts: Editing as Interpretation*, ed. George Bornstein (Ann Arbor: University of Michigan Press, 1991), 193–222 (204).

21 Gérard Genette, *Paratexts: Thresholds of Interpretation*, trans. Jane E. Lewin (Cambridge: Cambridge University Press, 1997), xviii, 372, 387.

22 Ibid., 344.

23 Ibid., 5.

24 As Silver writes of Virginia Woolf criticism, "Once we are aware of the manuscript versions […] it becomes impossible […] not to be conscious of their presence within the 'final' text." Silver, "Textual Criticism as Feminist Practice," 194.

25 Peter Handke, *Die Geschichte des Bleistifts* (Salzburg: Residenz, 1982), 63.

26 Handke, *Versuch über den geglückten Tag*, 7.

27 See note 19.

28 See note 10.

29 On Handke's reauraticization of the technical reproduction medium of the jukebox, see Ulrich Schönherr, "Die Wiederkehr der Aura im Zeitalter technischer Reproduzierbarkeit: Musik, Literatur und Medien in Peter Handkes *Versuch über die Jukebox*," *Modern Austrian Literature* 33, no. 2 (2000): 55–72 (63).

30 Kai Sina and Carlos Spoerhase, eds., *Nachlassbewusstsein: Literatur, Archiv, Philologie 1750–2000* (Göttingen: Wallstein, 2017).

31 Scott Abbott, "Handke's Yugoslavia Work," in *The Works of Peter Handke: International Perspectives*, ed. David N. Coury and Frank Pilipp (Riverside, CA: Ariadne, 2005), 359–86 (361–63).

32 Abbott, "Handke's Yugoslavia Work," 362; Huber, *Versuch einer Ankunft*, 393; Handke, *Die Wiederholung* (Berlin: Suhrkamp, 1986).

33 Handke, *Abschied des Träumers vom Neunten Land*, 13, 29, 49.

34 Handke, *Die Wiederholung*, 317; Peter Handke, *Repetition*, trans. Ralph Manheim (London: Methuen, 1988), 234.

35 Handke, *Abschied des Träumers vom Neunten Land*, 8.

36 Ibid., 21.

37 Martina Wagner-Egelhaaf, *Mystik der Moderne: Die visionäre Ästhetik der deutschen Literatur im 20. Jahrhundert* (Stuttgart: Metzler, 1989), 193.

38 Handke, *Die Wiederholung*, 298; Handke, *Repetition*, 220.

39 Huber, *Versuch einer Ankunft*, 390; Wagner-Egelhaaf, *Mystik der Moderne*, 173.

40 Wagner-Egelhaaf, *Mystik der Moderne*, 189.

41 Ibid., 190.

42 Ibid., 202.

43 Peter Handke, *Chronik der laufenden Ereignisse: Notizbuch suhrkamp taschenbuch* (Berlin: Suhrkamp, 2017).

44 Peter Handke, *Gestern Unterwegs* (Salzburg: Jung und Jung, 2005), 26.

Chapter 3

CONTRASTS IN THE BRAZILIAN BOOK MARKET IN THE EARLY TWENTY-FIRST CENTURY

Laura Rivas Gagliardi

The following chapter focuses on the emergence of deluxe book publishers in Brazil, where the book industry is clearly more vulnerable to the fluctuations and crises of the global book market than it is in other regions of the world. This vulnerability will be explained primarily through the lenses of historical, economic, and social inequality, which present fundamental problems for the book industry. They lead, for example, to higher book prices, higher printing and paper costs, and unfavorable delivery networks. These are limitations that affect not only authors but also publishers as well as the book market in general. These contrasts can be most clearly observed in the early twenty-first century, when a phase of stability and growth in the book trade was disrupted by economic downturns. Prior to that, a new publishing phenomenon had emerged in Brazil: for the first time, prestige was associated with the consumption of books.

My considerations are based on two historical facts that cannot be ignored. First, since the early twenty-first century there has been a new organizational form in the Brazilian publishing industry, which was previously unknown. The international tendency to transform publishing houses into media companies[1] and government policies to democratize access to education[2] have greatly contributed to this shift. These policies have been undertaken since the end of the military dictatorship (1964–1985), but the first signs of success only came with the economic upswing and the investments in book production and distribution that took place under the governments of President Luíz Inácio Lula da Silva (2002–2010) and President Dilma Rousseff (2011–2016).[3] Although Brazil plays a role in the global economic system, its role in the academic and cultural production of immaterial

goods, like books, remains marginal. Today, after a process of deindustriali-
zation from the 1990s onward, Brazil has become a supplier of raw materials
for the international market, and many of the books published in Brazil are
printed in China.[4]

The colonial past and the former opposition between the proprietors of
enslaved workers and the enslaved themselves created a brutal concentration
of wealth that is still evident today. This is illustrated by studies on income tax
data, which have recently been published for the first time.[5] This data shows
that 30 percent of the total wealth of the country is in the hands of 1 percent
of the entire population, which is one of the largest, if not the largest, con-
centrations of income in the world.[6] Another repercussion of being a former
society of slave holders is a correspondence between cultural and economic
property, as the possession of cultural goods tends to be limited to the ruling
class. Furthermore, any kind of physical labor is not only seen as undignified
but also poorly paid. A consideration of the relationship between prestige
and book consumption on a cultural level also requires a consideration on
these social conditions, which cannot be understood without looking at their
historical development.

Another preliminary remark also concerns the concepts of prestige and
consumption. These concepts are connected to books in the same way that
they are connected to any other commodity. The industrial production of
goods through new technologies and new methods of production has increasingly led to the formation of market niches, as certain material elements are
highly valued in an end product, and its retail price will depend on how it
compares to other mass-oriented products. The consumers of these products
also use them to acquire respect and admiration within their social spheres—
and they are willing to pay for it. In recent decades, these developments have
also begun to affect the book industry. If the production of books is viewed
from this perspective, however, then the price of books must now include the
profits; the increased production costs due to high-quality paper types, printing processes, and book design; and the prestige it affords its buyers. The
prestige granted to the owner through the magical sheen of the commodity
itself thus conceals the labor involved in these new sophisticated manufacturing processes and adds a surplus to the prices that does not represent a
surplus-value. This strategy of the book market to provide customers with
prestige by enabling them to differentiate themselves from others through
the production of deluxe editions with distinguished, exclusive properties—
similar to jewels, porcelain, Gobelin carpets, or other luxury products in
the past—can be traced back to the concept of the commodity fetish and
its social function.[7] This means that objects not only mediate and regulate
relationships between people but also denote a certain difference—a social

distance—between them. From this perspective, prestige is a social idea that serves to mark a particular social status.

I am assuming here that the relations between prestige and consumption in the realm of culture also provide insight into the relations between material and intellectual production more generally. This is especially true in a country like Brazil, which is culturally as well as economically seen as "underdeveloped." In the following, I will attempt to provide an overview of the contemporary Brazilian publishing industry within a global economic and sociocultural context. I will also focus on the contrasts within the Brazilian publishing industry by examining the emergence and the marketing strategies of two publishers—Companhia das Letras and Cosac Naify—which I consider paradigmatic for the dynamics of deluxe book production in the Brazilian literary book trade. I will then focus on the brief life of Cosac Naify, whose ultimate fate most clearly demonstrates the relations between prestige and consumption in contemporary Brazil. In conclusion, I will address the controversial ideas of "cultural weakness" and "underdevelopment" in a postcolonial context in order to consider their influence on literary creation itself.

The Book Market and the Reading Public in Brazil

As part of the national economy, the Brazilian book market experienced a boom in the late 1990s and has been in a state of political and economic crisis since 2014. A look back at the 1990s shows that the opening of the economy to mass consumer markets and the containment of hyperinflation emerged as a result of neoliberal policies that privatized state-owned enterprises and enabled the tremendous growth of the middle class. During the second term of Lula's government, for example, the middle class constituted 52 percent of the total population. However, this growth was achieved through the integration of the poorer classes thanks to emergency aid programs and the allocation of credit for consumption rather than through an actual redistribution of income and property. In this context, the so-called new middle class could afford books for the first time. There were many indicators of economic growth that could convince the national and international public of Brazil's economic progress between 2002 and 2016. The country was even called a new "global player," as it had the seventh-largest economic market and the eighth-largest book market in the world. This was the reason why Brazil was represented twice as a guest country at the Frankfurt Book Fair (in 1994 and 2013).

Lula's government fulfilled its educational mandate to acquire books and deliver them to the most remote libraries. In 2005 the government also implemented a campaign to promote reading in collaboration with private enterprises. The four pillars of this campaign were the democratization of access to education, the continuing education of mediators and multipliers, the opening of book centers, and the development of the book trade by offering cheap editions. According to a study of Brazilian book sales conducted by the Fundação Instituto de Pesquisas Econômicas (Economic Research Foundation), the Câmara Brasileira do Livro (Brazilian Book Chamber), and the Sindicato Nacional dos Editores de Livros (National Union of Book Publishers), the government purchased between 20 percent and 30 percent of the books produced in Brazil between 2011 and 2018.[8] In the context of the Frankfurt Book Fair, the German newspaper *Die Welt* reported on October 9, 2013, that "books are luxury goods for most Brazilians, yet the Brazilian book industry is nevertheless booming with undreamt-of sales figures [...] because the government is buying so many books."[9]

As an "emerging nation," Brazil has not yet freed itself from the old oppositions of the colonial past, which have been updated through new forms of subordination to the world market. Despite recent economic growth, urban living and transportation have become increasingly expensive, slums are constantly growing, the agricultural sector is increasingly dominated by agribusiness and soy monocultures, the national debt is higher, wages are still very low, and the stark contrast between the poor and the rich has led to so many social tensions in recent years that political impeachment proceedings were implemented and President Dilma Rousseff was suspended in 2016. The threatening crisis situation is related not only to the restructuring of the Chinese economy after 2008 and its reduced requirements for raw materials but also to the strengthening of conservative forces within Brazil and their desire to control the government. These political and economic fluctuations have dramatically influenced all aspects of the Brazilian publishing industry.

A recent study shows that there was no growth in the Brazilian book market between 2009 and 2015; in fact, the market shrank by 24.6 percent from 2009 to 2011 and by 22.8 percent from 2014 to 2015.[10] At the same time, the prices of books increased. These statistics thus show that the Brazilian book trade is still very fragile and that the purchasing power of the population must not be confused with their reading habits, as other factors may have an effect, such as access to books and reading behavior.

Comparing the reading habits of Brazilians with those of Germans and Americans can provide a general outline of book consumption, even though it is often misleading to compare figures without reflecting on the specific contexts in which they arise. According to the results of a very extensive study conducted by the Instituto Pró-Livro (Pro-Book Institute) in 2016, 56 percent of the population had read at least one book in the previous three months, and they read on average no more than five books per year (although they only read two books to the end).[11] In contrast, according to the results of a survey conducted by Forsa for the German magazine *Stern* that same year, 39 percent of Germans read up to 5 books per year, 19 percent read 6 to 10 books, and 27 percent read more than 10 books (only 14 percent did not read any books at all).[12] However, people read much less in the United States, as a study conducted by the Pew Research Center showed that Americans read on average only 4 books per year and 26 percent of the population do not read books at all.[13]

The problem of illiteracy was partially solved in Brazil, as the illiteracy rate was 33 percent in the 1970s and is now roughly 9 percent; however, this does not necessarily mean that an educated readership has emerged. In contrast, the literacy rate is 96 percent in Germany and 99 percent in the United States. It is also significant that there are roughly 800 publishers in Brazil, 2,200 in Germany, and 90,000 in the United States. Two companies in Germany (Bertelsmann and Springer) and three companies in the United States (Thomson Reuters, McGraw Hill, and Wiley) are also among the 10 largest book conglomerates in the world, while the largest Brazilian company (Somos Educação) is only in the 42nd place.[14] The sales of e-books in Brazil also do not cover the costs of their digital production, even though more tablets were sold in 2013 than desktop or laptop computers. Amazon also began selling e-readers in Brazil in 2012, although the cheapest Kindle device still costs roughly $100 USD or one-third of the minimum monthly wage, which is much more than in Germany or the United States. A study conducted in 2016 also found that only 37 percent of Brazilian publishers sold e-books and that e-book sales constituted only 1 percent of total book sales,[15] which is much lower than in Germany or the United States.[16]

Another problem in Brazil is that the book distribution process is not as dynamic as would be desirable. The connections between the actors involved in book production, such as authors, publishers, and readers, are often blocked, and the distribution of books and the range of available titles are particularly hindered by the absence of fixed prices or similar regulations. This results in a massive concentration of publishers and bookstores, which constitute the most important channels for book distribution, in the wealthiest cities of the southern and southeastern regions of the country.

The Book as a Consumer Good

I have selected Companhia das Letras and Cosac Naify from among the roughly 800 publishing houses in Brazil because they provide an accurate picture of the development and production of deluxe editions within the Brazilian book market. While they both benefited from the educational policies of the Lula and Dilma governments, they were established during successive historical periods, as Companhia das Letras was founded at the end of the democratization process of the 1980s and Cosac Naify was founded in accordance with the neoliberal orientation of the 1990s. They also developed in opposing directions. For example, Companhia das Letras was originally a small- to medium-sized publisher that was oriented toward a select readership but a series of mergers dramatically changed the profile of the company, and today it is one of the largest general-interest publishers in the country.[17] It earned tremendous intellectual and literary recognition among the educated public, although this only accounted for a small segment of the total population. The contemporary prestige of the publisher is primarily due to its impressive backlist of older titles. Unlike Companhia das Letras, Cosac Naify has maintained its elitist and cosmopolitan profile, which is associated with visual art, international literature, and the humanities. Both publishers served the same clientele until the first decade of the twenty-first century, but Companhia das Letras was then able to reach a wider readership through mergers with Brazilian and international publishing groups. A comparison of these companies will thus show how the fate of both publishers was influenced by the global crisis in the book market: while Companhia das Letras decided to merge with larger companies, Cosac Naify chose to close its operations in 2015.

Companhia das Letras was founded in 1986 by Luiz Schwarcz, who previously worked at the traditional leftist publishing house Editora Brasiliense, and his wife Lilia Moritz Schwarcz, who worked as a social anthropologist. Three years later, the management of the company fell to Fernando Moreira Salles, whose family controlled the Unibanco financial group. The company succeeded in attracting educated readers through extraordinary titles, beautiful designs, and high-quality printing processes. Their backlist includes 3,000 titles in the areas of fiction, philosophy, essays, and poetry in addition to 16 imprints for children's literature, graphic novels, textbooks, and paperbacks.[18] In 2011 the British media group Pearson purchased 45 percent of the company's shares, and since then the company has collaborated with the British publisher Penguin to produce cheap editions of literary classics. After Penguin merged with Random House in 2013, Companhia das Letras became part of Penguin Random House, which is currently the largest trade publisher in the world. In 2015 Companhia das Letras also merged with the Objetiva publishing house in Rio de Janeiro to become Grupo Companhia das Letras. The company now has roughly 250 employees and publishes about 30 books per month with an average print run of 4,500 copies, which is quite high compared to the usual print run of 1,500 copies.

Companhia das Letras was always known for its prestigious authors and titles. In 2010 the trade journal *Valor econômico* conducted a survey among professors and critics to determine the best publishers in Brazil, and Companhia das Letras was in first place with 81 percent of the vote.[19] The backlist also includes the most important classic and contemporary Brazilian authors, such as Hilda Hilst, Bernardo Carvalho, and Chico Buarque. The company also has roughly 2,000 e-book titles, which are up to 40 percent cheaper than the print versions.

The book *O desejo* (The Desire, 1990) provides an example of how Companhia das Letras innovatively shaped the design of books in the 1990s. This anthology contains various contributions to a public lecture series at the Funarte (National Foundation of Art). Under the leadership of Adauto Novaes, professors and intellectuals from Brazil and France were invited to address the topic of desire from different perspectives using examples from the works of Plato, Epicurus, Baruch Spinoza, Francisco Goya, António Vieira, Denis Diderot, Marquis de Sade, Marcel Proust, Georges Bataille, Karl Marx, Herbert Marcuse, and Walter Benjamin. The cover of the book, designed by Moema Cavalcanti, received the *Prêmio Jabuti* (Tortoise Prize), which is the most important prize in the Brazilian publishing industry. Book design was understood as both an independent art and an important component of the book as a whole, and it established a local tradition that Cosac Naify further developed. In this context, prestige and luxury were associated not with the cheap material properties of the book but rather with its use of visual art, which was largely due to the fact that most of the country's population had limited access to culture.

The Book as a Luxury Good

Cosac Naify was founded in 1997 by Charles Cosac, and it is impossible to separate the history of this company from that of its founder. Cosac's family came from Syria to Rio de Janeiro in the early twentieth century, and they became rich through the mining of quartz, crystal, iron, and manganese. Cosac had lived in various European cities for 15 years, as he studied mathematics in England and art history in France and Russia. He interrupted his doctoral studies on Russian avant-garde artist Kazimir Malevich in St. Petersburg in order to return to São Paulo and establish a fine art publishing house, which had never before existed in Brazil. Using his own capital and the financial support of the American media tycoon Marshall Naify and his son Michael Naify, who had made a fortune in the United States as owners of United Artists Theaters, Cosac not only published beautiful books but also created a publishing program that could itself be seen as a work of art. As a collector of religious art, he always furnished the company's offices with alternating pieces from his own valuable collection. This familiar atmosphere also shaped the company's work, although the results were initially negative from an economic point of view. In the beginning, for example, book prices were not precisely calculated but rather simply estimated, and an accurate calculation was not introduced until five years after the company was founded. As a result, the company's revenues never covered its expenses, and Michael Naify was forced to contribute millions of dollars every year. The founders never declared the exact amount of their investment in the company, but there are rumors that it was as much as 50 million USD. Cosac explained: "The publishing house has lived the life of books, not the life of the book market."[20]

Cosac Naify's impact on the Brazilian book market in the 2000s was comparable to that of Companhia das Letras in the 1990s, although it went much further. The company's publishing program was like a breath of fresh air, as it featured works by Brazilian and international authors, including classics that had never before been translated into Portuguese, and critical editions, commentaries, apparatuses, and paratexts written by distinguished Brazilian experts. The company also promoted a new concept of the book as an art object. The design team was extremely well-read, and in the spirit of Brazilian modernism of the 1960s they sought to surpass the normally low standards of book production by integrating the overall design of the book with its content through the format, layout, typography, binding, dust jackets, and paper stock. The books were beautiful in terms of their appearance as well as their material quality in general, as they not only attracted attention on bookshelves but were also a pleasure to hold in one's hands while reading. The senses of the reader were aroused using various techniques and design elements, which were mainly related to the decorative accessories of the text. Cosac Naify's first book, *Barroco de lírios* (Baroque of Lilies, 1997) by Brazilian sculptor, performer, and installation artist Tunga, was particularly impressive, as it featured 10 different types of paper, 200 illustrations, and a braided pigtail that was a meter long when unfolded. Another prominent example was the first Portuguese translation of Ivan Goncharov's novel *Oblomov* (2012), which was published in a deluxe edition in 2012. Because the protagonist was a rich landowner who hardly ever left his sofa, the cover displayed a cloth pattern used for nineteenth-century Russian sofas.[21] Cosac Naify never bothered to produce e-books, as the digital medium would not have enabled such luxury. The publishing house developed its prestige very quickly on this basis and was appreciated all over Brazil.

In November 2015 Cosac announced that the publishing house would cease its activities. This news was a huge surprise, even for his employees. Cosac claimed that he did not want to fire anyone or reduce the number of new releases. He also did not want to sell the publishing house, which was his life's work. Michael Naify briefly added that the publishing house would leave its mark on the cultural life of the country, as the material and intellectual quality of books had been quite low when the company was originally founded. After 19 years of an economically questionable yet nevertheless brilliant history, Cosac Naify thus came to a self-imposed end, and it was forced to close due to its atypical practices and the financial insecurity of the economic crisis that finally reached Brazil in 2014.[22] Furthermore, it did not have any of the stars of Brazilian literature under contract, such as Carlos Drummond de Andrade or Clarice Lispector, which could have increased the revenue from previously released titles for a broader readership. Cosac also stated bluntly that "the company closed because no one buys books and there is no interest in literature."[23] The production and distribution of beautiful books cost money, good design and excellent content cost even more, and the founder of the company could no longer afford these additional expenses.

The inherent contradictions of Cosac Naify ultimately reflect the contradictory dynamics of capitalism in Brazil and in the publishing industry more generally, as it can provide deviations from the logic of profit. The fetishism of commodities plays a role in raising prices, as seen earlier. In the case of Cosac Naify the prices were actually reduced, and the books were often sold at a loss despite the prestige represented by its books and the fact that its production costs were higher. Cosac himself was a fascinating figure, who acted as a kind of patron. Indeed, his appreciation of art was virtually limitless—up to the point where money became crucial, and the company was forced to conform to the rules of the book market. In order to avoid this conformity, Cosac decided to terminate the company instead, which was an unusual fate compared to other medium-sized publishing houses, like Companhia das Letras, which was able to continue operating through mergers with national and international companies. Cosac explained his reason for refusing to sell the company as follows: "It may be tremendously valuable, but the idea of selling Cosac Naify never crossed my mind. The name of the company is also my own name, and it would be humiliating to negotiate a deal for my own name."[24] This comment once again reveals the publisher's personal rather than commercial approach. The economic failure of Cosac Naify also reveals a lot about the education of the Brazilian elite, which was the company's target audience. Due to the fact that the books did not actually sell, they were distributed at reduced prices on various occasions, such as informal book fairs, so their main buyers consisted of humanities students, scholars, and professors—in addition to the government, which reduced the number of books it purchased. The company enjoyed an exceptional reputation among these social groups, which was also because its titles were exceptionally affordable in this irregular way. In any case, it definitely left an indelible imprint on the history of Brazilian book art.

Literature and Prestige

Based on the histories of these two companies, I would now like to present a few closing remarks on their methods of producing literary content in a country like Brazil. The debate among Brazilian intellectuals concerning the conditions for literary creation or the work of writers goes back to the 1970s, and it can be clearly explained using Brazilian literary critic Antonio Candido's essay "Literature and Underdevelopment." Candido's essay reassesses and redefines the concept of "backwardness" so that it takes on an emancipatory significance. For him, the condition of "underdevelopment" is neither a stage in a teleological development toward capitalist prosperity nor an essential episode in Brazilian history. Instead of reinforcing the constantly shifting expressions of subordination, depending on the historical moment, the idea of "underdevelopment" can be more clearly seen and understood as an integral part of the global economic system. Shortages and deficiencies produce poverty, powerlessness, institutional disorder, illiteracy, financial anarchy, and archaic working methods, which in turn produce material dependencies and cultural deficiencies. Candido thus situates "backwardness" within a world-historical context.[25]

Candido's terminology may seem unfashionable from a contemporary perspective, as the idea of "underdevelopment" can either evoke a developmental pattern that would be universally valid or be understood within a bourgeois framework that is not necessarily critical of capitalist modes of production, the division of labor, and property law.[26] However, Candido's focus was the ideological imperialist U.S. foreign policy that supported the military dictatorship in Brazil (1964–1985), whose economic and political interests in the country violated the basic rights of citizens through persecution, exile, torture, and censorship. From this perspective, Candido's views anticipate a theoretical postcolonial framework, and his essay "Literature and Underdevelopment" offers an insightful example of a radical process of decolonization in the field of Brazilian literature and scholarship. The central core of his argument also remains important, as people's lives are still conditioned by the negative aspects of the reality of Brazil, such as the concentration of income and the limited access to education. His method of connecting literature and society, as well as national and world literature, is thus intended to explain the impact of political and economic dependency on literary creation itself.[27]

These conditions still have an impact on literary creation today. This can be seen, for example, in Regina Dalcastagnè's study on how literary texts are produced, purchased, and read by members of a particular class, who disseminate their own values by determining and restricting the forms of literary representation. She notes that poor people are typically represented as marginalized social groups, which points to their exclusion from the field of literature—even though they constitute the largest portion of Brazilian society. As she observes, "The world of the contemporary Brazilian novel is the bourgeois world of the middle class."[28] In other words, authors create narrators who have the same socioeconomic characteristics as the authors themselves, and literary texts thus reproduce the same mechanisms of exclusion that affect other aspects of Brazilian society.

The histories of Companhia das Letras and Cosac Naify similarly show that the ruling ideas in Brazilian society correspond to the ideas of the ruling class, as this class controls the means of producing books.[29] In this sense, the different directions taken by these publishers are ultimately insignificant, as they both came up against the structural problem of income inequality and poverty, and the production and consumption of books remained inaccessible to the majority of the population, for whom books were not products of immediate necessity and for whom social prestige was derived from other sources. Despite their efforts to expand and consolidate the book market in Brazil, social and economic exclusionary practices imposed older mechanisms of domination. The fact that Cosac Naify worked in an anti-capitalistic way indicates that it could have performed a kind of compensatory function within the broader capitalist system, but even this function could not be fulfilled when the contradictions of the Brazilian book market imposed themselves, which led Charles Cosac to cease his activities as a publisher.

Translated by Anthony Enns

Notes

1 Sandra Siehe Reimão, "Tendências do mercado de livros no Brasil—um panorama e os best-sellers de ficção nacional (2000–2009)," *Matrizes* 5, no. 1 (July–December 2011): 194–210.

2 It is important to mention that during the government of President Fernando Henrique Cardoso (1995–2003) a certain number of slots at public universities were reserved for Afro-Brazilian students for the first time in history. In 2012, at the beginning of President Dilma Rousseff's government, a law also went into effect that reserved 25 percent of all slots in public institutions for Afro-Brazilian, indigenous, and ethnic minorities as well as students from public elementary schools whose families received less than one and a half times the minimum wage. Public elementary schools in Brazil had been neglected by the government for decades and were only attended by the poorest students, whereas public high schools were attended by a rich and privileged minority of students, who completed their basic education at expensive private elementary schools.

3 Bárbara Borges, *Um novo cenário para o negócio do livro* (São Paulo: COM-ARTE 2009); Galeno Amorin, ed., *Retratos da leitura no Brasil* (São Paulo: Imprensa Oficial, Instituto Pró-livro, 2008); Iara Augusta da Silva, "A conformação do mercado editorial brasileiro a partir das últimas décadas do século XX e anos iniciais do século XXI: o caso do grupo Abril," *Revista HISTEDBR Online* 60 (December 2014): 78–94.

4 Pedro Lovisi, "Importação de livros encomendados por editoras na China agrava crise," *Estado de Minas*, December 21, 2018, https://www.em.com.br/app/noticia/economia/2018/12/09/internas_economia,1011674/importacao-de-livros-encomendados-por-editoras-na-china-agrava-a-crise.shtml.

5 Pedro Herculano Guimarães Ferreira de Souza, "A desigualdade vista do topo: a concentração de renda entre os ricos no Brasil, 1926–2013," PhD diss. (Universidade de Brasília, 2016), 243–50.

6 Fernando Canzian, Fernanda Mena, and Lalo de Almeida, "Brazil's Super-Rich Lead Global Income Concentration," *Folha de São Paulo*, August 19, 2019, https://temas.folha.uol.com.br/global-inequality/brazil/brazils-super-rich-lead-global-income-concentration.shtml.

7 This is based on the Marxist concept of the fetish character of commodities, which is described as follows:

> [W]hen we bring the products of our labour into relation with each other as values, it is not because we see in these articles the material receptacles of homogeneous human labour. Quite the contrary; whenever, by an exchange, we equate as values our different products, by that very act, we also equate, as human labour, the different kinds of labour expended upon them. We are not aware of this, nevertheless we do it. Value, therefore, does not stalk about with a label describing what it is. It is value, rather, that converts every product into a social hieroglyphic. Later on, we try to decipher the hieroglyphic, to get behind the secret of our own social products; for to stamp an object of utility as a value, is just as much a social product as language.

From this perspective, prestige would be a hieroglyphic for advanced users. Karl Marx, *Capital: A Critique of Political Economy*, trans. Samuel Moore and Edward Aveling (New York: Modern Library, 1906), 85.

8 "Desempenho Real do Mercado Livreiro," *Sindicato Nacional dos Editores de Livros*, May 2019, https://snel.org.br/wp/wp-content/uploads/2019/05/histórico_pesquisa_preço_2018_final.pdf.

9 Holger Ehling, "Wie Brasilien zum weltgrößten Buchkäufer wurde," *Die Welt*, October 9, 2013, https://www.welt.de/kultur/literarischewelt/article120739558/Wie-Brasilien-zum-weltgroessten-Buchkaeufer-wurde.html.

10 "Série histórica '10 anos de produção e vendas do setor editorial brasileiro' é lançada no Snel," *Sindicado Nacional dos Editores de Livros*, August 24, 2016, https://www.snel.org.br/serie-historica-10-anos-de-pesquisa-producao-e-vendas-do-setor-editorial-brasileiro.

11 "Retratos da Leitura no Brasil," *Instituto Pró-livro*, March 2016, http://prolivro.org.br/home/index.php/atuacao/25-projetos/pesquisas/3900-pesquisa-retratos-da-leitura-no-brasil-48.

12 Werner Mathes, "Stern-Umfrage: 27 Prozent der Deutschen lesen mehr als zehn Bücher pro Jahr," *Presseportal*, March 11, 2015, https://www.presseportal.de/pm/6329/2969695.

13 Andrew Perrin, "Book Reading 2016," *Pew Research Center*, September 1, 2016, https://www.pewresearch.org/internet/2016/09/01/book-reading-2016.

14 A ranked list of the largest publishing companies in the world is jointly published by *Livres Hebdo* (France), *buchreport* (Germany/Austria/Switzerland), *BookDao* (China), *The Bookseller* (Great Britain), *Publishers Weekly* (United States), and *PublishNews* (Brazil).

15 "Censo do livro digital," *Sindicado Nacional dos Editores de Livros*, August 2017, http://cbl.org.br/site/wp-content/uploads/2017/08/Apresentacao-Censo-do-Livro-Digital.pdf.

16 According to the Börsenverein des Deutschen Buchhandels and the Association of American Publishers, e-books constituted 5 percent of all book sales in Germany and 13 percent of all book sales in the United States in 2018. "E-Books: Zahlen zum E-Book in Deutschland," *Börsenverein des Deutschen Buchhandels*, https://www.boersen-verein.de/markt-daten/marktforschung/e-books; "AAP Statistics," *Association of American Publishers*, https://publishers.org/data-and-statistics/industry-statistics.

17 It is not possible to separate fiction from nonfiction in the Brazilian book market, as all of the titles that are not included in the categories of "religious books" and "textbooks" are assigned to the category of "general titles."

18 "Institucional," *Companhia das Letras*, https://www.companhiadasletras.com.br/sobre.php.

19 Márcio Ferrari, "Críticos e professores de literatura elegem as melhores editoras do Brasil," *Valor econômico*, July 23, 2010: 4–11.

20 Adriana Abujamra, "A via-crúcis de Charles," *Piauí*, April 10, 2016: 38–46.

21 Elaine Ramos, "Oblomov," *Estúdio Gráfico*, https://elaineramos-estudiografico.com.br/Oblomov.

22 Although Brazil was affected by the economic crisis of 2008, like all countries in the world, it experienced a decisive recovery starting in 2010 thanks to commodity exports to China (mainly ore and agricultural products). Brazil's gross domestic product (GDP) increased by 7.5 percent per year during this period. The instabilities in the European economy between 2011 and 2013, especially in Portugal, Greece, Ireland, Spain, and Italy, caused Brazil's GDP to fall again to 2 percent per year, and this drop in growth caused inflation levels to rise to 10 percent per year. This resulted in a significant shrinking of the book market, especially because of the increase in debts. In this context, the economic crisis served as a trigger for the reorganization of conservative forces in opposition to the Workers' Party, which had been in the federal government since 2003. The impeachment of President Dilma Rousseff, who had been democratically elected in 2014, inaugurated a period of multiple crises, which culminated in the government of Jair Bolsonaro in 2018. For more information on the economy of Brazil, see "Séries históricas," *Instituto Brasileiro de Geografia e Estatística*, https://www.ibge.gov.br/estatisticas/economicas/contas-nacionais/9300-contas-nacionais-trimestrais.html?=&t=series-historicas&utm_source=landing&utm_medium=explica&utm_campaign=pib#evolucao-taxa.

23 Abujamra, "A via-crúcis de Charles."

24 Ibid.

25 Antonio Candido, *On Literature and Society*, ed. Howard S. Becker (Princeton: Princeton University Press, 1995), 119–41.

26 Concepts like the "third world" and "underdevelopment" are no longer used in postcolonial theory. See María do Mar Castro Varela and Nikita Dhawan, *Postkoloniale Theorie: Eine kritische Einführung* (Bielefeld: Transcript, 2015).

27 The diversity of Candido's work can be seen in various contexts, as Stefan Helgesson points out, "A towering figure in Brazilian intellectual history, Candido made a decisive impact not just on national literary studies but also, by extension, on international literary theory—his erstwhile student, Roberto Schwarz, provided Franco Moretti with some of the fundaments of his theory of world literature. I would even argue that Candido's work in the 1960s, notably *Literatura e sociedade*, prefigure some of Bourdieu's thinking in its combination of external and internal approaches to literature." Stefan Helgesson, "Fields in Formation: English Studies and National Literature in South Africa (with a Brazilian Comparison)," in *Bourdieu and Postcolonial Studies*, ed. Raphael Dalleo (Liverpool: Liverpool University Press, 2016), 159–74 (171).

28 Regina Dalcastagnè, *Literatura brasileira contemporânea: Um território contestado* (Rio de Janeiro: Eduerj; Horizonte, 2012), 147–97 (189).

29 This statement is based on the Marxist notion of the relationship between the ruling class and ruling ideas:

> The ideas of the ruling class are in every epoch the ruling ideas: i.e., the class which is the ruling *material* force of society is at the same time its ruling *intellectual* force [emphasis in original]. The class which has the means of material production at its disposal, consequently also controls the means of mental production, so that the ideas of those who lack the means of mental production are on the whole subject to it. The ruling ideas are nothing more than the ideal expression of the dominant material relations, the dominant material relations grasped as ideas; hence of the relations which make the one class the ruling one, therefore, the ideas of its dominance. The individuals composing the ruling class possess among other things consciousness, and therefore think. Insofar, therefore, as they rule as a class and determine the extent and compass of an historical epoch, it is self-evident that they do this in its whole range, hence among other things rule also as thinkers, as producers of ideas, and regulate the production and distribution of the ideas of their age: thus their ideas are the ruling ideas of the epoch.
>
> Karl Marx and Friedrich Engels, *The German Ideology*, trans. S. W. Ryazanskaya (Amherst, NY: Prometheus Books, 1998), 67.

Section Two

MATERIAL DISTINCTIONS IN POPULAR FICTION

Chapter 4

ONLY THE "OUTWARD APPEARANCE" OF A HAREM? READING *MEMOIRS OF AN ARABIAN PRINCESS* AS A MATERIAL TEXT

Kate Roy

"Mrs. Ruete, the Berlin-based sister of the Sultan of Zanzibar, will soon publish a two-volume work entitled 'Memoirs of an Arabian Princess,' which is said to contain both personal experiences and particularly impressive descriptions of Mohammedan [*sic*] culture in East Africa"[1] states a notice in a German illustrated magazine of April 1886, an example of the publicity preceding the publication of Emily Ruete's autobiography *Memoiren einer arabischen Prinzessin* (Memoirs of an Arabian Princess) that same year. The memoirs, written in German, primarily describe the childhood and young adulthood of their author, who was born Sayyida Salme, daughter of the sultan of Oman and Zanzibar, near Zanzibar Town in 1844, and who lived in Zanzibar until the age of 22, when she left the island after her relationship with her German neighbor was discovered. It is widely acknowledged as the oldest published autobiography of an Arab woman in existence.[2] The memoirs, extending from a personal life to "a meditation about the self" in history and culture,[3] also describe episodes from Ruete's later life, such as her journey to Zanzibar in 1885, where she and the inheritance she hoped to claim were used as a bargaining instrument, playing a central role in German colonial ambitions in East Africa. As the notice in the illustrated magazine heralds, they additionally discuss important aspects of Muslim and East African culture for her German readership, such as "The Status of Women in the Orient," "The Fasting Period," and "Slavery." "I don't want to write a scholarly book," writes Ruete, "I just want to try to make it possible for the European reader to have a correct understanding of the more important views and customs of the Orient."[4]

Before the publication of Ruete's memoirs, the Ruete's relationship and subsequent perceived flight from Zanzibar had proven enticing fodder for asides in the narratives of explorers and for articles in the illustrated magazines of the day. These imaginative retellings of this episode in Ruete's life read like a "fairytale from the *Thousand and One Nights* made real"[5] and have arguably provoked the distinctive sober language and style of the memoirs themselves, termed "ethnographic" by Annegret Nippa, editor of the contemporary modernized and somewhat abridged German version of the memoirs.[6] The memoirs' factual reporting disallows the previously established fantasy element, in turn enabling pithy comparisons between the constructs of East and West through the medium of the everyday and the author's appropriation and manipulation of the traditionally subordinate role of the "Oriental." The "love story," specifically, is impoverished and domesticated (in Tarek Shamma's strategic sense of the word)[7] in contrast to what has gone before, thereby moving this episode, and thus Ruete herself, until then so often represented, into the realms of the indescribable.[8]

Given the potential workings of the text as I have outlined them here, it is all the more telling, particularly in view of Gillian Whitlock's comments on the "cultural authority" of memoir writers,[9] that the memoirs should have gone through so many guises in their afterlife. In 2014, for example, they are available as an academic-style text, a romance novel, and a Victorian erotica Kindle book. Despite their different forms, however, all but the romance novel use the text of Ruete's original. Clearly, then, this is an instance of the book as "*un*stable physical form" with "multiple material lives" that has connected with its cultural contexts and discourses in varying ways over time.[10] Gérard Genette's analysis of the paratexts of a work is illuminating here in demonstrating how a text can engage with the world in multiple ways through its packaging[11]:

> Being immutable, the text in itself is incapable of adapting to changes in its public in space and over time. The paratext—more flexible, more versatile, always transitory because transitive—is, as it were, an instrument of adaptation. Hence the continual modifications in the "presentation" of the text (that is, in the text's mode of being present in the world).[12]

When Ruete published her memoirs, the material and paratextual elements that shaped them into a book—such as cover design, illustrations, and title page—and their provenance as a text by an "Oriental" woman writing about her life immediately entered them into the genre of harem literature, a genre Reina Lewis describes as inherently viable and marketable in the eighteenth and long nineteenth centuries: "[W]hether you wrote about living in one, visiting one, or escaping from one, any book that had anything to do with the harem sold. Publishers knew it, booksellers knew it, readers knew it and authors knew it."[13] In its "generically unstable and intrinsically porous" state, placement of the harem narrative, which encompassed women's popular (auto)biographical writing on this subject, vacillated between popular memoir and (romance) novel.[14] As one of the first of these texts to write back to the West from an "Oriental" point of view, the interaction between the linguistic style and the paratextual features of the memoirs conveys the tensions Lewis speaks of between the commercially driven need to satisfy and the simultaneous bid to defy the established paradigms that fed the market for harem narratives. Suggesting, therefore, that the packaging is shaped by and confirms genre expectations, even when the content of the text might tell a very different story, Lewis draws particular attention to the inclusion of genre-appropriate key words in the books' titles—in our case "Arabian" and "princess"—and to the associated images, most notably that of the books' authors in veils on the cover or frontispiece.[15]

Proceeding largely chronologically, my contribution aims to explore the material history of the memoirs in their German- and English-language contexts, that is, the history of the major elements that make them, in textual theorist Jerome McGann's understanding, a "bound, printed edition [...] 'held in the hand.'"[16] It is these aspects of a book's materiality—"its original matter of publication, its marks, deletions, binding and actual circulation"—that actively interact with the networks they propel themselves into with their publication, namely the public reading spaces I have labeled "the world."[17] Mapping the journey of the memoirs' materiality thus entails a focus not only on the manner in which the various editions have been materialized through their paratextual features—in particular, cover images, illustrations, and the so-called value aspect of the text (its physical format and corresponding cost)—but also on the "networks of resonance, action and circulation" they insert themselves into.[18] This journey will take us through the memoirs of 1886, the early translations, and the modern reprints, before I go on to briefly discuss and contrast the materiality of two very recent German rewrites of the memoirs: a postcolonial novel and a historical romance.

The ethnographic content and expression of the memoirs-as-book, I argue, do not preclude the book itself existing in a liminal space between autobiography and fiction and finally being subsumed by its popular fictional paratexts and becoming a novel in the German context. Indeed, the liminality that is produced via the book's materialization in paratextual effects is a further tension that has accompanied the reception and adaptation of Ruete's memoirs, most notably in their inclusion (surrounded by advertisements for corsets) in *Collier's Once a Week Library* in 1890 and their recent doubled high and low culture fictionalization in the German context. This chapter explores how the interplay of paratext and world, of two apparent outsides to the text in other words, could contribute to the production of genre(s), where "Context [could become] Content."[19] At the same time, it explores how this interplay may ultimately work to reterritorialize the memoirs more specifically in latent, popular cultural Orientalist discourses of their contemporary periods, citationary discourses that build on unconscious fantasies from the writing on and imagery of the "Orient" that have gone before, to shape and "deliver" the construct Orient to the construct West, their inherent "enunciative capacity" allowing for this exercising of power that can act to privilege context over content and that has a long material textual history.[20]

Thresholds of Book and World?

The intersection of the paratextual features of the memoirs and the reading public and contemporary discourses highlights the textual engagement of world and book. Here, I am interested in Genette's notion of a paratext, a "message that has taken on material form," as "a zone not only of transition but also of *transaction*" with the ability to interact with text and world and to make productive or not-so-productive connections [emphasis in original].[21] Yet Genette also describes this threshold more concretely as presenting or "making present"—in other words, functioning "to ensure the text's presence in the world" and that it is received as a book.[22] If we follow Michele Moylan's near contemporaneous reading of presentation as performance, this is a process that seems to imply the book's simultaneous insertion into "meaning" or discourse via the paratext, given that "texts 'mean' when they are performed" and that textual materiality constitutes an "interpretative performance" because it not only shapes the text but also introduces itself into the world as an "agent of change," encouraging others to read the text in the same way.[23]

McGann's discussions of the material text's interaction with the world and what this does—in other words, how the circumstances of its publication affect its literary meaning—are well-tailored to a text that has been multiplied as often as the memoirs, allowing, unlike Moylan's model, for editorial and not just authorial intervention. McGann has always insisted on the important role of the book's materiality in producing meaning, coining the term "textual field" to express the interaction of a text's material form ("paratexts, bibliographical codes and all visual features") and linguistic elements.[24] For McGann, the linguistic codes, or actual words, of a work could stay the same, yet it would still be capable of "chang[ing] its cultural meaning" through the manipulation of its bibliographic codes, its "typography, layout, paper, order, etc."[25] Importantly for our purposes, the McGannian material text is in this way always already unstable: any (editorial) attempt to stabilize it in fact results in the creation of a new version for its new context, for a text "is always a new (and changed) originality each time it is textually engaged."[26] Texts' meanings can thus be seen as created by their use, with the social relations they make resultantly a vital part of themselves, producing them, McGann argues, as "social *acts*," where the dynamics they model transform them into "the very events of time and history itself" [emphasis in original].[27]

In this sense, mapping the presentation history of a work alongside the world it inserts itself into unlocks the "semiotic potential" of the text's mate-riality, which takes center stage in McGann's *The Textual Condition*, where it is the structure "within which textuality is constrained to exhibit its transfor-mations."[28] Reading the semiotic potential of the materially different incar-nations of the memoirs in this way enables us to glean an understanding both of their production of liminality (their perceived instability as fiction/memoir) and of the implications of this liminality in their repeated textual engage-ment with (and by) popular culture as a narrative by an Arab woman that the Other Europe seeks to bring under control.[29]

Early Editions: Thresholds "Made Present"

Turning first to the early editions of the memoirs published in Berlin (1886), London (1888), and New York (1888), I begin by exploring how the cover—that most apparent "containing" feature—might be seen to function as a threshold in transaction with the world. Nicole Matthews argues that the materiality of a book's cover (fonts, illustrations, and the manner in which the cover elements are laid out) is central to the experience of the book, work-ing on readers both as a "visual object of pleasure" and as an "entry point into the text."[30] Color, design, and choice of image are, in this reading, the predominant actors in the book's reterritorialization in a genre, as they show how the content could be fixed in a different way, subsumed—at least tempo-rarily—by context.

Taking the earliest cover art of the memoirs, we find that the first three groups of readers effectively encountered a book that made present for them an image of a set of "non-Western" buildings, surrounded in some way by tropical plants and trees. In all three cases, I would like to explore what con-nections the cover art, and in one case the physicality of the cover itself, may have produced in readers through aspects of style, color, and material; what implications these connections may have had for the text's reterritorialization in overarching discourses from the world it enters into (here Orientalism); and in particular the effects of their unsettling of the text's status as memoir or popular fiction.

The cover art of at least one print run (the second) of the original German edition of the memoirs, which is also present in black and white as the title page of each of the book's two volumes, is a strikingly material, garishly tinted image of tropical plants and trees, framing a central, if distant, view of palaces on the shore (see Figure 4.1). Beit el-Sahel, the main Zanzibar palace building, known as the "harem" at the time, is recognizable on the left. Putting the accent firmly on palace life and suggesting a viewer—evocatively staged as a peeping Tom peering in from behind the bushes—being drawn in from outside, the cover art presents an intriguing insight into the perspective of the first readers, who Ruete herself claimed had previously only been able to read about the (inauthentic) "outward appearance" of a harem in the accounts of European commentators, male or female.[31] Taking Beit el-Sahel, the other palace buildings, and a harbor scene with a docked dhow, and surrounding them with detailed exotic foliage, the features of this image in their staged accuracy (their botanical and architectural precision) not only allude to the abovementioned publicity note, illustrating the suggestion that the reader will

Figure 4.1 Cover of Emily Ruete, *Memoiren einer arabischen Prinzessin* (1886). *Source*: © Herskovits Library of African Studies, Northwestern University.

benefit from Ruete's insider perspective, but also make connections both with German "knowledge" about Zanzibar and with familiar images of the exotic. At the same time, articles on Germany's "colonial endeavors" with similarly detailed pictures of Zanzibar were circulating in illustrated magazines,[32] and explorer Otto Kersten had already introduced Zanzibar to German readers in his 1869 volume on Baron Carl Claus von der Decken's expeditions, his book including descriptions of both plant life and palaces.

It seems by no means insignificant that Kersten's book is reputed to be the first to give the name Zanzibar a "lyrical ring" in German-speaking countries.[33] The garishness of the tropical vegetation on the German cover resonates with developments in printing at the end of the nineteenth century, which dramatically transformed the potential of fantasy illustration, as Terry Reece Hackford describes in his study of the *Thousand and One Nights*, by bringing with them more accurate, "intensified" colors paradoxically able to create a "mysterious, glowing universe."[34] For Richard van Leeuwen the use of the "dark, ominous colours" of this palette in particular both enhances the impact of the illustrations and lends them "a sense of Eastern mystery," ultimately producing an intertwining of documentary realism and "veiled exoticism," arguably akin to the thrust of Kersten's text, which similarly combines the authoritative display of knowledge and the appeal to fantasy that underpin Orientalism.[35]

Both Jonathan Hensher and John D. Mackenzie have commented on the practical function of exotic vegetation in Orientalist illustration and spectacle, Hensher identifying how palm trees and tropical plant life as "familiar indicators of unfamiliar places and climes" are used to conjure up an "exotic location" in the illustrations to Sinbad from *Le Cabinet des fées*.[36] Mackenzie, writing about a different visual dimension—that of stage design—but whose ideas are nonetheless applicable to textual histories, as will be shown, takes this interplay of knowledge and fantasy further to demonstrate how depictions of the exotic, be they architectural, botanical, or animal, and the desire to exercise (colonial) power went hand in hand on the nineteenth-century stage. These images, employed to give the impression of "an opulent fantasy world," functioned, he argues, to enable the "appropriation" of this world "through spectacle [..., a] spectacular novelty through which the audience could identify difference and potentially confirm their own supposed uniqueness in appearance, moral values and power."[37] That the exact depiction of such plant life also took on a documentary function again points toward the knowledge-representation-power nexus that Tarek Shamma identifies in the "exhibitionary complex" of Edward Lane's translation of the *Thousand and One Nights* and William Harvey's commissioned illustrations that accompanied it. Shamma considers that what readers encountered here "was not only the exhibition that was the East, but the East itself being fashioned into an exhibition to be experienced by the dominant European gaze."[38]

In the case of the German cover too, the fantasy foliage's framing of the ethnographically presented, "known" palace makes present an Orient that is appealing and consumable: exotic, yet reassuringly knowable. Appealing to fiction *and* to fact, the connections the image makes go above and beyond the dry narrative of the text itself, reterritorializing the book squarely as harem narrative, a "true fairytale" that is able to stoke the reader's everyday latent Orientalist fantasies—the banal and popular fantasies of the Orient, that, as Meyda Yeğenoğlu demonstrates, were so crucial in establishing manifest Orientalism, the "official knowledge" of the Orient, through the creation of a discursive field.[39]

The first English translation of the memoirs (unattributed) was published in two versions in 1888 by Ward and Downey of London and D. Appleton & Company of New York. The British publication is an attractive octavo volume, very similar in size and quality to the German original, and, priced at 6s, a decidedly middle-class volume.[40] The iconography of the cover suggests that it is a reworking of the German original (see Figure 4.2). It uses the same spatial configuration, but the buildings have multiplied, replacing the vegetation as a frame on the image's left-hand side, and have undergone a transition into forms more clearly recognizable in the popular cultural context. "Heaping on the viziers," as Jorge Luis Borges would term it,[41] these changes produce an image that now corresponds more clearly with Lewis's marketable title key words. The background on the British cover materializes the "fierce," "Oriental" light so beloved of Orientalist painters.[42] In the absence of most of the exotic botanical frame, this "Oriental" light works to enhance two dhows, more recognizable under sail, and arabesque buildings that outstrip their rather drab, stocky Zanzibari counterparts in Oriental codification.

In practical terms these changes allude to Orientalist painters' nineteenth-century ideas of the Orient, which then "meant first of all the Levant," later including the North African coast.[43] Such a Genettian threshold also patently transacts with the iconography of the *Thousand and One Nights*, a connection not only significant in its evocation of the popular cultural field surrounding the memoirs but whose own history of the interplay of text and paratext shows how the former can come to be outstripped by the latter. Robert Irwin has argued that from the seventeenth century on, book illustrators have been instrumental in the genesis and development of the iconography of the *Thousand and One Nights*, progressing this iconography from "ethnographic realism" to "stylized fantasy."[44] For van Leeuwen, too, the imagery of the *Nights* has come to govern our understanding of the stories themselves, as

Figure 4.2 Cover of Emily Ruete, *Memoirs of an Arabian Princess* (1888). *Source*: © The British Library Board.

"part of a broader, more universal layer in the tradition of visual culture, with a complex fabric of connotations," even subsuming them and "perhaps even *becom[ing]* the *Thousand and One Nights*" [emphasis in original].[45]

Charles Johanningsmeier uses the term "reading field" to describe the combination of the ideological, the textual, and the material connections a book makes.[46] I argue that the reading field of the late nineteenth century would have connected such a cover with the *Thousand and One Nights* and its "complex fabric of connotations," the *Nights* having iconographically caught the European popular imagination[47] and having already generated a craze for Oriental-style works that delivered the exotic East. Similarly, the fact that the memoirs' cover image has taken on a life of its own demonstrates a comparable dynamic to that of the transactions of the imagery of the *Thousand and One Nights* and the world, in that the memoirs' cover image, too, has created a world far removed from the linguistic codes "inside"—its own fantastical Arabian iconography as it were—by functioning in conjunction with paratextual elements, such as the title, rather than acting as any real illustration of the words of the memoirs themselves.

Moving from fiction/memoir crossovers provoked by the realm of fantasy paratexts to those provoked by a more physically present paratextual context, I suggest a reading of the cover apparatus of the American edition of 1888 as an extension of its material format. The American version offers, on a modest brown or blue clothbound cover, a small partial repeat of the German cover image in monochrome: a sketch in thick strokes, from a different angle, depicting a close-up of part of Beit el-Sahel, the tower, and a moored dhow, with a nod to the exotic vegetation (large palm leaves) functioning as a decorative extension of the image. Perhaps in keeping with the image's realism, the American version's title page prominently displays the genre specification "An Autobiography" and the author's name "Emily Ruete, née Princess of Oman and Zanzibar." Yet, like all the early editions, the interplay of paratextual elements is not as straightforward as it seems with regard to the book's cultural or genre status. Genette reminds us that the proclaimed markers of genre need not be accepted "without a mental reservation" and indeed that *Jane Eyre* was also initially presented as "An Autobiography."[48] In reading the "genre contract," the genre indication that heralds the so-called agreement between author and reader as to how the reader should approach the text's content,[49] the author's name is merely an element in the whole broad and potentially contradictory paratextual field of the title page; it is "caught up in a complex whole [the contract], whose boundaries are hard to trace and whose constituent parts are equally hard to inventory."[50] In combination with the author's name, her title too has a role to play, functioning as the "publisher's introduction"; here, as Lewis would no doubt agree, it is clearly "good for business."[51]

Appleton's edition, likely a corresponding (or possibly unauthorized) reprint of the 1888 British edition, was printed at a time when mainstream American book publishers had brought out libraries of inexpensive fiction to take on the issuers of cheap books.[52] While not a part of *Appleton's Town and Country Library*—the publishing house's "fiction publication,"[53] which was launched that same year—advertisements for fiction in the back of the memoirs provoke genre confusion, as empirical evidence shows Appleton primarily advertising like with like. Although it is important to remember that there was no clear fiction/fact binary in price, it is nonetheless interesting to note that the memoirs were sold at the same price—a modest 75¢[54]—as the clothbound versions of works from *Appleton's Town and Country Library*, also sharing their format: "cheap twelvemos," common in the period, were often works by "popular standard authors."[55] However, advertisements for the memoirs in other books published by Appleton—what Genette would term the publishers' "epitext"—speak against a fictional interpretation. Despite their contradictory tone (extolling the "entertainment" value of the text and promising a "picture of Oriental court life" from one "to the manner born"), they list the book under "publications" rather than "fiction" and surround the advertisement itself with others for clearly nonfictional books.

In this case, therefore, we could argue that the cover, in keeping with the entirety of the paratextual framework of Appleton's edition of the memoirs, is a site of transaction between popular fact (the cover image harking back to the ethnographic connotations of the German cover and all they imply) and—in its format—popular fiction. What all three covers then share is a liminal relationship between truth and fiction. The texts' varying covers, as thresholds on the world, are their "illustrated dimension," acting, as Margaret Sironval puts it, as "the expression of different readings [...] by contemporaries."[56] For John Mullan, in the fictional sphere at least, a cover not only tells us what is in the book but also expresses "its singular imaginative space,"[57] a space here clearly transacting with Oriental discourse and in particular with the everyday fantasies of latent Orientalism as fed by popular culture.

"Making Present" Without Pictures: *Collier's* and the Physical Text

Unlike the first three editions of the memoirs, the version published in 1890 by P. F. Collier of New York presents an imageless cover but one which suggests a sustained transaction between its elements and the world, providing us with an intriguing textual field. A reader can enter this field from the page functioning as the cover (itself only slightly thicker than the pages it encases), where the header and the title are jammed in above a much larger block of text advertising "Crosby's Vitalized Phosphites." In practical terms, Collier had no need to attract the attention of potential customers: the books published in *Collier's Once a Week Library* were sold twice-monthly to existing subscribers alongside the *Collier's Once a Week* magazine (the whole package cost $4.80 a year), guaranteeing them a circulation of 200,000 copies.[58] His print capacity clearly a source of pride, Collier writes, in a letter published in the *Athenæum*, that he has had a Hoe press built, able to "turn [...] out fifty thousand books a day, folded."[59] Approximately 10 million copies of these paperbound books were issued each year.

At the time the memoirs became part of *Collier's Once a Week Library*, the *Collier's Once a Week* magazine promoted itself as "a magazine of 'fiction, fact, sensation, wit, humour, news'" and was considered "a story paper [...] of good standards."[60] Johanningsmeier has analyzed the very different bibliographical setting of a work's appearance in *Collier's*: the printing of the magazine on paper that was "relatively cheap," for example, suggested it was not intended to last, and it employed many and varied illustrations and typefaces.

Its physicality, suggestively encompassing the transitory nature of the para-text, "encouraged its readers to read its contents quickly."[61]

With periodicals in general acting as "portals to fiction," and *Collier's* itself being popular for "traditional romances,"[62] we could argue that this context could also have had the effect of encouraging the memoirs to be read in this way, an effect arguably only enhanced by exploring other features of its textual field. Like many other paperbound books, the books in the *Collier's Once a Week Library* contained pages of nonliterary advertisements alongside advertisements for other texts by the same publisher (an eclectic mix of Dickens, encyclopedias, and previous *Library* volumes) at both ends to cover publishing costs. Robert Hertel provides a telling assessment of the likely market: "As she read her favorite paperback *novel*, the American housewife could become acquainted with the cleansing properties of Sapolio and Pears' soaps, the perfect fit of Ball's corsets and the miraculous cura-tive powers of many patent medicines."[63] Hertel's description is apt: Pears and Sapolio are both part of the memoirs' assemblage in *Collier's*, alongside Madame Warren's corsets and "Beecham's Pills for Bilious and Nervous Disorders," aimed specifically at "female sufferers." These elements give us an indication not only of the imagined readership for the memoirs but also of the *way* they may have been read—in other words, the connection between the artificiality of this advertising of everyday products and the idea that what was presented on the page was similarly everyday popular fiction. The publishers' epitext is much clearer in this respect, with notices inside the book itself guaranteeing the reader twice-monthly delivery of "one of the largest, newest and best of the famous Library of modern fiction in book-form" and explaining the selection of the library in a rather grandi-ose manner that belies the bibliographical context as "nothing in the way of prose fiction which has not been attentively read and heartily approved of by men thoroughly competent to detect the higher literary qualities whether they come accredited by famous names, or shrinking behind the modest mask of anonymity."

Precisely with regard to this anonymity, the paratextual features of the *Collier's Once a Week Library* volume suggest that it was almost certainly a pirated copy of the British version (if such a term could exist before the copy-right law of 1891). It uses an identical text, albeit formed into columns and thus giving it more of a magazine look, and reimagines the text/anonymity interplay of that version, where the publisher's presentation (and accompa-nying "guarantor" act) of the author was missing in the smooth, anonymous title page, an omission also functioning as part of the paratextual apparatus, unsettling the notion of autobiography. Conversely, with the introduction of "By Salme, *Daughter of the Sultan of Zanzibar*", the "pseudonym effect" of a romantic and exotic name chosen for these very particularities is techni-cally brought to bear, changing the text's author function. "If the name on the spine looked Oriental," writes Lewis, "the marketing opportunities were greater,"[64] a fitting transaction for a text as overwhelmingly materially com-mercial as the *Collier's* version of the memoirs.

Contraindications of Authenticity? The Visual Plane

The 1907 version of the memoirs, retranslated by Lionel Strachey and pub-lished by Doubleday, Page & Company of New York, is deserving of discus-sion despite (or perhaps because of) its predominantly historical-sociological staging, as it was the first to explicitly present the memoirs as a historical document, yet it was also the source for the Victorian erotica Kindle book I discuss later. In a text published when harem literature was still popular but was past its peak, both the doubled staging of the author image itself and its interactions with other images in the textual field suggest the production of not one but two genres—two contexts for the content—in an age when the book's colonial history is gaining in historical import.

The frontispiece in the memoirs' German original had continued the strange paradox of surfaces and drawing initiated in the cover art. It depicts Ruete in "the barbaric glory of her native costume" (as *The Times* reviewer put it in 1886), staring at us defiantly from a lavishly draped interior, which was in fact a Hamburg photographer's studio. Subsequently, this image of Ruete functioned evocatively either precisely in its absence or in the *man-ner* of its presence. It was absent in the British version of 1888 and the pre-sumably derivative *Collier's* version of 1890—both, as we have seen, verging paratextually on the fictional—while the Appleton version, an uncaptioned engraving, is a fittingly fictionalized repetition of the photoengraving that appeared in the German text, its illustrated nature tapping into what Lewis would call "another order of representation" to the "photographic codes of realism" of standard depictions of the author in harem narratives.[65] Tellingly, the 1907 version has both photograph and illustration.

Captioned for the first time in this edition—as "THE AUTHORESS Salamah bint Saïd, afterward Emily Ruete"—it is the frontispiece that stages the memoirs squarely within the conventions of harem literature through "the looked-for pleasures of Oriental dress," instantly readable in a market where the ability to be visibly, convincingly Oriental was any such author's unique selling point.[66] Yet the frontispiece is not the first image of Ruete encountered in the 1907 text: this image is located, for the first time, on the cover itself, a luxurious embossed gold and silver engraving of the contours and main features of the frontispiece in miniature, an image arguably staged for exotic appeal, particularly considering the absence of anything similar on the covers of other books from the *Memoirs of Charming Women* series to which it belongs.

Lewis has shown, in the case of Ottoman author Zeyneb Hanoum, how notions of authenticity can be (re)produced via the way the book's visual narrative is put together.[67] This idea meaningfully transacts with the 1907 version's newly included, unsigned introductory text "Authenticity of these memoirs." The translator felt, we are told, that the historical events depicted were well-known and could consequently have been written by anyone. The "intimate revelations," on the other hand,

> betoken [...] an extraordinary knowledge of Arab life in general and of Zanzibar royal harem life in particular. Was the alleged writer, then, actually a Sultan's daughter who escaped from her country and went to live in Germany as the wife of a German merchant? So romantic a supposal seeming to require confirmation, the translator wrote to an English government official well-versed in matters pertaining to the African colonies.[68]

The reply, also cited in the introduction, is in the affirmative and does not skimp on scandal: "Ruete was a German trader, and she unfortunately became *enceinte* by him."[69] I argue that it is precisely this intersection of authenticity and "romance" (or fantasy) that is staged in the visuals accompanying the narrative. Aside from the two images of Ruete, fictionalized and factual, 31 additional images have been introduced, falling, broadly speaking, into 3 categories: the ethnographic ("Type of Oman Arab," for example), the historical (historical figures with a role in the memoirs, such as Bismarck), and the "geographic" (scene-setting photographs of palaces and plantations). All of the images are captioned, and all but five display in addition a clear indication of their provenance; some even include copyright information.

In the midst of all this staged authenticity it is perhaps surprising to find as part of the same textual assemblage a fictional image that transacts with a popular and evocative material context. "Members of an Arabian Harem," the 15th image, is in fact the colonial postcard "Deux femmes arabes" (Two Arab Women; see Figure 4.3), which usually also carries its makers' label—"made for Arougheti Bros Suez"—but here is apparently cropped to exclude both the title and the origin. The manipulation of this image into a "purely" ethnographic illustration apparently achieves the transaction of two photographed veiled faces with Ruete's unveiled one in the frontispiece, a (face) veil of some description deemed necessary in harem literature to make visual "the ultimate sign by which the West distinguishes the Oriental woman from the Occidental."[70] Yet while ticking this box, the image nonetheless unconsciously underlines its unreality—the women wear veils but pose inside (in a

Deux femmes arabes.

Figure 4.3 Colonial Postcard (Author's Collection).

studio setting and against a faintly defined balustrade); these veils, with their distinctive strips joining the top and bottom sections, are Egyptian *burqu'* with no correspondence to the Omani masks Ruete describes, they reproduce a generic Orient.

French author Leïla Sebbar has further challenged the authenticity of collectible colonial postcards, her text accompanying a collection of postcards of "Women of North Africa" reflecting on the circumstances in which the pictures were taken (their studio construction) and the origins of the women who posed for these pictures (many of whom were prostitutes).[71] After the decline of Orientalist painting, the postcard experienced its "Golden Age" (1900–1930): utterly and deliberately consumable, peddled by photographers "thirsty" for the exotic and for folklore, it not only "[became] the poor man's phantasm for a few pennies, display racks full of dreams," as Malek Alloula puts it, but also produced "pseudoknowledge" and stereotypes through its types.[72] Gérard Guicheteau encourages us to remember that the photograph's materiality should not deceive us into thinking that these women actually existed; rather, we should see them as embodying a "virtual ethnicity" that belongs to Orientalist fantasy.[73] The textual engagement with the consumable material culture of colonial postcards—along with the more clearly fiction-alized cover image—thus destabilizes the framework of presentation of this 1907 version of the memoirs as a purely serious historical text, taking on a dynamic not unlike Alloula's description of the colonial postcard's multifari-ous function, "avowedly" ethnographic, but in fact a site of "repressed" (colo-nial/Orientalist) fantasy.[74]

New Iconographies? The "Veiled Female Face"

With postcard and frontispiece intertwined in the 1907 edition of the memoirs and the photographic version of the frontispiece image repeatedly reproduced on the covers of reprints of the memoirs since the 1980s, Pamela Pears's inter-pretation of book jackets of modern texts by Algerian women writing in French as capturing the shift between the colonial postcard of the past and the con-tinued "selling" of Arab women in the present seems particularly relevant. In our time, she writes, "this same desire to sell the [Arab] woman as the exotic other translates into a regressively monolithic project," a project that is depend-ent on "clichés or [...] audience expectations that can be traced back to the colonial era."[75] Certainly the covers of contemporary reprints of the memoirs appear overwhelmingly uniform, repeatedly making present the frontispiece image of Ruete, be it full-length or in various stages of close-up. In an all-too filial continuation from the original frontispiece above, I argue that the persis-tence of this particular image-as-photograph as lead-in to the modern reprints of the memoirs works to enter the text into the discourse surrounding modern memoirs—and indeed popular fiction—by Muslim women writers in Europe and North America. This reading field, through the marketing apparatus that encompasses it, functions to *present* such veiled cover images as a metonym for both the "act of exposé" and the "trope of 'oppressed Muslim woman.'"[76]

As a staged studio scene suggesting that Ruete will take on the role of the Oriental, the frontispiece transacts with the written text, combining compli-ance (through the clothing she wears) with noncompliance, a staunch and challenging "looking back": her return of the gaze of her viewer. Yet it also apparently transacts with what Marilyn Booth calls "the politics of presenta-tion" as a sociological act, where the author-narrator is generated, through the covers of modern popular Arab literature by women writers, "as [a] female face swathed in hijab, seeming to offer as direct and unmediated a gaze at the reader as she promises to direct at her society."[77] The veiled female face, Booth suggests, now has a "familiar" currency in visually presenting books from the Middle East for the English-language market, arguably bringing into line Booth's sociological act and McGann's idea of the material text as *social* act that models the dynamics of the network(s) in which it occurs.

Whitlock, Pears, and Booth all make reference to the impact of cover images of veiled women prominently displayed in bookshops. Whitlock and Pears draw attention to anonymous, standardized close-ups of the face of a woman with kohl-lined eyes, wrapped in a black veil and *niqab*, used to sell both memoirs and fiction by women from a range of different Arab countries, while Booth discusses the contemporary role of the "familiar" *hijab*, which contrastingly individualizes, "framing the face and offering a legible inter-locutor to the Western reader."[78] The standard black veil close-up provides the marketable face of the memoirs' 2010 Russian edition, with a nod to this referential image in the cover iconography of the Weltbild paperback edition of Nicole C. Vosseler's recent novel on Ruete, which includes a dark-haired woman with kohl-lined eyes returning our gaze from behind a flowing red veil that obscures her lower face. The veil's role is arguably filled by the stand-ard frontispiece image itself, with which Ruete has arguably undergone a contemporary-style framing or "Orientalizing celebrity-making"—a process, Booth warns, in which the author image, once "product of the work [, ...] takes control."[79]

For Whitlock, the covers of popular books by Middle Eastern women make present iconography, titles, and subtitles that "grab the Western eye with a glimpse of absolute difference, of the exotic" and that thereby reveal their strategic positioning for the market, as attractive for precisely these rea-sons.[80] Indeed, both Whitlock and Booth argue that any veiled cover image enters into a manufacturing of otherness that creates the exotic in Graham Huggan's sense,[81] where the image is simultaneously "strange and familiar," thus maintaining an "aura of mystery" and allowing an "imagined access."[82] The covers imply that the "Western" reader can gain access to this mystery via the popular bestseller as "window on the mysterious Orient," a generic exponent of an "Islamic-world crossover genre" in which the distinctions between fiction and (auto)biography are all but obscured, with both seen as a reliable source for "information" on the Arab world.[83] According to Booth, the "sociology effect" that publishers demand even from fictional works is thus made present in the books' paratextual framings, in particular, in their covers. In a McGannian reading, this enters them into a "politics or context that is always already *textual*" and that impacts on the activation of their liter-ary meaning [emphasis in original].[84]

The predominantly paratextual conflation of memoirs and fiction that this popular genre undergoes is of course reminiscent of harem literature where, as we have seen, romance and "the ethnographic rationale of classified local information" can be tantalizingly mixed.[85] Significantly turning on the same principle in the contemporary market, if functioning in the inverse, para-texts reshape the fictional as experiential, aligning it with the memoir genre.[86]

This paratextual blurring of fact and fiction arguably further confirms the memoirs in their commodified authenticity by the new transactions their cover image makes with the contemporary world. At the same time, however, the ramifications of the author's photograph taking center stage continue to generate them, within the popular "Islamic-world crossover genre," as the product of a marketable "Orientalized Other," a society, as Booth puts it, "'captur[ed]' [...] through the I/eye."[87] In such a reading field it is perhaps not surprising that more obviously fictional incarnations of this "I/eye" are simultaneously enabled and authoritatively circulated.

Subsumed by the Paratext? The Memoirs as Novel

From textual fields with novelistic leanings, the memoirs, in the German context at least, have *become* a novel in Nicole C. Vosseler's *Sterne über Sansibar* (Stars over Zanzibar, 2010) and Hans Christoph Buch's *Sansibar Blues oder: Wie ich Livingstone fand* (Zanzibar Blues or How I Found Livingstone, 2008). In the English-language context, the harem narrative framework has recently carried them into the world of Kindle, as *Dangerous Romance* (2011): an improbable staging as Victorian erotica that perhaps only a surface engagement with the material properties of the original could enable.[88] Briefly considering each of these very different formats, I will explore the functioning of their paratextual features.

The rather shambolic Kindle text, published by Erotic Evolution, seems to seek the "order making" McGann views as the task of readers of hypertexts.[89] We are presented with a reissue of the 1907 English translation, in electronic form, its ethnographic, historical, and geographical images, including the colonial postcard, now removed and replaced with what the publisher's epitext on amazon.com terms "beautiful nude art photography."[90] These 23 apparently Victorian images (although many, judging by clothing and hairstyles, seem to have been taken much later) are typically inserted at the beginning of chapters. Only three could be said to clearly transact with Ruete's narrative: an image of three near-naked non-European women chained together (presumably a reference to slavery), a naked dancer with a gauzy veil alongside a table holding a copper or brass plate and a water pipe, and a close-up of a woman's head with a headband fashioned from an "Oriental-style" scarf fringed with coins. The curious disjointedness of the text—the slavery image, for example, appears in the chapter on fasting—foregrounds its composition, predominantly transacting with the epitext, where its publisher declares:

> To bring you the best erotic stories and pictures we have reviewed several hundred famous romance and Victorian erotic novels (previous bestsellers and

banned books) and over 20,000 erotic images! This has allowed us to create a brilliant collection based on their beauty, sexual content, character and story development, quality of erotic literature, and types of sex scenes.[91]

The reconfiguring of the memoirs as *Dangerous Romance* (the title *Harem Romance* is allotted to another book in the series) demonstrates that the reissue both shares the genre confusion of its contemporaries and mines and repeats the latent Orientalist fantasies of the Victorian period (and beyond). It is, we are told, an "elegantly written and beautifully illustrated romantic novel, tell[ing] the true and daring tale of an Arabian princess forced to flee her native country with her German lover" and an "engrossing memoir reveal[ing] extraordinary insight into the life of women in Arabian society and harems."[92] The publisher's words, reminiscent of a reader's description of the recent Saudi Arabian novel *Girls of Riyadh* (2005) as "the best novel and memoir I have read this year,"[93] resultantly transact with the "Islamic-world crossover genre" and arguably (consequently) with Yeğenoğlu's conclusion that the Orient is simultaneously an object of knowledge and of desire.[94] *Erotic Evolution's* epitextual and paratextual framing of *Dangerous Romance*—the e-book contains three essays by the publishers on erotic art and censorship—concurrently reproduces precisely "the erroneous ideas of sex and violence" that the term "harem" evoked in the Western imagination and that Lewis describes the authors of harem narratives encountering on choosing their titles.[95] Arguably functioning as a hyped-up repetition of the romantic (and, courtesy of its introduction and colonial postcard link, arguably sexualized) leanings of the paratext of the 1907 edition, it perhaps serves as a reminder that Orientalism has persisted—particularly in its less easily confronted latent form as the "dreams, images, desires, fantasies and fears" of the Orient.[96]

Contrastingly, apparently modern preoccupations are produced by the textual fields of the two German novels, Nicole C. Vosseler's historical romance *Sterne über Sansibar*, which has Emily Ruete as its main character, and Hans Christoph Buch's *Sansibar Blues*, in which Ruete is one of many links between Zanzibar and Germany in a novel that aims to present "a German century in Zanzibar." Both could be described as adaptations, with substantial sections based on the memoirs, and both display the generic identifier "novel" prominently on the cover. In both cases, however, fictionality is also destabilized. The romance novel's epitext effects this through its back cover, which describes the book as "a fairytale in the style of the *Thousand and One Nights*—based on a true story," and the author's afterword, in which she speaks of her concern not to distort or embellish this "true story" in her novelistic retelling,[97] while *Sansibar Blues* has been described as documentary fiction.[98] As "entry point" into the text (to return to Matthews's term), both works visually repeat elements of the original cover (intense color, tropical vegetation, and Arab vessels) but suggest a different context in the nature of their photographic images: that of modern tourism and Zanzibar as exotic holiday destination. Dirk Göttsche has argued that it is the manner in which documentary images and exotically tinted 1970s-style tourist brochure images have been juxtaposed in *Sansibar Blues* that makes reference to that novel's artificiality and contrivance, while a glance at the cover of the historical romance returns us to Zanzibar Town's seafront and thus to a very similar scene to that of the original German version of the memoirs with which we began (see Figure 4.4).[99]

Hans Christoph Buch's *Sansibar Blues*—arguably not popular fiction but employing popular elements in its visual plane—has been described as a "bibliophile's treasure"[100] with its numbered editions, asymmetric slipcase, and wood- and acid-free paper. It interweaves the passages narrated from Ruete's perspective with those of other "I"s: fictional GDR diplomat Hans Dampf, nineteenth-century slave-trader Tippu Tip, and a contemporary narrator traveling in Africa who employs the second-person singular. Göttsche sees the framing of Buch's novel, with "picture galleries" (and the slipcase)

Figure 4.4 Cover of Hans Christoph Buch, *Sansibar Blues* (2008). *Source*: © Die Andere Bibliothek.

depicting black-and-white and sepia colonial photographs, juxtaposed with maps and "colour prints oscillating between the iconography of contemporary tourism and a dated modernity" as referencing the sedimentation of different times and events.[101] This effect, he argues, is "metareflexive," both suggesting the concept of historical reconstruction and, along with the text, fundamentally reshaping its historical subject matter from "a deliberately subjective contemporary perspective," its "postmodern" form challenging and interrogating "postcolonial and resurgent colonial fascinations."[102] I would take Göttsche's argument further to suggest that the repetition of tourist images in the book's textual field—particularly those taken from postcards—might take on a more active role than previously acknowledged in both the production of the book's self-reflexive artificiality (its "postmodern" form) and in the resultant self-conscious textual engagement, challenging the past and its reimaginations (its "postcolonial" field). In order to compare the functioning of tourist images with that in the historical romance, I will focus on the slipcase cover image.

The main image on *Sansibar Blues'* slipcase is from the studio of John Hinde—a studio considered to generate "instant nostalgia" with postcards staged as "idealised memories."[103] Known for the vividness of his color saturation, Hinde's images were further constructed in the sense that he added in brightly colored flowers (seen here in the foreground), deep blue skies, and sunsets, particularly to make the images look more exotic. Following Terry Barrett, the inclusion of photographic images presents a juxtaposition of what is "descriptively evident" in them (subject matter, medium, and the relations between these), the circumstances under which they were created (photographer and historical context), and the setting in which they are presented.[104] Here, the images work productively on each other in transaction with Hinde's already constructed image. Descriptively, Hinde's image depicts Mangapwani beach (site of the affecting "Slave Caves," paradoxically combined with lunch and a swim on contemporary tour itineraries), while the colonial postcards show Sayyid Hamoud bin Mohammed, sultan of Zanzibar; two cultural and commercial group scenes ("Swahili Dance" and "Ivory market and bargain"); an iconic image of two Swahili men holding elephant's tusks with the backdrop of an Arab door; and an image purported to be of Ruete that arguably repeats the composition of colonial postcards by depicting a reclining woman in pale-colored European clothes against a studio backdrop of a balustrade and potted tropical plants.[105] Created for the most part as postcards, they function as markers of popular culture that additionally transact with what Yeğenoğlu would term the "discourse of tourism,"[106] connecting the modern exotic (palm trees, a vessel resembling a dhow) and the colonial, thereby producing creative potential

with regard to their siting in the visual field of this book's cover. In this context, their presence (or presentation) transacts with Yeğenoğlu's ideas about
the primary output of the tourist industry, where "locality and authenticity" is "a set or stage, an entirely fantasmatic space" able to be consumed
by the "tourist gaze."[107] This gaze is in part brought into being through
Western fantasies about authentic natives (as nostalgia for the first encounter of the colonial past), where reencountering these natives reconfirms the
"sovereignty of the European self" that had been threatened by the migrant
presence in Western cities.[108] The textual field of Buch's slipcase, led by the
John Hinde image (both within and outside the cover itself), thus presents a
fantasmatic and staged ethnic authenticity, which in the very insistence on
the *production* of artificiality is used to discursively face the "European sov-
ereign gaze" with self-conscious and thereby challenging interwoven repeti-
tions of the objects of its consumption, past and present. This kind of textual
dynamic is compared by McGann to Brecht's alienation effect, and it is
here, he argues, that the material text can impact positively on the work's
linguistic codes, pulling the social and political, the "erstwhile 'content,'"
out through the "context," acting as a "mode of resistance."[109]

The cover of the most recent reincarnation of Ruete's life story, *Sterne
über Sansibar*,[110] also stages a tourist image—here travel photographer Bob
Krist's "Two Dhows Sail Past Stone Town"—but one that functions rather
differently in this variant textual field (see Figure 4.5). In foregrounding the
striking image, the cover also shapes it to fit the Nicole C. Vosseler brand,
with elements common to her series style—the peach-colored cover, the
flowers, the overall look—elements that, following Angus Phillips, would
work to reterritorialize it in the genre of popular fiction for women and, following McGann, would keep the reader bound up in the text.[111] The cover
thus functions as a repetition of an "author brand," and indeed publisher
Bastei Lübbe seems to give each of its authors a distinctive set of covers.
Sterne über Sansibar is Vosseler's third book with Bastei Lübbe and shares its
look with the previous two, which tell stories of young British women traveling to nineteenth-century India and Arabia. It also shares the concept of its
cover with the Indian historical romance: the repetition of a modern tourist
image for a historical setting, both images strikingly bathed in a peach-
toned sunset-like glow. The use of a modern image seems unusual given
that the cover of a work of popular historical fiction generally reflects its
"period and location." We could argue that instead of explicitly representing a *historical* location, its romantic sunset hue (concurrently working to age
the buildings and obscure modern features, such as the shore-goers T-shirts)
and Eastern connotations (the prominent dhows) combine and function suggestively to evoke a feeling in the reader that still presents the novel as exotic

Figure 4.5 Cover of Nicole C. Vosseler, *Sterne über Sansibar* (2010). *Source*: © Bastei Lübbe.

historical romance, albeit in a different way. Yet, as Booth might suggest, the manipulation of a modern photograph to serve as entry point into a historical romance could also function as a reminder of the lack of distinction between fact and fiction as a repository for information in reincarnations of harem literature in the present.

To take Barrett's approach again, the subject matter of the reworked photograph is a building from a different part of the seafront that resembles Beit el-Sahel,[112] which is surrounded by tropical vegetation and set against the backdrop of a minaret and cathedral spires. The most prominent features, however, are the two dhows sailing past the building. The colors of travel photographer Bob Krist's image, already intense, have been further heightened (in particular, the green of the vegetation, in keeping with the original cover image of the memoirs), and the bright blue sea is now peach, balancing the cover composition. Presented in this way, the image begins to transact similarly to Buch's novel cover, although it is quickly conjugated into a repetition of the same. Its repetition of a modern image of Zanzibar Town's seafront standing in for the German original creates a "temporal rhetoric" that "pushes the other back in time" in the manner of contemporary ethnic tourism.[113] It is arguably not only the elements of the original image that are repeated but also the imaginative space that goes with them, if we think back, for example, to the functioning of tropical vegetation. The materiality of the book's cover thus continues to play to the paradigms that fed the market for the popular genre of the harem narrative: the construct East, now staged both as "photo exhibit" and, with its unreal peach-sunset wash over the sea, as maintaining the "aura of mystery" important for the exotic, has become the object of the voyeuristic tourist gaze.

Conclusion

McGann reminds us that the instability of the physical text, its constant textual engagement and resulting mutation, is due to the production of its every edition as a (new) "event of time and history" on its entry into the world.[114] Historicizing textual relations, he argues, is a productive way of demonstrating the "textuality of meaning."[115] Mapping the material life of Ruete's *Memoiren einer arabischen Prinzessin* as it adapts to changes in its public over space and time—the different ways textual materiality has performed for the world— generates certain semiotic patterns. The "modulation" and manipulation of the material properties of the memoirs—their cover images, physical form and corresponding qualities and prices, and title page apparatus, to name just a few features—at their various points of entry into wider discourses see them functioning as "social acts" and generating (cultural) meaning and "status-as-genre" in their very attack on "the distinction between physical medium and conceptual message."[116] In each of its incarnations—from harem narrative to mass-market novel to the "Islamic-world crossover genre" of the marketable Orientalized Other—the memoirs-as-book has been part of a genre whose material features, reterritorialized in the popular discourse of latent Orientalism, were designed to sell. Arriving in the contemporary German context as a novel, "more of a 'seller' than any other genre" today,[117] only serves to underline tensions of fact/fiction that have been paratextually implicated throughout the memoirs' material life and that tie them tightly to the further weak binary of knowledge/fantasy in an Orientalist context. Indeed, if we see the material features of a book as an expression of its imaginative space, then the mechanisms of control become apparent, activated across the body of the tangible, bound work,[118] where the packaging, the "familiar indicators of unfamiliar places and climes"[119]—citationary and always already circulating in the latent Orientalist unconscious of popular culture—has barely changed at all.

Notes

1 *Illustrirte Zeitung*, April 24, 1886: 416.

2 Dwight F. Reynolds, ed., *Interpreting the Self: Autobiography in the Arabic Literary Tradition* (Berkeley: University of California Press, 2001), 8.

3 Gillian Whitlock, *Soft Weapons: Autobiography in Transit* (Chicago: University of Chicago Press, 2007), 20.

4 Emily Ruete, *Memoiren einer arabischen Prinzessin*, 2 vols. (Berlin: Friedrich Luckhardt, 1886), 1: 179.

5 Otto Kersten, *Baron Carl Claus von der Decken's Reisen in Ost-Afrika in den Jahren 1859 bis 1865*, 4 vols. (Leipzig/Heidelberg: C. J. Winter'sche Verlagshandlung, 1869), 1: xvi.

6 Annegret Nippa, "Nachwort von Annegret Nippa," in Emily Ruete, *Leben im Sultanspalast*, ed. Annegret Nippa (Frankfurt am Main: Athenäum, 1989), 269–88 (280).

7 Shamma sees domesticating tactics that enhance similarities, "magnifying [...] a shared ground of experience," as potentially creative, challenging, and subversive in the context of the translation of Arabic literature in nineteenth-century Britain. Tarek Shamma, *Translation and the Manipulation of Difference* (Manchester: St. Jerome, 2009), 5.

8 For a further discussion of the stylistic features in Ruete's memoirs and other works, see Kate Roy, "German-Islamic Literary Interperceptions in Works by Emily Ruete and Emine Sevgi Özdamar," in *Encounters with Islam in German Literature and Culture*, ed. James Hodkinson and Jeffrey Morrison (Rochester: Camden House, 2009), 166–80.

9 Whitlock, for whom memoir and testimony come from "different traditions of self-fashioning," contrasts the two, arguing that memoir, associated with "authoritative knowledge," is "traditionally the prerogative of the literate elite," while testimony, or "subaltern knowledge," denotes the way "disempowered experience" enters into the world "not necessarily under conditions of their choosing." Whitlock, *Soft Weapons*, 132 and 136.

10 D. F. McKenzie, *Bibliography and the Sociology of Texts* (London: British Library, 1986), 297; Michele Moylan and Lane Stiles, "Introduction," in *Reading Books: Essays on the Material Text and Literature in America*, ed. Moylan and Stiles (Amherst: University of Massachusetts Press, 1996), 1–15 (6).

11 In the English-language context the packaging is, in almost all cases, the sole aspect that has changed, although there has been, for example, a recent attempt to mediate Ruete's text as popular history in Christiane Bird, *The Sultan's Shadow: One Family's Rule at the Crossroads of East and West* (New York: Random House, 2010). For reasons of space, I am unable to detail the reshaping of Ruete's narrative in English translation or the individual packaging characteristics of the myriad of recently reprinted texts. Some have added more paratextual apparatus than others, most notably the 2008 version published by Trotamundas Press with a lengthened and further exoticized title and a cover that deviates from the pattern I will discuss, presenting us with the Frederick Arthur Bridgman's Orientalist painting *Women at the Cemetery, Algiers*. The chosen cover image is presumably intended to illustrate the plantation visits Ruete describes in her memoirs, but the women in the painting wearing the distinctive Algerian *haik* tell a different story—that of the interchangeability of "Oriental" images in this context.

12 Gérard Genette, *Paratexts: Thresholds of Interpretation*, trans. Jane E. Lewin (Cambridge: Cambridge University Press, 1997), 408.

13 Reina Lewis, *Rethinking Orientalism: Women, Travel and the Ottoman Harem* (London: I. B. Tauris, 2004), 12.

14 Ibid., 113.

15 Ibid., 17.

16 Claire Colebrook, "The Work of Art That Stands Alone," *Deleuze Studies* 1, no. 1 (2007): 22–40 (26).

17 Ibid., 27.

18 Ibid.

19 Jerome McGann, *The Textual Condition* (Princeton: Princeton University Press, 1991), 84.

20 Edward W. Said, *Orientalism* (London: Penguin Books, 2003), 221–22.

21 Genette, *Paratexts*, 1–2 and 4.

22 Ibid., 1.

23 Michele Moylan, "Materiality as Performance: The Forming of Helen Hunt Jackson's *Ramona*," in *Reading Books: Essays on the Material Text and Literature in America*, ed. Michele Moylan and Lane Stiles (Amherst: University of Massachusetts Press, 1996), 223–47 (224–25).

24 Jerome McGann, *Radiant Textuality: Literature after the World Wide Web* (New York: Palgrave, 2001), 11–12.

25 D. C. Greetham, "Foreword," in *A Critique of Modern Textual Criticism*, by Jerome McGann (Charlottesville: University Press of Virginia, 1992), ix–xix (xvii–xix).

26 McGann, *The Textual Condition*, 183.

27 Colebrook, "The Work of Art That Stands Alone," 28; McGann, *The Textual Condition*, 12, 16, and 186.

28 McGann, *The Textual Condition*, 16.

29 Said, *Orientalism*, 2–3.

30 Nicole Matthews, "Introduction," in *Judging a Book by Its Cover: Fans, Publishers, Designers, and the Marketing of Fiction*, ed. Nicole Matthews and Nickianne Moody (Aldershot: Ashgate, 2007), xi–xxi (xi and xix).

31 Ruete, *Memoiren einer arabischen Prinzessin*, 1: 62.

32 See Oscar Canstadt, "Deutschlands Kolonialbestrebungen. Sansibar," *Die Gartenlaube* 6 (1885): 96–102. Perhaps significantly, the picturing of Beit el-Sahel corresponds with these images (themselves fashioned from photographs). In Ruete's childhood, for example, the external "Sultan's Pavilion" visible in the memoirs' cover image had not yet been built. We could thus argue that the cover illustrator was offering the German public a recognizable image rather than an image that aimed to serve Ruete's text.

33 Nippa, "Nachwort von Annegret Nippa," 273.

34 Terry Reece Hackford, "Fantastic Visions: Illustration of the Arabian Nights," in *The Aesthetics of Fantasy Literature and Art*, ed. Roger C. Schlobin (Notre Dame: University of Notre Dame Press, 1982), 143–75 (168 and 172).

35 Richard van Leeuwen, "The Iconography of the *Thousand and One Nights* and Modernism: From Text to Image," *Relief* 4, no. 2 (2010): 213–36 (223–24).

36 Jonathan Hensher, "Engraving Difference: The Representation of the Oriental Other in Marillier's Illustrations to the *Mille et Une Nuits* and Other *Contes orientaux* in *Le Cabinet des fées* (1785–1789)," *Journal for Eighteenth-Century Studies* 31, no. 3 (2008): 377–91 (380).

37 John M. Mackenzie, *Orientalism: History, Theory and the Arts* (Manchester: Manchester University Press, 1995), 181.

38 Shamma, *Translation and the Manipulation of Difference*, 45.

39 Meyda Yeğenoğlu, *Colonial Fantasies: Towards a Feminist Reading of Orientalism* (Cambridge: Cambridge University Press, 1998), 23.

40 Simon Eliot argues that prices like 6s, which have traditionally been looked upon as cheap by book historians, actually represented a "substantial" expenditure for a single book in the nineteenth century and "were, in practice, almost certainly middle-class prices." Simon Eliot, "'Never Mind the Value, What about the Price?': Or, How Much Did Marmion Cost St. John Rivers?," *Nineteenth-Century Literature* 56, no. 2 (2001): 160–97 (167).

41 Jorge Luis Borges, "The Translators of *The Thousand and One Nights*," trans. Esther Allen, in *The Translation Studies Reader* ed. Lawrence Venuti (London: Routledge, 2000), 34–48 (43).

42 Van Leeuwen, "The Iconography of the *Thousand and One Nights* and Modernism," 226; Mackenzie, *Orientalism*, 65.

43 Kazue Kobayashi, "The Evolution of the *Arabian Nights* Illustrations: An Art Historical Review," in *The Arabian Nights and Orientalism: Perspectives from East and West*, ed. Yuriko Yamanaka and Tetsuo Nishio (London: I. B. Tauris, 2006), 171–93 (174).

44 Robert Irwin, *Visions of the Jinn: Illustrators of the Arabian Nights* (Oxford: Oxford University Press, 2010), 10 and 239.

45 Van Leeuwen, "The Iconography of the *Thousand and One Nights* and Modernism," 235.

46 Charles Johanningsmeier, "The Devil, Capitalism, and Frank Norris: Defining the 'Reading Field' for Sunday Newspaper Fiction, 1870–1910," *American Periodicals* 14, no. 1 (2004): 91–112.

47 Leigh Hunt, writing in 1839, termed it "the most popular book in the world." Qtd. in Shamma, *Translation and the Manipulation of Difference*, 40.

48 Genette, *Paratexts*, 95–96.

49 Ibid., 11n15. Genette draws his understanding of the genre contract from Philippe Lejeune's work on autobiography.

50 Ibid., 43–44.

51 Ibid., 54.

52 Charles Johanningsmeier, *Fiction and the American Literary Marketplace: The Role of Newspaper Syndicates, 1860–1900* (Cambridge: Cambridge University Press, 1997), 14.

53 Robert Russell Hertel, "The Decline of the Paperbound Novel in America, 1890–1910," PhD diss. (University of Illinois, 1958), 205.

54 At 75¢ it was well below the average price of $1.25 for hardcover works during the late nineteenth century. American (reprint) editions of British books could be sold much more cheaply, as publishers were not obliged to pay the authors prior to the introduction of copyright protection in 1891. As a result of the lack of copyright protection, several publishers might publish the same book simultaneously and would therefore need to keep prices competitively low, as could have been the case with Appleton's (1888) and Collier's (1890) editions of the memoirs. See Johanningsmeier, *Fiction and the American Literary Marketplace*, 12.

55 Raymond Howard Shove, "Cheap Book Production in the United States, 1870 to 1891," PhD diss. (University of Illinois, 1937), i–xi.

56 Margaret Sironval, "The Image of Sheherazade in English and French Editions of the *Thousand and One Nights* (Eighteenth-Nineteenth Centuries)," in *The Arabian*

Nights and Orientalism: Perspectives from East and West, ed. Yuriko Yamanaka and Tetsuo Nishio (London: I. B. Tauris, 2006), 219–44 (240).

57 John Mullan, "When It's Acceptable to Judge a Book by its Cover," *The Guardian*, October 18, 2003, http://www.guardian.co.uk/books/2003/oct/18/art.

58 Hertel, "The Decline of the Paperbound Novel," 94.

59 P. F. Collier, "To British Authors," *The Athenæum*, March 12, 1892: 328.

60 Frank Luther Mott, *A History of American Magazines*, 5 vols. (Cambridge, MA: Harvard University Press, 1957), 4: 453–54.

61 Charles Johanningsmeier, "Determining How Readers Responded to Cather's Fiction: The Cultural Work of *The Professor's House* in *Collier's Weekly*," *American Periodicals* 20, no. 1 (2010): 68–96 (92).

62 Charles Johanningsmeier, "Welcome Guests or Representatives of the 'Mal-Odorous Class'? Periodicals and Their Readers in American Public Libraries, 1876–1914," *Libraries & Culture* 39, no. 3 (2004): 260–92 (285); Johanningsmeier, "Determining How Readers Responded to Cather's Fiction," 75.

63 Hertel, "The Decline of the Paperbound Novel," 97 (emphasis mine).

64 Reina Lewis, "'Oriental' Femininity as Cultural Commodity: Authorship, Authority, and Authenticity," in *Edges of Empire: Orientalism and Visual Culture*, ed. Jocelyn Hackforth-Jones and Mary Roberts (Oxford: Blackwell, 2005), 95–120 (115).

65 Lewis, *Rethinking Orientalism*, 228.

66 Ibid., 231 and 245.

67 Lewis, *Rethinking Orientalism*, 212 and 225.

68 Emily Ruete, *Memoirs of an Arabian Princess*, trans. Lionel Strachey (New York: Doubleday, 1907), vi.

69 Ibid., vi.

70 Lewis, *Rethinking Orientalism*, 231.

71 Leïla Sebbar, Christelle Taraud, and Jean-Michel Belorgey. *Femmes d'Afrique du Nord: Cartes Postales (1885–1930)* (Saint-Pourçain-sur-Sioule: Bleu autour, 2006).

72 Malek Alloula, *The Colonial Harem*, trans. Myrna Godzich and Wlad Godzich (Minneapolis: University of Minnesota Press, 1986), 3–5.

73 Gérard Guicheteau, "Modèles orientaux," in *Rêves mauresques: de la peinture orientaliste à la photographie colonial*, ed. Safia Belmenouar (Paris: Hors Collection, 2007), 87–111 (87).

74 Alloula, *The Colonial Harem*, 28.

75 Pamela Pears, "Images, Messages, and the Paratext in Algerian Women's Writing," in *Judging a Book by its Cover: Fans, Publishers, Designers, and the Marketing of Fiction*, ed. Nicole Matthews and Nickianne Moody (Aldershot: Ashgate, 2007), 161–70 (162).

76 Marilyn Booth, "'The Muslim Woman' as Celebrity Author and the Politics of Translating Arabic: Girls of Riyadh Go on the Road," *Journal of Middle East Women's Studies* 6, no. 3 (2010): 149–82 (160).

77 Ibid.

78 Ibid.

79 Ibid., 158 and 166.

80 Gillian Whitlock, "The Skin of the Burqa: Recent Life Narratives from Afghanistan," *Biography* 28, no. 1 (2005): 54–76 (67).

81 Despite Huggan's focus on postcolonial literature, Anastasia Valassopoulos points out that his ideas could also be applied to popular fiction. Anastasia Valassopoulos, *Contemporary Arab Women Writers: Cultural Expression in Context* (London: Routledge, 2007), 173n29.

82 Whitlock, "The Skin of the Burqa," 61.

83 Booth, "'The Muslim Woman' as Celebrity Author and the Politics of Translating Arabic," 157.

84 Colebrook, "The Work of Art That Stands Alone," 27; Jerome McGann, *Byron and Romanticism*, ed. James Soderholm (Cambridge: Cambridge University Press, 2002), 77.

85 Lewis, "'Oriental' Femininity as Cultural Commodity," 106.

86 Booth, "'The Muslim Woman' as Celebrity Author and the Politics of Translating Arabic," 149–51.

87 Ibid., 151.

88 The continued inclusion of the captions to the images from the 1907 Strachey edition on which it is based—after the images themselves were removed—supports the notion that this was a hurried publication inspired by a cursory search for Lewis-style key words.

89 McGann, *Radiant Textuality*, 71.

90 "Dangerous Romance (Historical Romance & Adult Fiction)," *Amazon.com*, http://www.amazon.com/Dangerous-Romance-Historical-Fiction-ebook/dp/B004Q9TWGY.

91 Ibid.

92 Ibid.

93 Qtd. in Booth, "'The Muslim Woman' as Celebrity Author and the Politics of Translating Arabic," 178n14.

94 Yeğenoğlu, *Colonial Fantasies*, 23.

95 Lewis, *Rethinking Orientalism*, 212.

96 Yeğenoğlu, *Colonial Fantasies*, 23.

97 Nicole C. Vosseler, *Sterne über Sansibar* (Cologne: Bastei Lübbe, 2010), 534.

98 Paul Michael Lützeler, "Sansibar Blues: Das Blut der frühen Jahre," *Der Tagesspiegel*, December 14, 2008, http://www.tagesspiegel.de/kultur/literatur/sansibar-blues-das-blut-der-fruehen-jahre/1396032.html; Martin Lüdke, "'Sansibar Blues': Wie bei den Hottentotten," *Frankfurter Rundschau*, April 6, 2009, www.fr-online.de/literatur/-sansibar-blues--wie-bei-den-hottentotten,1472266,3079098.html.

99 Dirk Göttsche, "Hans Christoph Buch's *Sansibar Blues* and the Fascination of Cross-Cultural Experience in Contemporary German Historical Novels about Colonialism," *German Life and Letters* 65, no. 1 (2012): 127–46.

100 "Hans Christoph Buch über Sansibar und die Deutschen," *Mitteldeutsche Zeitung*, January 27, 2009, http://www.mz-web.de/kultur/hans-christoph-buch-ueber-sansibar-und-die-deutschen,20642198,18206472.html.

101 Göttsche, "Hans Christoph Buch's *Sansibar Blues*," 136–37.

102 Ibid.

103 Michael L. Collins, "Blown Up Out of All Proportion," *The Telegraph*, July 13, 2002, http://www.telegraph.co.uk/culture/3580036/Blown-up-out-of-all-proportion.html.

104 Terry Barrett, *Criticizing Photographs: An Introduction to Understanding Images* (London: McGraw-Hill, 2000), 96–98.

105 Attesting to the constructedness of images, Buch begins Ruete's first-person narration with a tour of the family photo album, a "word photo gallery," where he explicitly intertwines text and paratext in his narrative repetition of the familiar frontispiece image (also part of *Sansibar Blues*' own paratextual apparatus), a

repetition that does not correspond exactly with the "real thing" and instead incorporates "exotic scenery [...] which seemed to be borrowed from the Palm House at the Botanical Gardens," perhaps a transaction with the "Ruete" image from his own cover. Like the images purported to be of Victorian porn in *Dangerous Romance*, this image is to my mind unlikely to be Ruete, as clothing, backdrop, and the similarity to Zanzibari postcards of the early twentieth century all arguably suggest it was "composed" much later. Hans Christoph Buch, *Sansibar Blues oder: Wie ich Livingstone fand* (Frankfurt am Main: Die Andere Bibliothek /Eichborn, 2008), 43.

106 Yeğenoğlu, *Colonial Fantasies*, 41.

107 Ibid.

108 Ibid., 18 and 43.

109 McGann, *The Textual Condition*, 85–86.

110 There are to date at least three cover images for different imprints of the German original of Vosseler's novel and another for the Czech translation. Given space constraints, I am only able to discuss the first and most widely available.

111 Angus Phillips, "How Books are Positioned in the Market: Reading the Cover," in *Judging a Book by its Cover: Fans, Publishers, Designers, and the Marketing of Fiction*, ed. Nicole Matthews and Nickianne Moody (Aldershot: Ashgate, 2007), 19–30 (23); McGann, *The Textual Condition*, 119–20.

112 Beit el-Sahel was all but destroyed in the Anglo-Zanzibar War of 1896.

113 Yeğenoğlu, *Colonial Fantasies*, 41.

114 McGann, *The Textual Condition*, 186.

115 Ibid., 15.

116 Ibid., 77.

117 Genette, *Paratexts*, 97.

118 Colebrook, "The Work of Art That Stands Alone," 26.

119 Hensher, "Engraving Difference," 380.

Chapter 5

HIDDEN CODES OF LOVE: THE MATERIALITY OF THE CATEGORY ROMANCE NOVEL

An Goris

For the past few decades romance has been the popular genre par excellence in the English-speaking world. With sales figures that average around $1.36 billion a year, a readership of nearly 75 million people in the United States alone, and a 13.4 percent share of the American consumer book market in 2011, the popular romance novel is by far the best-selling genre in America.[1] In 2010 a staggering 8,240 new romance titles were released in the United States, and 469 of these novels became national or international bestsellers. Harlequin, the most important romance publisher in the world, "publishes more than 100 titles a month, in both print and digital formats, in 17 countries and 16 languages," and since its inception in the mid-twentieth century an astounding total of over 6.8 billion popular romance novels have been sold by this publisher alone.[2]

While these impressive numbers indisputably establish the widespread popularity of romance, the genre has been studied very sparsely. Even though the scholarly examination of popular culture has become a respectable and well-established academic pursuit, few scholars turn their critical gaze toward this most popular (and feminine) of genres. Studies of the popular romance novel are consequently few and far between, and within this relatively small body of work attention to the material aspects of the genre has been very limited despite the fact that the material conditions of popular novels are of major importance since they function as sites of intense debate concerning the status, meaning, and identity of the books.

This lack of critical attention paid to the romance novel in general and its material characteristics in particular may be a consequence of the widespread cultural prejudice that all romance novels are essentially the same.

Although academics are generally taught to be critical of cultural stereotypes, in the case of the popular romance novel the academy seems to overwhelmingly buy into—and frequently even be at the origin of—the ingrained stereotypes of conventionality, formula, and simplicity that surround the genre. As a result, the popular romance genre is largely ignored by academics, who deem books that are supposedly all the same unworthy of their critical attention. Somewhat surprisingly, a similar mechanism plays out *within* the developing field of popular romance studies with regard to the genre's materiality.[3] Underlying this disregard is, I believe, the tacit assumption that the romance novel's materiality, which even more than other aspects of the genre is imbued with stereotypes and conventions, is a relatively simplistic and straightforward aspect of the genre that is free of the interpretative complexities romance scholars now regularly (and, notably, against the cultural grain) uncover in the genre's texts.

In this chapter I examine if this tacit assumption remains valid when the romance novel's materiality is subjected to in-depth analysis. This analysis focuses in particular on the format of the category romance—the most conventional kind of romance novel—to uncover the fact that the genre's materiality is fundamentally and functionally marked by tensions between conventionality and originality, pattern and deviation, and simplicity and complexity. The double reading of the category romance novel's materiality that is developed in this chapter and the perhaps surprisingly intricate relation between this materiality and the reader/public that is uncovered not only offer an overdue and innovative discussion of the category romance's materiality but also develop interesting wider perspectives for the study of the complex relation between genre and materiality in popular culture more generally.

The Category Romance Novel

This chapter focuses on a particular kind of romance novel—namely, the so-called category romance. As the name implies, category romances are popular romance novels that are published in a category or series (also called a line or imprint), which groups together similar types of romance stories.[4] Examples of category romance lines include the *Blaze* series (featuring sensual romances), the *Intrigue* line (featuring romances with a suspense subplot), or the *Medical Romance* imprint (featuring romances set in a medical context). Series membership traditionally determines a large part of the category romance's identity, which is reflected in the prominent place the series imprint takes up on the category romance's front cover. The front cover is also traditionally dominated by the eye-catching image of a couple (often partially undressed) locked in a passionate embrace. This image, known within the romance community as the "clinch," has become an iconic visual marker for popular romance in our culture and renders the novel's generic identity unmistakable.[5]

Category romances are published in the mass-market paperback format that is typically used for genre fiction in the English-speaking world. The category romance is an (in)famously cheap book that is available "wherever women shop" (as Harlequin's decades-old tagline boasts). This includes venues outside of the traditional literary circuit, such as supermarkets, grocery stores, newsstands, and gas stations. Almost all category romances are published by the Canadian publisher Harlequin (or its subsidiaries Silhouette and Mills & Boon), which releases over a hundred category romances each month in a wide variety of lines all over the world.[6]

The system of lines defines the category romance format in many ways and is perhaps more intricate than it seems at first sight. Each category romance is published in a series or line that has a particular narrative profile. Although these profiles appear to be characterized by a single defining trait (*Blaze* novels are erotic, *Intrigue* novels feature a suspense storyline, and *Medical Romance* novels are set in a medical context), they are in fact composite and are made up of a conglomerate of narrative features. For example, *Blaze* novels are not only characterized by a high level of sensuality but are also always set in a contemporary (usually North American) setting, feature a heroine who is between 25 and 33 and a hero between the ages of 28 and 38, and have an average word count of 60,000 words.[7] Each line is thus differentiated from others via this conglomerate of primary and secondary line characteristics. Although the lines may appear simplistic to the outside world, the finely tuned differentiation between lines is very important within the genre's system, as the (commercial) viability of a line depends in part on the extent to which it can be differentiated from another line.

One of the consequences of this system is that category romances are highly conventional. All category romance novels share the overall conventions of the romance genre,[8] but within this encompassing generic framework each category romance also incorporates the conglomerate of conventions that characterize the line in which it is published. As a result, conventionality is pivotal to nearly every aspect of the category romance story and text. These conventions are, moreover, strongly enforced by editors and publishers, who act as gatekeepers guarding the genre and line profiles. Narratives that do not incorporate the various conventions are simply not published in the category romance system.[9] The strong conventionality that consequently marks the category romance novel is often interpreted as a characteristic that renders the category romance an aesthetically inferior form, and it is frequently cited as one of the main reasons for the format's low cultural status.[10]

Materiality and the Category Romance Novel

Category romance novels are marked by a very typical look; their visual and material properties are instantly recognizable to almost everybody, romance readers and nonreaders alike. Indeed, regardless of our interest in or knowledge of the genre, most of us are able to instantly recognize a category romance novel when we see one. The question arises why the genre consistently chooses to adopt such material uniformity. What are the functions and effects of this remarkable semiotic strategy? That the visual and material design of a book is anything but a meaningless matter has been argued convincingly by French theorist Gérard Genette, whose seminal study *Paratexts* examines the role that such features play in the reception and interpretation of a book. He defines the paratext as

> a zone not only of transition but also *transaction*: a privileged place of pragmatics and strategy, of an influence on the public, an influence that—whether well or poorly understood and achieved—is at the service of a better reception of the text and a more pertinent reader of it (more pertinent, of course, in the eyes of the author and his allies).[11]

In other words, Genette suggests that the book's materiality has two main functions: it is a zone in which the book's producers and consumers negotiate the identity, meaning, and interpretation of the text—a process that mainly consists of the producers' attempts to direct the consumers' reception of the text—and it serves to locate and reach the text's primary target audience. These functions are the paratext's main raison d'être; indeed, as Genette remarks at the end of his study, *functionality* is "[t]he most essential of the paratext's properties":

> Whatever aesthetic intention may come into play as well, the main issue of the paratext is not to "look nice" around the text but rather to ensure for the text a destiny consistent with the author's purpose. To this end, the paratext provides a kind of canal lock between the ideal and relatively immutable identity of the text and the empirical (sociohistorical) reality of the text's public [...] the lock permitting the two to remain "level."[12]

Following this reasoning, analyses of the paratext should primarily focus not on questions of aesthetics (is it beautiful or appealing?) but rather on questions of functionality (what purpose does it serve, and which effects does it attempt to produce?).

This functionality should be understood in relation to the consumer of the paratext. In this regard Genette makes what to me appears to be a fundamental distinction between what he calls "the public" and "the reader":

[T]he public is not the totality of the sum of readers. [...] For a book, however, it seems to me that the public is nominally an entity more far-flung than the sum of its readers because that entity includes, sometimes in a very active way, people who do not necessarily read the book (or at least not in its entirety) but who participate in its dissemination and in its "reception." [...] The reader as conceived by the author [...] is, to the contrary, [...] a person who reads the text *in toto*. [...] The public as defined here, therefore, extends well and often actively beyond the sum total of readers.[13]

Genette thus identifies a crucial difference between the reception and interpretation of the (narrative) text and the (material) paratext of a book. Whereas the former is targeted at a very specific (and ideal) kind of reader, who has the background knowledge necessary to understand and unlock the text, the latter is directed at a far more substantive and heterogeneous group of consumers without a clear-cut profile.

This distinction between public and reader plays a crucial role in the category romance's materiality. As a book that circulates in a large number of widely varying cultural and commercial spaces—from the grocery store to the independent book store, from the gas station to the airport newsstand—its materiality is encountered and interpreted by a huge audience that entails both (potential) readers and (a majority of) nonreaders. In order to communicate with these two types of consumers, the category romance novel's materiality adopts a double semiotic code: one targeted at the public and one aimed at the (romance) reader. As the analyses in this chapter illustrate, these two codes contain two different messages about the book's identity and its desired interpretation. The public code consistently suggests a uniformly generic interpretation of the text as a popular romance novel. This interpretative suggestion is created by the repeated invocation of a number of stereotypical images of and associations with the genre, which in turn perpetuate the public image of the romance genre as homogeneous, formulaic, and clichéd. The reader code, by contrast, advocates a more specific and even idiosyncratic interpretation of the text that aims to distinguish the individual text from the generic group in which it is situated.

This double semiotic codification—and its concomitant potential for divergent interpretations—is present in nearly every aspect of the category romance novel's materiality. To illustrate how the dual semiotic decoding of these properties may work, I will focus on three illustrative examples in the rest of this chapter. These analyses focus on three standard elements of the category romance's paratexts: the front cover iconography, the line template in the design of the category romance's material packaging, and the preview scene that is routinely printed on the first page of a category romance novel.

Front Cover Iconography

The category romance's front cover is visually dominated by an image that takes up a focal point in the cover composition. In the majority of cases this is an image of a (scantily clad) man and woman locked in a passionate embrace.[14] This image, known in the romance jargon as the "clinch," graces the front cover of an endless series of category romance novels in always changing but essentially similar variations. It appears to be a very apt visual representation of what the romance genre is all about. Depicting a man and a woman in an intimate and often explicitly passionate clinching embrace (hence the name), the image is made up of visual renderings of the nuclear elements of the conventional romance narrative: the hero, the heroine, and their romantic (sexualized) interactions with each other. In a way it also offers a visual representation of what is arguably the core fantasy offered by the genre—namely, that of an overwhelming and passionate love affair, in which the lovers are focused absolutely on one another.

The clinch image carries a double semiotic code and has the potential to be interpreted differently by the public and the romance reader. To the public at large, the clinch image likely signifies simply the genre identity of the popular romance. This interpretation is based on the strong semantic connection between this image and the popular romance genre that exists in our culture as a result of the incessant reformulation of this type of image on the front cover of category romance novels since the 1970s.[15] As a visually striking and instantly recognizable image with only a limited range of potential variations, the clinch quickly attained an iconic status and has become the cover design shorthand par excellence for popular romance. Although the constant reformulations of the image on a seemingly endless string of category romance front covers reinforce and perpetuate a number of cultural stereotypes about the romance genre, including interpretations of the genre as formulaic, overly sexualized, and more than a little ridiculous, the category romance is steadfast in its love for the clinch cover.[16]

Of course the clinch image is, much like the narrative it so strikingly represents, a generic type. Each individual execution of the type is slightly different but essentially—*typically*—the same. This typicality functions as the basis of the public's interpretation of the clinch image—that is, the public perceives the *type* of image and interprets this image as signaling a stereotypical kind of romance genre identity. This interpretation is based on the widespread cultural codes that regulate the semiotic functioning of cover iconography, which hold that a clinch image equals the generic identity "romance." In this interpretative act, the public overlooks the individual execution of this type—an execution that, for all its typicality, still has individual traits. These traits are, however, precisely the focal point of the romance reader's semiotic decoding of the image and suggest a somewhat different interpretation of the text's identity. They not only individuate the image but also do so according to a set of (generic) codes shared by the novel's producers and its target audience of romance readers. On the basis of these codes, the romance reader is able to learn more about the novel's specific characteristics.

Various elements of the clinch image are subjected to this genre-internal system of secondary codification. For example, the attire worn by the cover models can function as a code for the novel's subgenre. That models on the cover of historical category romances wear clothes that are instantly recognizable as period costumes comes as no big surprise and is a fairly obvious example of such a secondary codification of the clinch image. Other clothing-based codifications that are common in the romance genre are perhaps less obvious to the public at large. The relatively recent trend in paranormal romance to deck out cover models (particularly women) in leather clothing is probably not well-known outside the genre. Nonetheless, as romance bloggers Sarah Wendell and Candy Tan have observed, within the romance genre a female cover model dressed in leather or spandex-like clothing serves as a reliable semiotic sign that the novel in question features a paranormal storyline.[17]

The relative state of dress or undress of the cover models is another coded element of the clinch. Although in the past this code seems to have been stricter than it is today,[18] as a rule of thumb we can still assume that the more flesh is visible on the cover, the more sexually explicit the love scenes in the narrative are. The style in which the clinch image is drawn or photographed as well as the fashion and hairstyle worn by the cover models—all of which are cover elements that have been subjected to significant evolutions over the course of the past three decades—are yet other coded parameters of the clinch that provide the experienced romance reader with additional information about the individual characteristics of the narrative—in this case, the date of publication. All of these parameters—time of publication, level of sensuality, and subgenre—in fact serve to specify and singularize the text in the eyes of the romance reader. They function as important parameters of (narrative) differentiation within the romance genre's system and thus give the romance reader significant information about the particular qualities of the text.

The same clinch image is—or at least has the potential to be—interpreted rather differently by the public and the romance reader. Whereas to the former it likely functions as a code that signifies a very stereotypical, internally homogeneous kind of popular romance generic identity, to the latter the same image signals various kinds of specifications within this generic identity and essentially provides a message of generic heterogeneity. This semiotic mechanism of one material element simultaneously containing two codes or two layers of codification that mean different things to different consumers (the public vs. the reader) is essential to the semiotic functioning of the category romance novel's materiality. It is a core principle that, as the rest of the analyses illustrate, underlies nearly every aspect of this materiality.

Design Template

One of the most visually striking and remarkable characteristics of the category romance's material packaging is the dominance of a standard design template that all novels published in the same line share. While each line or imprint has its own characteristic template, most of these templates also have certain elements in common (e.g. the spatial placing of certain elements). The line-imposed design template determines the look of nearly every aspect of the category romance's materiality and is as such quite an invasive material and visual presence. It is perhaps most noticeable on the front cover, where its dominant color scheme, prominent imprint logo, and overall composition create an extreme sense of similarity between individual category romance novels published in the same line. The placing and (stylistic) execution of almost every element of the cover composition is thus determined by the line's design template.

However, the impact of the line template extends far beyond the front cover. The back cover is designed in a very similar fashion, which makes for books that look altogether very similar. Indeed, it is hardly possible to visually distinguish between the individual books in a series from their back covers. This imposing visual similarity seems to stifle any claim to a more singularized interpretation that a book's back cover traditionally develops. The same compositional principle also applies to the material features inside the books, which, like their covers, are designed on the basis of a line template. Category romances published in the same line consequently share the same font, font size, composition of the title page, foreword, and so on. In other words, they all look quite similar.

The predominant effect of such an invasive design template is a very strong sense of standardization. It makes category romance novels look like uniform assembly-line products that lack the individuating and unique characteristics that we as a culture tend to value—particularly in art and literature. Instead, category romances all look the same and appear to be mutually interchangeable. This dominant impression of interchangeability is amplified by the fact that the elements that traditionally signify the book's individual identity, such as its title, the name of the author, and the summarizing blurb on the back cover, are also slipped into the line's design template, which almost completely mutes their message of idiosyncrasy. Instead, these elements appear to be merely (insignificant) variations on an already existing pattern that appears to be more meaningful. In the public's interpretation of the category romance's design template, this message of standardization is likely dominant, and the line template in effect serves as a code signifying extensive similarity and lack of singularity.

Romance readers are, of course, not blind to the impression of similarity created by the line template, but they are nonetheless able to ascribe to it a different meaning. This interpretative difference is located in two aspects. First, whereas the public tends to interpret the extensive visual and material similarity of the line template in a rather negative way (category romances are generally considered inferior forms of literature because they are—or at least materially appear to be—so similar), romance readers are inclined to interpret this similarity more positively as a code for the strong conventionality that is part and parcel of the category romance format and that its target readers appreciate. Second, romance readers again, as in their reading of the clinch, detect a number of coded information parameters in the line template that in their eyes convey a more specific textual identity. For example, the template's dominant color scheme is often a code for the tone or subgenre of the line, as red signifies sensual lines, purple is conventionally reserved for suspenseful lines, white is typical of medical lines, and so on. The line number printed on the spine of each category romance further reinforces the public's interpretation of the category romance novel as a standardized assembly-line product,[19] but to romance readers this number denotes information about the line. The higher the number, the older the line is; the older the line, the more likely it is to have proven its (commercial) success, but, by the same token, the more risk it runs of being outdated in the fast-changing, trend-sensitive popular romance genre.

The line name is yet another element that is interpreted differently by the public and by romance readers. While the name denotes a simple narrative profile for the public, it functions as a code for a more complex and composite narrative profile for readers familiar with the romance genre's refined system of lines. This difference in interpretation or codification of the line name is particularly important in lines that appear to be quite similar. For example, Harlequin currently publishes two sensual lines: *Harlequin Blaze* and *Harlequin Desire*. The public is presumably unable to differentiate between these two lines since the names suggest similar erotic profiles, but experienced readers are aware of the differences in the lines' respective compound narrative profiles.[20] Whereas the public interprets these names as a codification of similarity, romance readers interpret the line names as a codification of difference.

The Preview Scene

This brings me to what I call the preview scene, which is the third and final example of the double semiotic codification of the category romance's materiality. The preview scene is a scene (or more often part of a scene) printed on the first page of the category romance novel. It is a brief piece of text (usually about 5–10 lines) that is placed before the title page, colophon, foreword, or any other kind of introductory page. Following immediately on the book's front cover, the preview scene is usually the first page of the book the reader encounters. It consists of a partial scene that is extracted from the main narrative and that functions somewhat like a trailer for a film. Although the scene is presented without any explicit framing, its strategic placement at the beginning of the book sets up a metonymic interpretation of the scene as representative of the narrative from which it is extracted. The scene then functions to provide a first, very brief, but supposedly representative taste of the narrative that follows a few pages later in the same volume:

> *"Now, If You'll Excuse Me—"*
> "Not Yet." The soft demand froze her in place. In that moment she registered that Constantine wasn't just angry, he was furious. She had seen him furious only once before—the day they had broken up—but on that occasion he had been icily cool and detached. The fact was that his formidable control had finally slipped and he was clearly in danger of losing his temper ratcheted the tension up several notches. A heady sense of anticipation gripped her. She had the feeling that for the first time she was going to see the real Constantine and not the controlled tycoon who had a calculator in place of a heart. His gaze dropped to her mouth and she was suddenly unbearably aware that he intended to kiss her.[21]

> *"My price is a date with you, Marissa."*
> Marissa gazed up at Kyle and slowly shook her head. "I can't. What kind of matchmaker would swoop in and take the prize catch for herself? No client would ever trust me again." Upping his game, Kyle raised a finger to her face and sketched a soft stroke down the length of her throat. Her eyelids fluttered, her lips parting of their own accord. "What are we doing?" she whispered helplessly, clutching his shoulder as if she were hanging on for dear life. "Being impulsive." He licked his way into the curve of her shoulder and she shivered. "Isn't it the best?" "I'm not impulsive," she said, even as she arched her neck to give him more room to work. He ran his tongue along the same spot over and over until she trembled. "You are now."[22]

As we can see in these examples, these scenes are marked by a strong sense of conventionality. This is no coincidence; indeed, scenes that are selected

as preview scenes usually depict a narrative moment that is instantly recognizable as a conventional part of a traditional romance plot. These scenes
frequently zoom in on feelings of sexual attraction and/or romantic conflict
between the protagonists and depict events such as the erotically charged
moments preceding the characters' first kiss or their first time making love.
Invariably ending on an (erotic) cliff-hanger, the preview scene is often a kind
of narrative equivalent of the clinch image and is charged with the same
sense of expectation, (sexual) tension, and narrative determinism that marks
the clinch. Like the clinch, the preview scene also represents a stereotypical
image of the romance genre not only because it depicts a very clichéd moment
in the romance narrative but also because this representation is rendered in a
highly conventionalized, even hackneyed discourse.

Even more so than other material aspects of the romance, the preview
scene is marked by a double codification and is accordingly interpreted rather
differently by the public and by romance readers. In the public's interpretation, the extreme conventionality of the scene is the dominant feature, and the
scene is consequently interpreted as yet another code that signifies the novel's
popular romance identity. Because the scene explicitly evokes stereotypes of
the genre that are particularly widespread in our culture—the first kiss, the
typical tension between conflict and attraction that is widely associated with
popular romances, the clichéd and euphemistic language describing sexual
attraction, and so on—this interpretation is guaranteed irrespective of the
reader's profile. Indeed, even a reader who is only aware of the most basic
cultural stereotypes surrounding the popular romance genre will recognize
in this scene the genre's conventions and will correctly interpret it as a code
for the narrative's popular romance genre identity. In this process the preview
scene not only invokes but also reinforces and perpetuates a number of the
stereotypes already surrounding the genre, much like the clinch that is its
visual equivalent.

Although romance readers are obviously aware of the scene's strong conventionality and, like the public, interpret it as another element inscribing
the novel in the popular romance genre, as members of the romance genre's
interpretive community they also have the ability to develop a different interpretation of this scene. In fact, when romance readers read these scenes *as
romance readers*—that is, using the interpretative strategies particular to the
genre—they are able to gain crucial new knowledge about the text and its
specific, individual poetic properties. This is due to the fact that in the eyes
of experienced readers the preview scene functions as a conceptual prefiguration of the creative interplay between conventionality and variation that is
pivotal to the category romance's poetic functioning. This creative dynamic
goes unnoticed by the public (and most of the genre's critics) because of their

one-dimensional assessment of the genre's strong conventionality as only creating a pervasive sense of repetition and similarity between individual romance texts. However, this interpretation of conventionality fails to recognize how the web of conventions also creates a context in which every minute variation upon the convention stands out.[23] This kind of variation—the brief deviation from the norm, the minor adaptation of the convention—represents a fundamental pillar of the category romance's poetic functioning and of the aesthetic pleasure the romance offers its readers. This particular creative dynamic is prefigured in the strongly conventional preview scene, which illustrates for romance readers precisely how the author deals with the central creative task of the category format of fusing various sets of conventions with the appropriate amount of creative variation. Since a thorough knowledge of the conventions of the genre (and the line) is necessary to develop this interpretation, only generically initiated readers pick up on this dynamic and read the preview scene as something other than a pure reconfirmation of the novel's clichéd generic identity.

In a similar vein, the preview scene also allows romance readers to get a first sense of what in the romance community is often referred to as the author's voice. In this context, the term "voice" refers to the conglomerate of elements that characterize an individual's writing.[24] Voice is determined by both narrative and linguistic elements and includes such things as the rhythm of the text, the cadence of the dialogue, the pace of the story, the tone of the narrative, the development of the characters, and so on. As I have pointed out elsewhere, voice is an important evaluation criterion in the popular romance genre and one that both editors and readers frequently cite as a potentially decisive factor in their evaluation of a particular romance novel.[25] Although voice is a fluid and compound notion, the preview scene provides the romance reader with a first impression of the author's voice, which in many ways functions as the primary parameter of singularity in the category romance novel. Given the importance of the voice in the reader's enjoyment of the narrative, this impression is likely to factor into the reader's decision to read (and buy) the novel, and it thus bestows a commercially important function on the preview scene.

These latter two interpretations of the preview scene require extensive familiarity with creative dynamics and codes that are specific to the category romance format and are hence only developed by readers initiated in the popular romance genre—in other words, the category romance's target audience. For these readers, the preview scene functions not only as a code signifying the novel's romance generic identity (as it does to the public) but also as a codification of the novel's singularity. As with the clinch and the design template, these different interpretations of the category romance's materiality are also fundamentally tied to the public's and the reader's respective degrees of knowledge of, and experience with, the particular codes of the popular romance genre. Romance readers are able to develop a more complex and layered interpretation of the category romance's materiality than the public because their extensive knowledge of the genre's conventions and codes enables them to see differentiation where the public only sees similarity.

Functions and Effects

These analyses of three aspects of the category romance's material packaging indicate the systematic manner in which a double codification of this materiality is created. The potential for a double interpretation is a semiotic pattern that is present in nearly every aspect of these material conditions and that is implemented in a coherent and coordinated way. This suggests that far from being a random or coincidental effect, this semiotic pattern is a deliberate strategy on the part of the category romance novel's producers, who seek to influence the reception and interpretation of their books.

The stereotype-driven character of the category romance's materiality ensures that the public is likely to follow the producers' primary suggestion and interpret the books in generic terms as popular romance novels. This interpretation is achieved via the repetitive material invocation of numerous widespread stereotypes that surround the genre in our culture. Although this strategy reinforces and perpetuates a very clichéd cultural image of the genre, one of its major interpretative benefits is that such stereotypes can be interpreted or decoded by a huge and diversified audience. This public intelligibility of its material code is an important commercial consideration for a book that circulates in a wide variety of cultural and commercial spaces frequented by a wide variety of consumers.

That the public codification of the category romance novel's materiality revolves around a *generic* interpretation is no surprise given the commercial character of popular fiction. As scholars such as John Cawelti and Ken Gelder have argued, the field of popular fiction is much more preoccupied with the notion of genre than that of literary fiction:

> One of the most productive ways to think about popular fiction is in terms of genre, a term that simply means—in our case—the type or species of fiction being written. The entire field of popular fiction is written for, marketed and consumed generically: it provides the primary logic for popular fiction's means of production, formal and industrial identification and critical evaluation.[26]

Genre is thus one of the most important organizational and interpretative pillars of the field of popular fiction, and it steers the mass communication that marks this field in the right direction. Given the industrial, commercial, and communicative prominence of genre in popular fiction, it is in fact only logical that the category romance novel—one of the most (in)famous examples of genre fiction—emphasizes this generic identity in the public codification of its materiality.

As noted in the above analyses, this is hardly a subtle process. On the contrary, the category romance is very obvious in its material genre performance. This generic blatancy is, as Gelder has pointed out, another characteristic element of popular fiction, in which "generic identities are always visible. This is how it differs from Literature. Popular fiction announces those [generic] identities loudly and unambiguously."[27] Although it is precisely this very emphatic generic conventionality that gives rise to the stereotypical interpretation of genre literature in general and the category romance novel in particular as a kind of literature that is repetitive, formulaic, and inferior to literary fiction, this is the price that the category romance novel is apparently willing to pay in order to achieve the generic transparency that is the commercial bread and butter of popular fiction.

Such a manifest material performance of the novel's generic identity is functionally important not only to the vast public of nonreaders but also to the book's target audience of self-identified category romance readers. Like the public, romance readers recognize the stereotype-driven public code as signaling the romance-generic identity. This generic identification of the novel triggers, as has been established by Janice Radway's seminal study of romance readers, a set of generic expectations on the part of the reader.[28] When the text meets these generic expectations—as the strongly conventional and carefully controlled category romance specifically aims to do—the reader is satisfied. This interplay between the creation of generic expectations, the fulfilling of these expectations, and the resulting reader satisfaction is of vital commercial importance to the category romance novel, as it provides the core impetus for readers to want to repeat the reading experience by reading—that is, buying—other category romance novels.

However, this ostensibly homogeneous generic identity is thoroughly complicated in what I have called the secondary codification of the category's materiality—a genre-specific code that only readers familiar with the genre can detect and decipher. Via these coded elements, the category romance's materiality suggests a more refined and singular interpretation of its text that is essentially designed to indicate how it is different from its generic colleagues. This hidden layer of the semiotic code not only allows romance readers to develop a secondary set of textual expectations but also thoroughly complicates the homogeneous image of the genre that is painted in the primary (public) layer of the book's material codification. Instead of further

supporting the stereotype-based public interpretation of generic standardization, this (hidden) secondary layer of the material code consistently signals
ways in which romance novels develop a more specific identity. As illustrated
in the analyses above, the degree of specificity of this identity increases gradually. Whereas the front cover is often still concerned with suggesting shared
identity traits, such as subgenre, level of sensuality, and line identity, the first
page inside the book resolutely focuses on the text's singularity by showcasing
the manifestation of authorial voice in the narrative text.

Conclusion

The apparent simplicity of the category romance novel's materiality conceals
a complex semiotic system of double encoding. The strong conventionality
that marks the material packaging of the novel functions in a complex way
that defies the stereotypes of simplicity, formula, and repetition that surround
the genre even as, on its surface level, it reinforces and perpetuates these same
stereotypes. Whereas the public relies on this stereotype-confirming surface
level to simplistically interpret the book as a formulaic instance of popular
genre fiction, romance readers are able to understand and decode the hidden
complexities of the underlying secondary semiotic layer due to their extensive
knowledge of both the romance genre's overall conventions and those that are
specific to the category romance format. Only on the basis of such generic
knowledge can this seemingly overwhelming conventionality be perceived
and recognized as markers of variation and deviation instead of repetition
and similarity.

The semiotic craftiness of this strategy lies not only in the duality of the
codification but also in the subtlety of its secondary layer. In fact, the stereo-
type-laden surface layer is such a strong visual and material presence that the
category romance novel actively courts the clichéd interpretations that this
surface codification gives rise to and effectively invites the public to interpret
its generic identity in a stereotypical manner. The secondary layer remains
hidden from view and can only be perceived by those who always already
know it is there. Although this strategy is a testimony to the predominance of
genre classifications in popular fiction, it also raises new questions about the
accuracy and effectiveness of such simplifying classifications.

The core interpretative mechanism uncovered in the material analyses in
this chapter—the notion that generically initiated readers interpret conventionality differently from readers who are not familiar with the genre's codes
and conventions—has the potential to shed new light on the broader discussion of the role that conventionality plays in the reception of romance fiction
in general. It stands to reason that the dynamics uncovered in the category

romance's materiality also apply to the text this materiality encloses and represents. Indeed, if we consider this materiality to be a physical manifestation and performative representation of the identity and characteristic traits of the text, as I have implicitly done throughout this chapter, then the implications for the role of conventionality in the category romance genre are potentially far-reaching, and they call for a renewed examination of the poetic functioning of both the romance genre and other genres of popular fiction.

Notes

1 "About the Romance Genre," *Romance Writers of America*, https://www.rwa.org/Online/Romance_Genre/About_Romance_Genre.aspx.

2 "About Harlequin," *Harlequin.com*, https://corporate.harlequin.com.

3 Although academic work on the popular romance genre remains minimal in comparison to the academic work being done on other popular genres, a relatively small number of studies on the genre have been completed since the early 1980s. Academic attention has particularly increased in recent years due to the establishment of the International Association for the Study of Popular Romance in 2009 and the launch of the academic peer-reviewed *Journal of Popular Romance Studies* in 2010. For more on these recent developments and an overview of the history of the burgeoning field of popular romance studies, see Kay Mussell, "Where's Love Gone?," *Paradoxa: Studies in World Literary Genres* 3, no. 1/2 (1997): 3–14; Pamela Regis, "What Do Critics Owe the Romance Novel? Keynote Address at the Second Annual Conference of the International Association for the Study of Popular Romance," *Journal of Popular Romance Studies* 2, no. 1 (2011), http://www.jprstudies.org/2011/10/%e2%80%9cwhat-do-critics-owe-the-romance-keynote-address-at-the-second-annual-conference-of-the-international-association-for-the-study-of-popular-romance%e2%80%9d-by-pamela-regis; An Goris, "Matricide in Romance Scholarship? Response to Pamela Regis' Keynote Address at the Second Annual Conference of the International Association for the Study of Popular Romance," *Journal of Popular Romance Studies* 2, no. 1 (2011), http://www.jprstudies.org/2011/10/%e2%80%9cmatricide-in-romance-scholarship-response-to-pamela-regis%e2%80%99-keynote-address-at-the-second-annual-conference-of-the-international-association-for-the-study-of-popular-romance%e2%80%9d; Eric Murphy Selinger and Sarah S. G. Frantz, "Introduction," in *New Perspectives on the Popular Romance Novel*, ed. Selinger and Frantz (Jefferson: McFarland, 2012), 1–20.

4 Within the contemporary popular romance genre the category romance is differentiated from the so-called single title romance, which is a longer romance novel that is not published in a series.

5 Jennifer McKnight-Trontz, *The Look of Love: The Art of the Popular Romance Novel* (Princeton: Princeton Architectural Press, 2002), 17.

6 For more on the global distribution and consumption of category romances in different linguistic and cultural contexts, see Eva Hemmungs Wirtén, "'They Seek It Here, They Seek It There, They Seek It Everywhere': Looking for the 'Global' Book," *Canadian Journal of Communication* 23, no. 2 (1998), https://cjc-online.ca/index.php/journal/article/view/1034/940; Peter Darbyshire, "Romancing the World:

Harlequin Romances, the Capitalist Dream, and the Conquest of Europe and Asia," *Studies in Popular Culture* 23, no. 1 (2000): 1–10; George Paizis, "Category Romance in the Era of Globalization: The Story of Harlequin," in *The Global Literary Field*, ed. Anna Guttman, Michel Hockx, and George Paizis (Newcastle: Cambridge Scholars, 2006), 126–51; An Goris, "Romance the World Over," in *Global Cultures*, ed. Frank Salamone (Newcastle: Cambridge Scholars, 2009), 59–72.

7 "Harlequin Blaze," *Harlequin.com*, https://www.harlequin.com/shop/brand/harlequin-blaze.html. The precise narrative profile of a line is stipulated in the so-called writing guidelines, which is a document for novice romance authors in which the publisher specifies the particular characteristics and conventions of a line. These writing guidelines are available on Harlequin's website.

8 Although it falls outside the scope of this chapter to give a complete overview of the romance genre's conventions, the most important of these have to do with the basic plot of the romance narrative. An authoritative account of this plot is articulated by Pamela Regis, who claims the romance narrative has eight conventional elements: "a *definition of society*, always corrupt, that the romance novel will reform; the *meeting* between the heroine and the hero; an account of their *attraction* for each other; the *barrier* between them; the *point of ritual death*; the *recognition* that fells the barrier; the *declaration* of heroine and hero that they love each other; and their *betrothal*" [emphasis in original]. Pamela Regis, *A Natural History of the Popular Romance Novel* (Philadelphia: University of Pennsylvania Press, 2003), 14.

9 For an account of how this particular system of publication might give rise to an interpretation of romance publishing as a form of constrained writing, see Dirk De Geest and An Goris, "Constrained Writing, Creative Writing: The Case of Handbooks for Writing Romances," *Poetics Today* 31, no. 1 (2010): 81–106.

10 This negative appreciation of strong (generic) conventionality is something that affects the cultural status of all so-called genre fiction but that is particularly strongly associated with the popular romance genre, which is often considered the most conventional and conservative genre of popular fiction. For more on the connections between genre, conventionality, and popular fiction, see John Cawelti, *Adventure, Mystery, and Romance: Formula Stories as Art and Popular Culture* (Chicago: University of Chicago Press, 1976); Ken Gelder, *Popular Fiction: The Logics and Practices of a Literary Field* (London: Routledge, 2004).

11 Gérard Genette, *Paratexts: Thresholds of Interpretation*, trans. Jane E. Lewin (Cambridge: Cambridge University Press, 1997), 2.

12 Ibid., 407–8.

13 Ibid., 74–75.

14 While the clinch image is the most common image on the front cover of the category romance novel, other types of images include an image of a single person (most frequently a man) or a more domestic image of a couple with children or pets. For further discussion of these other types of romance front cover iconography, see Sarah Wendell and Candy Tan, *Beyond Heaving Bosoms: The Smart Bitches' Guide to Romance Novels* (New York: Fireside, 2009), 176–77.

15 Images of embracing couples have been appearing on the covers of popular romance novels since British publisher Mills & Boon developed the format in the 1930s and 1940s, so the semantic association between an embracing couple on the front cover and the generic identity romance is long-standing in our culture. Still, the more sexualized version of the embrace did not become commonplace in the popular romance

genre until the 1970s, when the so-called "bodice ripper" romance started featuring more sensual embraces on the front cover. See McKnight-Trontz, *The Look of Love*, 23–24.

16 It is interesting, however, that in the Romance Writers of America's 2005 market study only 12 percent of romance readers indicated a preference for "romantic covers" while 35 percent indicated a preference for "sedate or abstract covers." The matter does not seem to be a potential deal breaker, however, as 53 percent of readers indicated that they "prefer both types of covers."

17 Wendell and Tan, *Beyond Heaving Bosoms*, 178.

18 Margaret Ann Jensen suggests that the category romance cover is composed according to a very strict code in order to indicate the narrative's level of sensuality: "The position of the hero and heroine on the books' cover is a good indication of how much sex there is in the romance. If they are not touching at all, the story does not have any sex scenes. If they are touching, the degree of sexuality escalates, with different touching positions symbolizing the amount of sexual involvement." The pictures also tell the readers how sexually responsive and aggressive the heroine is, as there are two types of embrace—the "hesitant heroine's" and the "cognizant heroine's": "The first kind is the more traditional portrayal of female sexuality and indicates that the hero pursues the heroine, who resists and perhaps capitulates, against her better judgment. The second kind of embrace is a departure from traditional sexual encounters and indicates that the heroine is responsive and probably even active in the pursuit of romantic-sexual gratification." Margaret Ann Jensen, *Love's Sweet Return: The Harlequin Story* (Bowling Green: Bowling State University Popular Press, 1984), 62–63. Although Jensen's observations might have been accurate in the late 1970s and early 1980s, category romance novel covers are no longer composed according to such strict rules. Still, the observation is indicative of the highly coded nature of the romance novel cover.

19 Jayashree Kamble, "Uncovering and Recovering the Popular Romance Novel," PhD diss. (University of Minnesota, 2008), 181.

20 For experienced romance readers the difference between these particular lines is in fact even more complex since the line that is now called *Harlequin Desire* used to be called *Silhouette Desire* and was published by Harlequin's subsidiary Silhouette. This subsidiary had a somewhat different profile than Harlequin itself, which was the result of the complex institutional history of the category romance market. Silhouette was originally founded in the early 1980s as a separate publisher and one of the main competitors to Harlequin in the category romance market. This competition ended when Torstar, Harlequin's parent company, acquired Silhouette in 1984. Although from then on the two publishers essentially belonged to the same business conglomerate, Silhouette continued to be developed as a separate brand name with a somewhat more modern, progressive, and specifically American profile than the Canadian Harlequin. Over time, the differences between the two brands became less and less pronounced, and in April 2011 the Silhouette brand was discontinued and the imprints published under this brand, such as the *Silhouette Desire* line, underwent a slight name change. The distinction between Harlequin and Silhouette (or between such lines as *Harlequin Desire* and *Harlequin Blaze*) may seem insignificant to readers who are unfamiliar with the category market and its complex institutional history, yet it is highly significant to experienced romance readers, as is indicated by the fact that the two brands existed side by side within one publisher for 25 years. For more

on the complex institutional history of this company, see Paul Grescoe, *The Merchants of Venus: Inside Harlequin and the Empire of Romance* (Vancouver: Rainforest, 1996).

21 Fiona Brand, *A Breathless Bride* (Toronto: Harlequin, 2012), 1.

22 Joanne Rock, *One Man's Rush* (Toronto: Harlequin, 2012), 1.

23 This interpretation of the category romance's poetic functioning is in line with suggestions made by Thomas Roberts, who compares the often misconceived aesthetic mechanisms underlying popular fiction (which he refers to as "vernacular fiction") to those at play in canonical poetry (such as the Spenserian stanza): "As suggested earlier, the pattern seems to play much the same role in vernacular fiction that the metrical scheme plays in a poem. In both cases, readers sense the formal scheme as the norm that permits them to appreciate the figural variations. The writers are like the jazz musicians who give us a familiar melody at the opening of the piece so that we understand the variations that follow. We do not listen for that melody. We listen for the variation." Thomas Roberts, *An Aesthetic of Junk Fiction* (Athens: University of Georgia Press, 1990), 165–66.

24 An Goris, "Loving by the Book: Voice and Romance Authorship," in *New Perspectives on the Popular Romance Novel*, ed. Sarah S. G. Frantz and Eric M. Selinger (Jefferson: McFarland, 2012), 73–83 (80).

25 For more on the different definitions of voice that circulate in the romance community and the decisive role it plays in evaluations of romance novels by both readers and editors, see Jane Little, "Authorial Voice: The Many Hued Definitions," *Dear Author*, October 26, 2010, https://dearauthor.com/features/letters-of-opinion/authorial-voice.

26 Gelder, *Popular Fiction*, 40.

27 Ibid., 42.

28 Janice Radway, *Reading the Romance: Women, Patriarchy, and Popular Literature* (Chapel Hill: University of North Carolina Press, 1984).

Chapter 6

STEPHEN KING'S *THE GIRL WHO LOVED TOM GORDON*: A RHETORICAL READING OF THE SCHNEEKLUTH EDITION DUST JACKETS

Thorsten Bothe

The book as an object is comfortingly substantial in its content and its material presence. At a time when so much information is dispersed in virtual form, it is especially important to examine the book as a distinctive object reflecting a marriage of authors' words and designers' vision.
—Ned Drew and Paul Sternberger, *By Its Cover: Modern American Book Cover Design* (2005)

It is rarely found in libraries and archives—at least not in one piece. If it is, then it is usually in a special location or an archival storage box, provided there is enough space to store it. It is rarely preserved in research libraries, as it is usually removed from the book and discarded without—or in some cases with—an understanding of its cultural significance. Research libraries discard it because a book must be loaned and used as a single material unit; to use Foucault's terminology, it is a "parallelepiped."[1] Public libraries also tend to discard it, although they sometimes cut it up, paste the more or less important additional information that it contains onto the cover of the book, and then—if they can afford it—laminate the cover so that this additional information, such as a blurb, is preserved more or less permanently. Dutch book collector Albert Samuel Abraham Struik used surveys to determine that only two libraries had ever purchased a book because of it.[2] I am talking here about the dust jacket.

In the case of the German translation of Stephen King's novel *The Girl Who Loved Tom Gordon* (1999), published by Schneekluth in 2000, the popular saying "never judge a book by its cover" was carried too far and became ironic,[3] as this edition forced readers who typically ignore covers and dust jackets to make a decision. It definitely put their taste and judgment to the test and thus differentiated itself enormously from more conventional book editions.

The same company had also published the first edition of the German translation of Stephen King's novel *Carrie* (1974) with a dust jacket, and the publication of the German translation of *The Girl Who Loved Tom Gordon* seemed to reflect a desire to continue this tradition.[4] The book was also shrink-wrapped, as usual, but the shrink-wrap was so large that the process of shrink-wrapping was almost parodied. It was as if the shrink-wrap was supposed to simulate old wrapping paper or an old wrapper. The most surprising aspect was that the publisher offered two variants of the book—one with a white dust jacket and one with a black dust jacket (see Figure 6.1)—yet the covers remained black in both cases, so they appeared identical after the dust jackets were removed.[5] It is important to note that today, in the age of online bookstores, such a marketing strategy only works in physical bookstores, which allow customers to hold books in their hands.[6] This is the only way to

Figure 6.1 Covers of Stephen King, *Das Mädchen* (2000). *Source*: © Schneekluth Verlag.

evaluate a book in its entirety as a material object and to evaluate how the material form in which the book is presented appeals to the taste of readers and influences their purchasing decisions. Even if the shrink-wrap is an obvious marketing gag[7] (I can only vaguely recall the condition of the wrapping),[8] this is only partially true of the dust jacket. Despite their identical content, the customer is essentially purchasing a different book.[9] As Gérard Genette points out, "Simply the color of the paper chosen for the cover can strongly indicate a type of book."[10] In such cases, the number of copies sold or pulped is often not released, even if it exists. Were more white copies sold than black copies? Were more white copies left than black copies? Stephen King's name usually evokes gloomy associations, so a black dust jacket might actually seem more suitable. Was it no longer possible for customers who arrived later to choose between these two variants, or did one of them suddenly become more valuable than the other due to an imbalance in the number produced or a lack of availability in particular regions? Although it is conceivable from an economic perspective that a few fans and collectors may have purchased both variants, it seems probable that customers normally chose one or the other when first purchasing the book. The decision to purchase a white or black dust jacket is thus a question of taste, and the decision to purchase a black dust jacket might also leave the bitter taste of not having chosen the white dust jacket, or vice versa. Once the reader knows that there are two variants, it is as if one always calls to mind the other, as they form a contrasting pair in terms of their color symbolism. Black suggests death and evil, for example, whereas white suggests innocence and hope (I will come back to this). The fundamental distinction of the printing press is also invoked, as printed texts are usually black on white.

If it is true that the dust jacket and the cover enclosed within it semiotically constitute a parasynonymy of the text[11] and that they really count as much as the supposedly mere "content" of the book,[12] then the individuality of the parallelepiped, based on its materiality, must have a decisive influence not only on the expectations of readers, as it informed their purchasing decisions, but also on their interpretations. It may be argued that in many cases the author is not directly involved in the design of the jacket, which particularly applies in this case due to the vast number of editions of Stephen King's books. And if the author is not directly involved, then this raises the question as to whether the jacket is actually part of the text.[13] According to Genette, the jacket belongs to the publisher's peritext, which the author can potentially but not necessarily influence, though he also differentiates between the jacket, band, and slipcase.[14]

Nevertheless, the question as to whether the jacket and cover are part of the text and whether the author is more or less responsible for them hardly seems to lead in the right direction. It is possible to refer to the designers of paperback jackets as partial graphic coauthors of the books or simply to allocate them to the side of the reader within the framework of the literary communication model of author, reader, and text, as they are excluded from the full significance implied by the literary concept of the "author." The design of a dust jacket would then represent one possible reading of the text, and the designers would represent readers who have prepared an interpretation through their designs and whose interpretations prefigure those of the customers or potential readers. The jacket could also be described as a form of secondary literature, although the term "secondary" seems rather inaccurate in this context. This theory of the dust jacket as a reading implies that any interpretation of a text would have to take into account the dust jackets of every hardcover edition as well as the covers of every paperback edition, which are so commonplace nowadays. This might well be the case in a few scholarly articles on literary texts. Marco Sonzogni described designers as translators, for example, and he used as examples the many variant covers for Umberto Eco's *The Name of the Rose* (1980), which originated from a design contest.[15] He thus took into account selected entries of cover proposals that various designers had produced for the competition. This seems to suggest that the designer is summarizing the text for the customer and that the dust jacket represents a kind of abstract of the text itself, but it says little about the taste of the reader or the underlying cause of the reader's purchasing decision.

Although Sonzogni's theory is very convincing from a semiotic perspective, and it is highly innovative for translation studies,[16] his focus on signs misses something. Jack Matthews proposed that the jacket should be seen as a specific memory of the book—that is, the memory of the jacket designer.[17] It seems reasonable to understand the jacket of the Schneekluth edition of *The Girl Who Loved Tom Gordon* as a mnemotechnical operation. Since the *Ad Herennium* and Quintilian, the fourth part or canon of rhetoric, *memoria*, has always used semiotic processes, even if they were not explicit.[18] Matthews then asked what actually remains of the book:

> [B]ut what, exactly, becomes of my memory of that story? Somehow, I find this *a profoundly mysterious question*; and yet it seems to me that at the heart of many stories there is a still point—an image, a tableau, a gesture that may be said to contain the rest of the story *by implication*. This is not entirely unlike a story's opening, in which the entire narrative seems to be implicit. In one sense, it is the opening which is the story's origin, the seed out of which all the events grow. But the central image, the symbol, I am thinking of is buried somewhere within the story; it is to the story's theme what the opening is to its plot. This central image I am thinking of occupies that place in the story where the story becomes most intensely and most unmistakably itself. I believe this

somewhat reflects the function of memory, which is a narrative text as surely as any made-up story. Narrative texts are designed by omitting all but a small part of any event, that small part becoming its synecdoche or *envoy*.[19]

It could be further argued that the design of the jacket is a kind of rhetorical envoy of the designer's reading of the story and that it functions synecdochichally as the transmission of a *pars pro toto*. This seems to explain precisely how the exclusivity of the dust jackets of the Schneekluth edition of *The Girl Who Loved Tom Gordon* influences the customer's purchasing decision and reflects the reader's taste, and it actually does this in the form of a metalepsis that merges into the materiality of the book. To be more exact, "Metalepsis refers to the subsequent condition of a cause that is retroactively closed in that a phenomenon is conceived as its effect and can be deduced retroactively as constituting something that preceded and preconditioned it."[20] The sophistication of this rhetorical phenomenon, which merges the content of the book into the typographical design and possibly even turns the trivial into the highbrow,[21] seems to become material, as the reading that invites the purchase in the bookstore is the distillation of a process that has not yet occurred for the customer. If the customer accepts a particular dust jacket when purchasing the book—black or white—then (by implication) the jacket reflects the customer's own anticipated reading. It does not matter if this reading is fictitious.[22] The suspense of the reading would also involve a determination as to whether or not the book satisfies the customer's anticipation.

It would be easy to claim that a cheap paperback edition does the same, as the purchase of this exclusive edition cannot be explained by the mere content of the book—that is, its story, which focuses on a girl named Trisha, who gets lost while hiking in the woods, becomes convinced that she is being hunted by a supernatural entity, and attempts to defend herself by emulating a famous baseball player named Tom Gordon. That is the story the buyer hears before reading the book, and many editions of *The Girl Who Loved Tom Gordon* have understandably chosen a forest[23] or some form of baseball game as the central cover motif that embodies the designer's reading, although the baseball game only really structures the design of the English-language editions. A black-and-white dust jacket thus alone already significantly stands out from other editions, which all seem somehow similar on closer inspection, as they tend to feature a forest, a woman, and so on.

In this case, what constitutes the rhetorical envoy or epitome of the designer's exclusive reading, which appeals to the reader's taste, is not the mosquitoes, which typographically accompany the openings of the chapters and also adorn the cover (one of many allusions to William Golding's *Lord of the Flies* [1954]), the exclusive ribbon marker or hidden adhesive, which simulates a well-bound book, or even the superior quality of the paper or the font in which the text of the story is set in both variants, but rather primarily the black or white dust jacket. These colors emphasize the idea that Trisha's odyssey is one of life and death, black or white, as she must either win or lose her struggle against the harsh environment. In other words, the choice of a black or white dust jacket becomes a discriminating purchasing decision, and the act of carrying the book home after the purchase is a performative gesture that displays qua experiential literature whether Trisha's story turns out good or bad—that is, whether she lives or dies. It would be unnecessary to perform a classical analysis of the corpus to show, for instance, how often the adjectives "black" and "white" occur in the text and which semantic fields are involved when they occur; in any case, a smart reader eventually notices that the text is saturated with color symbolism, so the jacket designer's immensely productive trick more than suffices for the purchasing decision of the potential reader. The book can then also be prominently shown as exclusive, when socially necessary, as its materiality is the basic condition of its simulated display of highbrow values. "Judge the book by its cover."

Because the book in general is a product of evolution—and I do not mean here Hans Blumenberg's prominent metaphor of *evolutio*—it must be assumed that certain rules also apply to deluxe editions, and the Schneekluth edition of *The Girl Who Loved Tom Gordon* is a deluxe edition at least within the context of German-language Stephen King editions. In the late eighteenth and early nineteenth centuries, for example, the "look of luxury" was mainly characterized by three elements—paper, typography, and illustrations[24]—which meant that a book had to be opened before its value could be ascertained, and there were extensive discussions as to whether luxury was even necessary. In the twentieth and twenty-first centuries, however, hardly anyone is still discussing whether luxury is acceptable. "[T]he consumer's desire for singularity and uniqueness"[25] no longer reflects a position on the question of whether everyone should be fed first[26] and luxury should come later or whether a customer could care less about the needs of others. We live in a luxury society that also culminates in the hyper-individualization of the consumer as reader who, in turn, conceals different economies that cannot be further examined here.[27]

What would be more luxurious or more appealing to the individuality of the reader than creating the impression that two different editions of a book were being released on the market at the same time so that they could be distinguished in this way? If the choice of a particular edition anachronistically reflects the taste of the reader through its material quality, then is this choice intended to produce the reader's affinity for a book culture from the past through its material simulation, and does it once again offer a contradictory differentiation for the reader due to the modern dust jacket? In other words, what are the rules according to which the self-presenting bibliophile and the book *The Girl Who Loved Tom Gordon* converge? What makes this edition a possible status symbol? What makes it—black or white—attractive?

What follows is based on three assumptions that connect in a potentially illuminating way the material culture of the book and the taste of the reader (even if it is a taste that the reader only wants to display outwardly in society)[28] as well as the representation of the jacket or cover and the rhetorical translation (and thus the epitome) that it communicates as the content of the book. In popular culture, Stephen King's works are usually cheap paperbacks. The Schneekluth edition is thus a deviation in terms of its materiality, and it also deviates once again from itself at a second level through the dust jacket variants. The rhetorical tradition has developed countless systematizations of linguistic deviation, such as the enallage as a figure of speech that describes intentional grammatical deviation.[29] It would thus be reasonable to inquire about the possible extension or application of textual rhetoric to material culture. The four categories of change in rhetoric (addition, subtraction, permutation, and substitution) seem particularly well-suited to such an extension.[30]

The formation of certain attractors appears to explain what appeals to readers and what corresponds to their taste over the course of book history and the genealogy of its materiality as well as what is able to catch on better than other products or to import older modes of representation into the current discourse, and these attractors are also more or less apparent for the dust jacket. Evolutionary psychology offers a way to define this more precisely.[31] The most complex problem is ultimately the transfer of the translation of the story—"a profoundly mysterious question"—into the materiality of the jacket or cover, which performs the mnemotechnical operation. If it is true that memory cannot be reduced to a single concept, then it appears that the distillation of the jacket as a rhetorical transmission cannot dissolve into logicality or even be defined. Instead, it must be conceived from a thoroughly metaphorological perspective[32] that extends beyond the "dust jacket," which is literally speaking nothing more than a duly forgotten catachresis, as the covering of the book hardly still fulfills its protective function. Perhaps only this perspective could ultimately explain a purchase and the taste of the reader. This can only be outlined in the following, but it cannot be fully executed, which is why these considerations are limited to a few examples.

The "novelty" of the dust jacket of the Schneekluth edition of *The Girl Who Loved Tom Gordon* at least provisionally and partially shows how the jacket can be conceived as a deviation within the context of its genealogical series or evolution (a history that would still need to be written) and how this deviation celebrates beauty and influences the taste and purchasing decision (and thus selection) of the reader through ornamentation, regardless of whether this ornamentation is minimal or frightful in the deviation (like a genetic vari-ation).[33] Indeed, this thesis appears not to be contradicted but rather to be reinforced by the fact that the black-and-white jackets culminate in an "aston-ishing extreme" and assume an excessive form that greatly surpasses the clas-sical protective function of the jacket.[34] In terms of rhetoric, it is a material hyperbole of the jacket's function that consequently leads to a purchasing decision, which is analogous to forms of sexual display behavior:

> Beauty arouses desire—and thus approaching behavior. In the case of sexual bodies, the goal of the approach often goes beyond aesthetic contemplation; in the case of artworks and other beautiful objects, the consequence of the action consists in preferring beautiful objects of all kinds, contemplating them for a longer time than others, seeking to repeatedly look at them, and eventually also *acquiring* them.[35]

Taken to its logical conclusion, such a history of the evolution of the jacket would also require a formulated rhetoric of the work of the graphic designer, whose sales rhetoric moves into the field of dark rhetoric, which particularly in self-help literature culminates in the highly controversial area of neurolin-guistic programming aimed at sexual attention.[36] It is irrelevant here whether the designer consciously or unconsciously mirrors such strategies in the prod-uct (i.e., the book).

This area also includes other differentiating characteristics that can be clearly visible as distinctive features of the accessories to the book and their respective work or text. In the case of the Schneekluth edition of *The Girl Who Loved Tom Gordon*, for example, this would include the typography and the ribbon marker, which enhances the value of the otherwise trivial content. The Trajan font was chosen for the jacket, and the not uncontroversial Rotis Serif font was chosen for the book itself. The latter can ensure an almost singular reading experience, as it is considered artistic rather than mainstream. The size of the book, which is a contributing factor in the design of the jacket, is also immediately recognizable as larger than a normal paperback, as it measures 21.5 centimeters from head to foot and 13.5 centimeters from the binding to the outer edge.[37]

Biologically formulated, the dual variants of the dust jacket represent a transgression of the preceding features and even of the normal presence of only a single jacket in a single edition.[38] This excessive feature forces black and white to compete with one another, and the simultaneous presentation of both variants shifts the "promotional behavior" of the book from the marketplace to an almost closed differentiating system of variation by drawing the atten-tion of the potential customer from other editions that could be purchased, such as an English-language paperback, to the specially designed German translation. Variation is thus produced rhetorically in a sophisticated way, but from the publisher's perspective the customer is purchasing the same book, regardless of which variant is taken home. The value of the jacket variation is also based not on the print run but rather on its material uniqueness, as it produces scarcity for the taste of the reader when compared to other paperback editions. It is thus a matter of purchasing something quite particular that one believes is a better or truer variant of the same book.

The black jacket is the antithesis of the white jacket in terms of its design, and it allows the customer to purchase the repugnance of the interpretation of the story along with the book. It is a rhetorical representation through opposition, as readers do not know before reading the book whether the woman survives or dies, and they can opt for a good or bad outcome by choosing a particular color. Readers also cannot know whether the woman survives after reading the teaser presented on the jacket in the bookstore, as the information there is kept as open as possible. Even in the case of used copies or sample copies without any wrapping, the blurb on the jacket would not provide any useful hints as to how the story turns out, and the reader could still be disappointed with the story afterward. It would be a scholarly gamble to relate the phenomenon of white and black jackets to Charles Darwin's theory concerning white and black swans or even to predict a gender-specific taste.[39]

The approach of systematic rhetoric[40] is based on the violation and observation of norms (through reinforcing repetition) as well as the distinction between literal and figural meaning. Shifts in grammaticality and rhetoricity are easy to notice in language. In the case of semantic figures, the antithesis "syntagmatically relates not synonyms but rather antonyms," and this syntagmatic relation "usually forms a parallel sentence."[41] Plett cited an example from Georg Büchner's *The Hessian Courier* (1834)—"Peace to the huts! War to the palaces!"—that invokes the quality of value in the semantic field, as houses are poor and palaces are not poor.[42] Just as the linguistic antithesis only comes into being through the textual comparison of both sentences (such as by writing one below the other), so too is the chromatic oxymoron of this special edition only made possible through the textual comparison of the black-and-white jackets. Perhaps this edition is even the only example of a paratextual oxymoron on the basis of the color of the dust jacket. The taste of the reader emerges from this situation, as it is only realized after one or the other edition is purchased, and it is thus unavoidably secondary.

Once the semantic field of black and white is opened, it is hard to say when rhetorical substitutions should stop. The fifth chapter of Arthur Quinn's *Figures of Speech* (1982), which is titled "Reds in the Red," includes the following discussion of this "red" chapter title:

What this title means depends upon how we interpret "red" and "reds." The interpretations that come most readily to mind are probably those in which at least one of these words is taken as a substitute for an associated word. "In the red" frequently means financial loss, the color of the ink used to record the loss being used to indicate the loss itself. Then again, red is also associated with blood; and so through ferocious battles rivers of red routinely flow. Red is the color of the Russian flag, and hence a country can endure a red scare, or be subverted by reds. Red is a distinctive human hair color, and those who have it are often known by it. It is also the distinctive pigment in the plumage of Rhode Island chickens and Cincinnati baseball players. And when we get very angry, it is all that we see. On the other hand, we sometimes see nothing clearly after eating a bowl of red, on account of the tears the chili provokes. This string of reds could be continued indefinitely. Once you start substituting, it is hard to know where to stop.[43]

Black can stand for darkness, death, grief, and depression; white can stand for purity, peace, freedom, and innocence. There is thus an infinite number of possible ways to anticipate the story through the color of the jacket that embodies it: whether Trisha dies or survives, whether she falls into a depression or soars once again, whether she wins the match against her environment (i.e., the forest), or even the oscillations between the protagonist's psychic states. The choice of a jacket variant is like love at first sight.

The jacket deserves special attention precisely because it represents a more or less variable envoy of the content of the book (i.e., the story). In this particular case, it seems that both jacket variants seem to represent the story better collectively than they could individually.[44] This might also be the special attraction of the Schneekluth edition, as the combination of two contradictory jackets expresses a preconceptual understanding that a normal, individual jacket would never be able to express. The unique materiality of each black or white edition is also perceived as a distinctly unique object. For example, a bisected design (half white and half black) would not be able to produce this effect. The rhetorical representation of the story through the jacket thus also alternates between a mnemotechnical operation that combines both jackets and their individual components (black or white). The materiality of the book becomes a metonymy of a reading that has not yet been realized. This edition might also be appealing because it maintains a permanent undecidability, which it performatively exhibits through its materiality, and the reader is thus occupied with it for a longer time or many times.

The problem of the examples of such a rhetoric of the jacket is the same as that of all rhetorical figures: their definitions are often undermined by the realizations on which they are based. In the case of a rhetoric of the jacket, which is intended here, the example is thus not an insurmountable enemy but rather an opponent that needs to be taken into consideration. In this example, the figure of the chromatic oxymoron is at best a provisional "figure of thought,"[45] which initiates a rhetoric of the jacket and can perhaps be applied to other figural forms.

In order to develop a rhetoric of the dust jacket or cover, it thus seems necessary to borrow all of the figures of opposition and differentiation, to apply systematic rhetoric to paratextuality, and to question what a jacket actually represents. This can occur within the context of a single edition, it can include all of the jackets and covers of a particular title, or it can even have a bearing on certain types of books and their historical manifestations through epochs. In the end, the demand for a "pragmatic concept of figural interpretation" is only made possible by a rhetoric that "judges a book by its cover."

Translated by Anthony Enns

Notes

1 Michel Foucault, *The Archaeology of Knowledge and the Discourse on Language*, trans. A. M. Sheridan Smith (New York: Pantheon, 1972), 23.

2 A. S. A. Struik, "The Dust-Jacket: Cloth of Gold in the Auction Room," *Quaerendo* 28, no. 3 (1998): 185–214 (207). For more on dust jackets, see George Thomas Tanselle, "Dust-Jackets, Dealers, and Documentation," *Studies in Bibliography* 56 (2003/2004): 45–140. For more on the "physical presentation of texts," see George Thomas Tanselle, "Analysis of Design Features," in *Bibliographical Analysis: A Historical Introduction* (Cambridge: Cambridge University Press, 2009), 61–88.

3 Stephen King, *Das Mädchen*, trans. Wulf Bergner (Munich: Schneekluth, 2000).

4 A copy of the Schneekluth edition of *Carrie* in good condition with a dust jacket is now sold in antiquarian bookstores via Amazon for up to 1,000 euros. This high price is presumably related to the dust jacket, although this cannot be confirmed due to its scarcity.

5 *The Girl Who Loved Tom Gordon* was also published as a pop-up book in English as well as German, which seems very interesting from a material culture perspective. See Stephen King, *The Girl Who Loved Tom Gordon: A Pop-Up Book* (New York: Simon & Schuster, 2004). A comprehensive examination of the history of the pop-up book has yet to be done in the context of material culture studies.

6 It is actually possible today to inspect new books online using the "look inside" function on Amazon, but the Schneekluth edition of *The Girl Who Loved Tom Gordon* was published so long ago that only used copies are still available.

7 Such marketing strategies are not unusual. A famous example from the realm of middlebrow culture is the combination of Shakespeare and candy—a case in which the thoroughly discriminating customer sought to combine the purchase of a book with a special kind of gift: "In 1916 the Whitman Candy Company of Philadelphia marketed a Library Package, uniting a large box of candy with a small, leather-bound book. The promotional strategy clearly imagined the existence of discriminating buyers who might want to endow a gift of caramels and chocolate-covered maraschino cherries with the tony aura of high culture. Whitman obliged by offering its own product in conjunction with one of fifteen Shakespearean plays collected in a series

called the Little Leather Library." Janice A. Radway, *A Feeling for Books: The Book-of-the-Month Club, Literary Taste, and Middle-Class Desire* (Chapel Hill: University of North Carolina Press, 1997), 127.

8 The function of the wrapping is usually just to convey a sense of otherness, but it may substantially distinguish a book from others on display in the bookstore, as it directs the attention of the potential customer to the object. In such cases, research on material culture is confronted with the irretrievable loss of the materials, as the wrapping was almost invariably disposed of in waste bins. There is said to have been another book by Stephen King on the American market whose wrapping was designed like skin, and the unwrapping of the book was supposed to have been a "dramatic" experience for the reader (the title could unfortunately not be identified).

9 One is in fact purchasing a different book, as they are assigned different ISBN numbers.

10 Gérard Genette, *Paratexts: Thresholds of Interpretation*, trans. Jane E. Lewin (Cambridge: Cambridge University Press, 1997), 24. Genette is referring here to French "yellow" books, which for historical reasons indicated explicit sexual content by means of their color.

11 See Marco Sonzogni, *Re-Covered Rose: A Case Study in Book Cover Design as Intersemiotic Translation* (Amsterdam: John Benjamins, 2011).

12 "Content" here does not refer to the familiar and highly questionable difference between "content" and "form"; rather, it refers to the question of what constitutes a (material) book, which must be naively asked anew here.

13 If I talk about the dust jacket as a paratext, then I am obviously not following Genette's terminology, which to me is actually not precise enough for bibliology. Genette himself also admitted that this was never his intention: "[T]hese technical givens themselves come under the discipline called *bibliology*, on which I have no wish to encroach." Genette, *Paratexts*, 16. Tanselle provides a more precise differentiation of the dust jacket: "I use 'dust-jacket' and 'book-jacket' interchangeably; but I never use 'wrapper' for 'jacket,' reserving 'wrapper' for paper covers that are attached to a book or pamphlet." Tanselle, "Dust-Jackets, Dealers, and Documentation," 45. "Cover" is also too imprecise, as it is also used for paperbacks that do not have a dust jacket.

14 Genette, *Paratexts*, 32.

15 Sonzogni, *Re-Covered Rose*, 37–149.

16 See María López Ponz, Review of *Re-Covered Rose* by Marco Sonzogni, *The Journal of Specialised Translation* 18, no. 7 (2012): 224–25.

17 Jack Matthews, "Dust Jackets and the Art of Memory," *Logos* 14, no. 3 (2003): 155–58.

18 See Bettine Menke, "Mneme, Mnemonik—Medien (in) der Antike," in *Medien der Antike*, ed. Lorenz Engell, Bernhard Siegert, and Joseph Vogl (Weimar: Verlag der Bauhaus-Universität, 2003), 121–36 (125).

19 Matthews, "Dust Jackets and the Art of Memory," 157 (emphasis mine).

20 Bettine Menke, "Zur Evidenz—der Stigmata," in *Rhetorik und Religion*, ed. Holt Meyer and Dirk Uffelmann (Stuttgart: W. Kohlhammer, 2007), 134–51 (137).

21 As is generally known, Stephen King has always been derided by professional literary critics. His entry in the *Lexikon der phantastischen Literatur* (Lexicon of Fantastic Literature, 1998) might be considered an especially negative example: "When an author becomes a literary phenomenon, it is difficult to make a judgment about him, as phenomena, whether natural or supernatural, must first be accepted. [...] While the number of individual novels can probably be attributed to the willingness of the

word processor, their flat style, which skillfully blends colloquial language and poetic clichés, leaves little room for aesthetic reflection." Rein A. Zondergeld and Holger E. Wiedenstried, "Stephen King," in *Lexikon der Phantastischen Literatur* (Stuttgart: Weitbrecht, 1998), 191–93 (191). It is thus particularly interesting that such supposedly trivial content would be sold in such an exclusive book format.

22 Many graphic designers obviously do not read the books whose jackets they design. In the case of the Schneekluth edition of *The Girl Who Loved Tom Gordon*, however, it is hard to conceive of any specifications from the editorial office that would summarize the story in the way implied by the dual jacket variants. If one were to think of the most minimalistic guideline for the designer, then it would definitely include the forest theme, which is pushed to the background in the form of a small detail on the back of the jacket. This is only conceivable through a conscious decision, as the central theme of the book is the disappearance of a woman in a forest. It can thus be assumed that Matthews's argument is indeed valid: "[A]fter dust jacket artists have spent hours reading and studying a book, they will go over the notes they have taken along the way (either explicitly or in their memories) and will test them according to their own sense of what the book is—their memory of the book—as that sense intersects with their own artistic values." Matthews, "Dust Jackets and the Art of Memory," 158.

23 See, for example, the American paperback edition: Stephen King, *The Girl Who Loved Tom Gordon* (New York: Pocket Books, 2000). The jacket of the Schneekluth edition only cites the forest in the form of a round telescopic detail of a piece of bark in the middle of the back, which serves as a synecdoche for the forest as a whole.

24 Matt Erlin, "How to Think about Luxury Editions in Late Eighteenth- and Early Nineteenth-Century Germany," in *Publishing Culture and the "Reading Nation": German Book History in the Long Nineteenth Century*, ed. Lynne Tatlock (Rochester: Camden House, 2010), 25–54 (29).

25 Ibid., 48.

26 See Johann Gottlieb Fichte, *Ausgewählte politische Schriften* (Frankfurt am Main: Suhrkamp, 1977), 79.

27 Passable examples include the unreflective users of Google and Amazon, who have still not grasped that they are not the customers or users of companies but rather their products. See Jaron Lanier, *Who Owns the Future?* (New York: Simon & Schuster, 2013).

28 This would obviously also include the taste of literary scholars as readers, even if they only want to determine in their academic culture whether the rhetorical synecdoche of the jacket is an accurate envoy of the book, but that is another story.

29 See Arthur Quinn, *Figures of Speech: 60 Ways to Turn a Phrase* (Salt Lake City: Gibbs M. Smith, 1982), 49f.

30 See Heinrich F. Plett, *Systematische Rhetorik: Konzepte und Analysen* (Munich: Fink, 2000).

31 See Winfried Menninghaus, *Wozu Kunst? Ästhetik nach Darwin* (Berlin: Suhrkamp, 2011); and Winfried Menninghaus, *Kunst als "Beförderung des Lebens": Perspektiven transzendentaler und evolutionärer Ästhetik* (Munich: Carl Friedrich von Siemens Stiftung, 2008).

32 Hans Blumenberg, *Paradigms for a Metaphorology*, trans. Robert Savage (Ithaca, NY: Cornell University Press, 2010), 2f.

33 Menninghaus, *Wozu Kunst?*, 34f.

34 Ibid. Menninghaus cites antlers as a classic example that reaches such extremes that they are actually more of a hindrance to the struggle for survival.

35　Ibid., 32 (emphasis mine).

36　When read using rhetorical theory, self-help literature appears to be a practical consequence of the laws of "mating strategies" discovered by evolutionary psychology, which enable the formulation of instructions on the wearing of flashy clothes and jewelry. See, for example, Neil Strauss, *The Game: Penetrating the Secret Society of Pickup Artists* (New York: Regan Books, 2005), 17–23; David M. Buss, *The Evolution of Desire: Strategies of Human Mating* (New York: Basic Books, 2003), 97–122.

37　The Heyne Verlag implemented this on the German market by publishing Stephen King's novels in the jumbo format. These are volumes that are almost reminiscent of typescript books, as in the prominent case of *Es* (It, 1996).

38　"Edition" is a problematic term here, as it is clear from the perspective of bibliology that both variants have different ISBN numbers and that they are thus actually two different editions that were released simultaneously. However, this is opposed to the perception of the reader engaged in a textual comparison of both variants, which were also sold at the same time. It is therefore necessary to adopt a phenomenological perspective.

39　With regard to "sexually attractive [...] color and sound ornaments," Menninghaus mentions Darwin's "examples of bird species that developed contrasting color extremes but were otherwise the same, such as black and white swans." Menninghaus, *Wozu Kunst*, 38. Darwin explained this phenomenon as follows:

> As sexual selection depends on so fluctuating an element as taste, we can understand how it is that within the same group of birds, with habits of life nearly the same, there should exist white or nearly white, as well as black, or nearly black species—for instance, white and black cockatoos, storks, ibises, swans, terns, and petrels. Piebald birds likewise sometimes occur in the same groups, for instance, the black-necked swan, certain terns, and the common magpie. That a strong contrast in colour is agreeable to birds, we may conclude, by looking through any large collection of specimens or series of coloured plates, for the sexes frequently differ from each other in the male having the pale parts of a purer white, and the variously coloured dark parts of still darker tints than in the female.

Charles Darwin, *The Descent of Man, and Selection in Relation to Sex* (Princeton: Princeton University Press, 1981), 230.

40　Plett, *Systematische Rhetorik*, 21f.

41　Ibid., 206.

42　Ibid.

43　Quinn, *Figures of Speech*, 49.

44　There is a certain appeal to the idea of seeing a book produced with a changeable jacket that could be used entirely according to taste.

45　Eva Horn and Michèle Lowrie, "Vorwort," in *Denkfiguren: Figures of Thought*, ed. Eva Horn and Michèle Lowrie (Berlin: August Verlag, 2013), 11–21 (11).

Section Three

CULTURAL PRESTIGE AND GRAPHIC NARRATIVES

Chapter 7

THE PRINTING OF PHANTASMS: THE ILLUSTRATIONS OF NINETEENTH-CENTURY SERIALIZED NOVELS AND THEIR APPROPRIATION IN MAX ERNST'S COLLAGE NOVEL *UNE SEMAINE DE BONTÉ*

Philipp Venghaus

In 1933 German artist Max Ernst created his third collage novel, *Une semaine de bonté* (A Week of Kindness),[1] which consists of 183 collages divided into 5 booklets whose differently colored covers identify the days, elements, and examples to which each chapter is dedicated. The structure can be best represented in the form of Table 7.1:

Booklet	Color	Day	Element	Examples	Collages/Chapter
First	violet	Sunday	mud	The Lion of Belfort	35
Second	green	Monday	water	Water	27
Third	red	Tuesday	fire	The Court of the Dragon	45
Fourth	blue	Wednesday	blood	Oedipus	28
Fifth	yellow	Thursday	black	The Rooster's Laugh	16
				Easter Island	10
		Friday	sight	The Interior of Sight: Three Visible Poems	First poem: 6 Second poem: 4 Third poem: 2
		Saturday	unknown	The Key of Songs	20

If the popular serialized novels whose illustrations Ernst used as the basis for his collages were already forgotten in 1933, as German art historian Werner Spies claims,[2] then this only applies to the individual novels. His contemporaries would have still remembered the serialized novel as a genre "that belonged to the world of the parents of Max Ernst's generation," as German philosopher Theodor Adorno said.[3] The narrative model and illustrations of nineteenth-century serialized novels still shaped the collective unconscious of the younger generation that grew up during World War I. In his introduction to Ernst's previous collage novel, *La femme 100 têtes* (The Hundred Headless Woman, 1929), French Surrealist André Breton even said that they "might reveal better than all else the special nature of our dreams."[4]

The form and content of the serialized novel were closely interwoven with the technical means and economic conditions of its printing. In the nineteenth century the newspaper became the primary medium for the mass distribution of popular literature, and the serialized novel marked the beginning of the modern press.[5] The conditions of production of the serialized novel, to which Ernst's collage novel refers, cannot be separated from the conditions of production of the myths and phantasms to which the illustrations testify, as they depict a world in which people are both threatened by mythical powers and subjected to industrially rationalized exploitation—a subjection that culminated in the first industrialized world war.

Ernst's unusual artistic appropriation of the serialized novel foregrounds images of crime and violence. Instead of glorifying violence, instinct, and the unconscious, however, it seems to reflect on the prehistory of fascism by critiquing the need to display one's own sophistication (which was particularly prevalent during the interwar period), attacking the fascist logic of distinguishing between friends and enemies, and demonstrating the absurdity of distinguishing between good and bad violence. Ernst's appropriation of the serialized novel, which was one of the most important popular genres of the nineteenth century, for a collage novel, which was a product of the art publishing system, thus went far beyond the mere use of a fund of spectacular visual material.

Ernst's collage novels present the serialized novel as a mirror of its time, yet they make this mirror readable not as a realistic but rather as a phantasmatic genre that becomes clear through defamiliarization. The technical craftsmanship with which Ernst appropriates not only the illustrations of serialized novels but also the outer appearance and characteristic features of this mode of publication can be appreciated as a milestone in the development of artistic techniques, as it represents the merging of "high" and "low" art. The defining principles of collage, such as fragmentation and juxtaposition, also suggest that this merging resembles a collision that leaves neither of them unscathed.

The Production Conditions of the Serialized Novel and Its Illustrations

Ernst evokes the tradition of the serialized novel through the subtitle, *Les septs éléments capitaux* (The Seven Deadly Elements), which alludes to the seven deadly sins.[6] Even if Ernst was not familiar with French novelist Eugène Sue's *Les sept péchés capitaux* (The Seven Deadly Sins, 1847–1849), his subtitle clearly referred to the popular titles of serialized novels, which were often advertised with the words "misdeed, sin, or crime."[7] Even the font used for the titles of the booklets was designed to draw attention by evoking the familiar "typography of horror."

Assigning a particular day of the week to each booklet can also be seen as an allusion to the many serialized novels published on a weekly schedule.[8] Like a serialized novel, Ernst's collages were originally supposed to have been issued in seven consecutive booklets. Their binding and their 9x11-inch format also recalled the bound collections that were published after a novel had been successfully serialized in a daily or weekly newspaper in the latter half of the nineteenth century.

The first two booklets were published by French gallerist Jeanne Bucher in April 1934; however, they apparently did not attract the subscribers he had hoped for, despite various advertisements in magazines like *Minotaure* (1933–1939), as an advertisement posted in May only mentioned six installments. The last three days were eventually combined into a fifth and final booklet, which was not released until December.[9]

Ernst's collages served as templates for etchings, and 800 copies were printed on "Papier Navarre" by Georges Duval in Paris. According to the May advertisement 12 special editions on "Papier d'Arches" were supposed to be forthcoming, but of these only 5 were printed and numbered from 0 to 00000. In addition, 16 roman numbered copies were also created. The booklets were accompanied by a slipcase that was decorated with etchings on both sides, and the special editions included a soft-ground etching specially created by Ernst himself. In 1934 the 125 subscribers each paid 400 francs for the booklet series.

The illustrations that Ernst used for his collages were woodcuts from the period 1860–1900, which were taken from newspapers that had specialized in the publication of serialized novels. However, early serialized novels were usually printed without illustrations, as they often appeared in the bottom third of the newspaper, which was separated from political journalism by a clear dividing line. The space below this line was commonly reserved for travel reports, reviews, glosses, commentaries, and entertainment.

Nonpolitical serials became increasingly important as restrictions were placed on political journalism at the end of the French Revolution.[10] Large print runs also became possible in the nineteenth century through the introduction of fast yet expensive rotary presses.[11] Until then newspapers had served as a medium of communication for small groups of politically interested intellectuals, but with the rise of serials and new methods of mass production newspapers began to address a broader, less homogeneous, and less politically engaged public.[12] This new public consisted of the urban middle class and the growing industrial proletariat, which had better access to education than the rural population. However, they could only be reached after a significant price reduction. This gave rise to an innovative concept of production and distribution, as the serialized novel was seen as a means of "systematically conquering the popular marketplace."[13]

French publisher Émile de Girardin's newspaper *La presse* (The Press) first appeared on June 15, 1836. With a price of 40 francs for an annual subscription, instead of the usual 80 francs, other newspapers were soon forced to follow this concept. Any publication that wished to survive was required to lower its cover price, defray its production costs through advertising, and increase its distribution as much as possible.[14] French writer Alphonse Royer's novel *Patrona Calil* (1836) was first serialized in the newspaper *Le siècle* (The Age, 1836–1932) beginning on September 30, 1836. French writer Honoré de Balzac's novel *La vielle fille* (The Old Maid, 1836) was also serialized in *La presse* beginning on October 23, 1836. French journalist Alfred François Nettement already noted in 1845 that

> [i]n order to offer a journal for 40 or 48 francs, it is necessary to have lots of advertisements. In order to have lots of advertisements, it is necessary to have lots of subscribers. In order to have lots of subscribers, it is necessary to address all opinions at once and to substitute an interest of general curiosity for the political interest of a particular group. [...] As soon as journals were offered for 40 francs and included advertising, it was almost inevitable that they would publish serialized novels and "immoral serials"—two words for the same idea.

With the expansion of readership, serialized novels became synonymous with the industrial production of literature on a mass scale[15]; they were mass-produced commodities for the "illiterate" masses.[16] The classification of people as either literate or illiterate thus shifted to a distinction between readers with taste and an anonymous mass audience[17]; however, "high" literature was still related to the serialized novel, as the reading public was given access to many books that later became classics through their serialization in newspapers and respected authors often wrote serialized novels or were inspired by them.[18] Serialized novels also borrowed elements from "high" literature, although these elements were mostly reduced to stereotypical set pieces.[19]

Serialized novels were also closely related to popular science and *faits divers* (various facts) or human-interest stories. Indeed, literary and scientific articles were often difficult to distinguish from one another in journals like *La science populaire* (Popular Science, 1880–1884). In addition to practical knowledge from the fields of medicine or agriculture there were also adventurous reports from explorers and inventors, which were full of spectacular accidents and killings. Although popular science journals presented themselves as *bonne lecture* (good reading), as they offered an alternative to reading bad novels, their crossover to printed adventure novels was quite fluid. These journals had been founded in order to democratize science, but in the face of the increasing "professionalization and commercialization of the media landscape" at the end of the nineteenth century, contributions were only printed "if they conformed to the logic of the media and were able to attract the attention of readers and potential buyers."[20]

The first illustrated newspaper, *Illustrated London News* (1842–2003), originally used woodcuts to illustrate news stories, as they were quick to produce, wear-resistant, and easy to modify.[21] Woodcuts were soon adopted by newspapers to illustrate serialized novels, and publishers often reused the printing plates produced for new stories about murders, accidents, or mass unrest. Novel illustrations also influenced the aesthetics of news illustrations:

> [T]he new style of dense, dramatically lit engraving with high articulation of emotions was firmly established as a part of fiction and in social reportage. Thus the reader, in his or her experience of the discourse offered in such material, is not only presented with visual styles which may be very similar in both "fact" and "fiction" passages; he or she also encounters a relationship between word and image which is fundamentally the same in both, and thus a type of discourse is shared between notional "fact" and "fiction" which colours and in many cases directs the reader's approach to the outside world.[22]

Popular science journals also employed the methods of novel illustration by featuring full-page illustrations that presented dramatic moments, like the collapse of a lighthouse or the death of an explorer. It is no surprise, then, that Ernst also used these illustrations for his collages in *Une semaine de bonté* in the same way that he used illustrations from serialized novels.

The argument that serialized novels shaped their readers' views of the world and the thinking of an epoch[23] is corroborated by their close proximity to *faits divers* and popular science, which "intensified the literary parallels between news stories, sensationally written and occasionally even fictionalized, and feuilleton novels in which crime was an ever-present element."[24] *Faits divers* and serialized novels also followed the same aesthetic of sensations and tension, all the more since the cases of *faits divers* were often explained incrementally and in episodes.[25] While serialized novels offered a narrative model for the presentation of news and discoveries, their proximity to *faits divers* and popular science made it credible that they were about real-life events. The illustrations also lent additional credibility to the events, as they were closely related to the didactic engravings found in popular science journals and they were thoroughly realistic due to the "pin-sharp" woodcut technique.[26]

The Freedom and Order of Serialized Novels

Serialized novels had a certain freedom, as feature sections were subject to less strict censorship than political journalism,[27] and they often included material that was forbidden in the main body of the newspaper on moral grounds, such as reports on crimes and scandals. Serialized novels also became a place where women's interests were publicly articulated, as they attracted a larger proportion of female readers and writers than other areas of literature.

If literature can be conceived as "an expression of personal, social, or in any case historically contingent hopes and illusions, predilections and fears,"[28] then the novels serialized in daily newspapers were not least designed to serve the daily interests of the broadest possible audience.[29] The speed required for the repeated extensions of some successful serialized novels, like Sue's *Les mystères de Paris* (The Mysteries of Paris, 1842–1843), "was particularly conducive to a liberation of fantasies and an explosion of images and scenes that seem to speak freely the language of the unconscious—and that is primarily why they were of interest to the Surrealists."[30]

British literary critic David H. Walker sees the violence and excess that characterized the feature section as the expression of an untamed and resistant reality that penetrates the surface of the ruling order and threatens to disrupt it,[31] although I find this argument overly simplistic. Walker relies on the work of French philosopher Michel Foucault, but he overlooks the fact that Foucault saw *faits divers* as not opposed to but rather an instrument of discipline. According to Foucault, for example, *faits divers* helped to spread the fear that the threat of crime was ever-present, which encouraged readers to accept the establishment of the police in the nineteenth century as well as the classification of certain people as inherently criminal. It was thus part of a productive order that had long subjected undefinable human life to a system of classification.[32]

The discussion of a few "monstrous" cases in the 1820s and 1830s seems to have been important for early serialized novels.[33] As Spies explains, "The main goal of these serialized stories [...] was to show crimes in order to punish them. We are miles away from the criminalistic metaphysics that established the *roman noir* [crime novel] as a bulwark against the Enlightenment."[34] In other words, crimes were perceived not as an expression of the mysterious depths of human existence but rather only as a breach of order and a confirmation that order needed to be maintained and expanded through sanctions.[35] The evil and monstrous criminals, who are associated with cosmic counterforces and still populate the *roman noir* today, were downplayed in the nineteenth century as individuals who exhibited deviant behavior and were in need of correction.[36]

The narratives of serialized novels mostly featured "stock characters," as they were limited to sets of distinct and familiar types.[37] Considering that physiognomy and phrenology were attempting to identify dangerous types at this time,[38] the illustrations could be seen as "encyclopedias of atrocities"[39] as well as their perpetrators. Following this idea, it can be assumed that *faits divers* and serialized novels contributed to these efforts "to impose a pattern on the perception of delinquents."[40] Serialized novels thus revealed the hidden machinations of evil and assigned clearly recognizable faces to the criminals, and the illustrations played a key role in mediating this visual, spatial order.

Phantasms of Violence in the Illustrations Used by Ernst

Images of collapsing bridges and lighthouses, mass unrest, and train accidents reflected the horror and fascination of a century that was shaken by technical and social revolutions. Serialized novels chronicled the uncertain divisions between the new urban classes, offered readers a panoramic view of a demimonde full of criminals and prostitutes, and provided a glimpse into the homes of wealthy social climbers threatened by moral decline.[41] It can thus be claimed that serialized novels "are dominated more by what they fear than by what they want to keep safe."[42] However, these elements were integrated into the familiar framework of a mythical battle between good and evil, which exonerated everyday reality.[43]

Ernst presents two figures of fear and fascination in the collage novel: an amorphous woman[44] and a man who does not bow to any laws. In the second booklet, for example, water penetrates the bourgeois world and for the most part directly into the bedroom. However, page 23 raises the question as to whether this disruption originates with a man pulling aside the curtain in his wife's room, from which water gushes forth. A crowd seized with revolutionary fervor causes a bridge to collapse, while a woman rests peacefully on the waterfront (in other images she is sleeping in a bed buffeted by waves). She thus becomes the embodiment of the water, the hysterical masses, and the elementary powers of chaos.

The second disturbing yet fascinating figure is the lion-headed protagonist of the first booklet. The lion is an allusion to Frédéric Auguste Bartholdi's statue in Belfort, which was a monument designed to commemorate the city's resistance against a German siege during the Franco-Prussian War (1870–1871) and the heroic defense of French civilization. Ernst added a citation from French writer Alfred Jarry in the 1963 German edition: "The ermine is a very dirty animal. In itself it is a precious bedsheet, but as it has no change of linen, it does its laundry with its tongue."[45] The tension between repulsive bestiality and erotic attraction should not be underestimated. The lion was identified by its medals as a representative of the church and the state who nevertheless violates their moral standards,[46] and Ernst used this figure to polemicize against the corrupting power of institutions. His blasphemy was also an examination of the fascination that emanates from religious and political power, which was much more powerful than the "enlightened [...] anti-clericalism" of the other Surrealists.[47]

The appeal of the protagonist of a serialized novel is particularly fascinating when he is elevated by religious elements. Consider, for example, the protagonist of Alexandre Dumas's novel *Le comte de Monte-Cristo* (The Count of Monte Cristo, 1844–1846), who stands like a god above the masses and the laws that govern them. This allows him to fight the villains with their own weapons without appearing immoral.[48] At the same time, readers are also able to identify with this superhero of the latter half of the nineteenth century, as he himself rose up from the lower middle classes to become a hero.[49] Ernst's lion-headed protagonist represents a "new type of power seeker,"[50] who conceals his lower-middle-class status under his lion mask. It all comes together in the closing image of the booklet, as three lions rest on platforms with the inscription *Laudate pueri dominum* (Praise the Lord, Children) and the "emblems of his authority"[51] or the insignias of a militarized bourgeois society lying scattered about, such as a wallet, a watch, cannonballs, and medals: "The '*pueri*' [children] are the respectable bourgeois, whose collective portrait emerges in the background [and vanishing point] as a calf's head."[52]

Italian philosopher Antonio Gramsci noted that the reading of serialized novels allowed the lower middle classes to escape the constraints of their living conditions through violent fantasies veiled in morality.[53] These fantasies, along with the "hero and leader cult" of the late nineteenth century, were apparent in the illustrations that Ernst appropriated for his collage novel.[54] The superhero can thus be seen as a prefiguration of the fascistic version of German philosopher Friedrich Nietzsche's *Übermensch* (overman).[55] The image of Napoleon on the first page of the collage novel can also be read as a reference to the popular Napoleon cult in serialized novels, which according to Gramsci became a model for the leader cult of Italian fascism. Ernst was very familiar with the political situation in Italy, as he traveled there in 1933–1934, and it was there that he created *Une semaine de bonté*.[56]

The lion-headed protagonist looks up to the image of Napoleon, as if he wants to emulate him, and he turns his back on the naked "lioness," who is smitten with him. Ernst thus opens the novel with a turn away from the liberation of animality toward the paternalistic model.[57] Some of the images also show the lion as a protective husband, in accordance with the paternalism of the superhero.[58] The growth of nationalism was also reflected in serialized novels around 1900, and it became particularly aggressive on the eve of World War I. Under its influence, violence and chaos were often blamed on evil conspirators like Jews or Jesuits, who sought to weaken the unity of the nation and who were defeated by the protective heroes.[59] For example, page 32 depicts the execution of French serial killer Jean-Baptiste Troppmann "in the claws of the 'tiger,' Georges Clemenceau's nickname at the time": "Clemenceau was responsible for the French negotiations at the treaty of Versailles and was thus also associated with the punitive retribution exacted upon the German people for the sake of French pride. Troppmann, the Jewish criminal, signifies the outsider: widely blamed in antisemitic discourse for crime and disorder since Dreyfus."[60] On page 33, the sad conclusion of the booklet, the lion gathers his victims in a dark, desolate landscape. This image shows what is left of the heroic European nations at war: "Night, chaos, escape from guilt and skulls. A hand indicates the direction to the container, which is full of bones, stamped with state medals, and represents the remains of modern civilization."[61]

The Collage of "High" and "Low" Art

The Surrealists were fascinated by the violence of serialized novel illustrations, as they recognized its disruptive potential, but they still presented this historical material in a distorted form. Gerd Bauer sees Ernst's use of representations of violence as a glorification of "anarchistic power," which "threatens the established order."[62] It is uncertain, however, whether it is the violence of the representations or their violent distortion through collage that threatens the established order. As Ernst remarked, "It's not the glue that makes the collage."[63] Spies concludes that the principles of collage as a technical process, such as fragmentation and collision, also affect the meaning of their content.[64]

The process of collage is directed against painting. In his writings, for example, Ernst polemicized against the representatives of the academy who promoted painting *d'après nature* (from nature).[65] First and foremost, however, he criticized his own father, Philipp Ernst, who was not seized by nature but rather subjected nature to his own ordering gaze when he painted. Ernst was opposed to this form of painting, which fanatically fought against disorder.[66] In his first "Manifesto of Surrealism" (1924), Breton similarly criticized "the incurable mania of wanting to make the unknown known, classifiable."[67]

Ernst's discovery of collage took him in the opposite direction, as he sought to uncover the aspects of product catalogues, clichés, and serialized novel illustrations that subverted order: "The catalogue of a provider of school supplies attracts attention. [...] The items are of such a diverse nature that the absurdity evoked by their accumulation disturbs the gaze and the senses, creating hallucinations and endowing the represented objects with new senses that change rapidly."[68] He also revealed the product catalogue's affinity to the cabinet of curiosities, as it resisted any kind of overview and demanded a gaze that adapted itself to things. Spies also compares Ernst's collages with the cabinet of curiosities: "These representations of the miracles and monsters of the world are not only about the registering of phenomena. They also seek to achieve astonishing effects through contrasting juxtapositions that attempt to present what has never been seen before."[69] The combination of objects in the cabinet of curiosities could not be explained on the basis of measurements and systems; rather, it reflected the fascination that the objects exerted on their collector. Ernst also discovered these "contrasting juxtapositions" in product catalogues, as the "confusing equivalence" with which the catalogue brought things together constituted its fascination and subverted its order, which led to his discovery of collage.[70]

In his book *Écritures* (Writings, 1970), Ernst described one of his father's paintings of a forest, in which the trees are trapped in their own "singularities," separated from each other and deindividualized in their arrangement.[71] A monk sitting amongst the trees is immersed in a book and closed off from the experience of his surroundings. This is contrasted with the experience described shortly afterward of "little Max," who feels "rapture" and "oppression" when entering the forest.[72] Unlike the monk, Ernst could not close himself off from the impressions of the forest. A distant gaze at objects is thus replaced by direct contact with things, and the skin—the surface of the body—becomes a contact zone. The subject has no control over this contact, as it seems to come from the things themselves. This idea culminates in the collage technique, which "announces a sensuality [...] that in a thirst for knowledge strives to touch everything that exists."[73]

Ernst used collage to challenge his father's notion of art as the creation of a new universe according to the genuine rules of nature.[74] Instead of creating something *ex nihilo* (out of nothing)—that is, something that negates what came before—he demanded its transformation. In his essay on *bricolage* (handicrafts), French anthropologist Claude Lévi-Strauss described the mechanisms of mythical thought by comparing engineers and handymen: unlike the engineer, who controls his material and shapes it entirely according to his plan, the handyman is content with what is found by chance.[75] In the same way, Ernst was a collector toward whom fascinating "finds" radiated through the dark uniformity of things.[76]

Just as the handyman makes use of "the remnants of events,"[77] the collagist uses the woodcut not as a method of artistic production but rather as a remnant, like used printing blocks and obsolete novels and catalogues. And while the engineer seeks to discover a genuine nature behind "the constraints that express the state of civilization,"[78] the collagist recognizes that reality is always shaped by culture and that his methods have a history, whose traces are stubbornly reflected in the entirety of his works. He thus enters "into a kind of dialogue" with his material,[79] and the result is "always a compromise": "[By the time the collagist's project] is realized, it has inevitably shifted from its original intentions—an effect that the Surrealists appropriately called an 'objective accident.'"[80] The collagist cannot entirely evade the material's existing relations of sympathy, as similarities can determine the compositions. This can be seen on page 29 of "The Court of the Dragon," where a woman in a quilted dress nestles an armadillo whose scales resemble the dress pattern.

The dialogue provoked by collage, which Ernst described during his time as a Dadaist, is a struggle to change the relationship between the subject and the object. In the Dada exhibition of 1920, for example, destroyed artworks were replaced as a matter of course, as if they had no other purpose, for, according to the text that accompanied the exhibition, "if [the visitor] falls prey to the delusion of Anti-Dadaism too late, he notices the personal union of the butcher and the sacrificial lamb."[81] This dialogue thus challenges the sovereignty of the viewing subject and the sanctity of "high" art,[82] and a similar technique can be seen in the collage novel. For example, the second image presents a naked woman exhibited like a sculpture on a pedestal. However, the classical pose of the figure is inconsistent with the objects on her lower abdomen and legs, which recall prostheses. The many wounded bodies in the novel are references to World War I, which Ernst experienced firsthand,[83] and the fact that the prosthetic is set against the classical pose shows that the Surrealists refused to idealize the war.[84] Ernst chose to place a wounded body on the pedestal instead of a soldier, and he thus attacked the exaltation of man as a hero whose body is a first layer of armor. This image visualized the shameful "wounded organic substance of the creature, who was supposed to conceal its armor."[85]

Many of the figures in the novel are also headless or animal-headed, which shows how the head is disempowered and confronted with a proliferating body. Beings with wings emerge, who blend into screens and folds almost as an accessory to flowing clothes. The clothing, which itself becomes a body part, also merges with its surroundings. Snakes, bats, armadillos, and grasshoppers swarm in the corners and folds, as if arising from the patterns on the wallpaper, fabrics, and ornaments. According to

Bauer, the central principle of the collage novel is the production of hybrid creatures, which accompanies the dissolution of people's identities.[86] The figure of the monster represents the destruction of people, and the collage novel can be seen as an attack on the idealism that caused people to over-look this destruction. It is also an attack on sexual morality, which distin-guishes between moral and monstrous forms of contact in order "to set in motion a multiplying machine, to provide [...] countries with fit individuals to meet the requirements for production and military service."[87] In contrast, Ernst created fantastic collages in his Dadaist phase that juxtaposed pieces of military equipment without any sense or purpose. In his Surrealist col-lage work, and above all in his collage novels, there are no machines but rather countless combinations of organic creatures and inorganic technolo-gies, which are reminiscent of French philosophers Gilles Deleuze and Félix Guattari's schizophrenic "organ-machines."[88]

Ernst thus took the technique of *bricolage*, which had a long tradition in folk art, and introduced it to the realm of "high" art, where it had previously been seen as inappropriate. It even became a central technique in Dadaism and Surrealism, where it was seen as an "ontological condition for work in gen-eral,"[89] and it reached its peak with Ernst's elaborately designed and exqui-sitely printed collage novels. Collage was thus rooted in folkloric traditions, which according to German art historian Herta Wescher "remained on the sidelines of artistic development and did not exercise any influence on [the collages of recognized artists]."[90] However, Ernst's collage novels helped to "ennoble" this technique while simultaneously challenging everything noble about "high" art, and they thus called into question the strict division between "high" and "low" art.

Conclusion: Disorder

If Ernst presents the reader with images shaped by the thinking of his father's generation, then this does not mean that he wanted to restore the order of time around 1900. The violence depicted in serialized novel illustrations was clearly part of this order, so it is understandable that the Surrealists saw the killing of the war—"the most grandiose manifestation of modern folly"[91]—as motivated not by an outbreak of the irrational but rather by this order itself, which was supposed to be preserved and maintained by violent heroes and their followers.[92]

The Surrealists' "cult of evil"[93] was supposed to undermine the division between good and evil violence, and Ernst was similarly opposed to a war waged in the name of progress and freedom: "By visualizing the atrocities that were committed to serve these ideals, Max Ernst demanded the admission that the real perpetrators were those who wielded power and yearned for counterviolence."[94] The Surrealists countered good violence with collages that fomented monstrosity and disorder. They did not respect the boundaries between good and evil, humans and animals, or "high" and "low" culture.

Une semaine de bonté can inspire such considerations, but it cannot thereby be decoded. Whoever attempts to read it will be irritated, distracted, and exasperated by associations, which will cause them to turn back and eventually lay the book aside. The collage novel repeatedly shows readers that it cannot be resolved through a preconceived idea of an organizing subject; intertextuality and materiality remain all the more present.

The collage novel constitutes a materially comprehensible entity in a network of relations: a *petite machine* (little machine) that is connected to others, like organ-machines, for the hand that strokes the paper is also interacting sensually—"How autoerotic is such rubbing?"[95] Ernst would have nothing against this. Is the novel therefore a *machine d'amour* (love machine)?[96] Perhaps. Rosalind Krauss describes how Adorno kept one of Ernst's collage novels "spread across his knees" as he "looks back at surrealism."[97] The weight of the book and the touch of the paper are not without meaning.

In contrast to posters, magazine covers, or films, however, such an elaborately designed book is less appropriate for reaching and politically agitating large numbers of people. Instead, it invites bibliophiles to forget the world around them. A departure from the "language of instruction"[98] of the left and right avant-gardes is inherent in the choice of the novel form. Instead, readers are inspired to question the myths and phantasms that might underlie their own political convictions. *Une semaine de bonté* proposes an engagement in mythical and phantasmatic ways of thinking while at the same time undermining them and thus disrupting the current order, for whoever observes the images cannot immediately find the appropriate repressive compartment.

Whoever undertakes a reading of the collage novel does not create a new world or enter into a fantasy world in which it would be possible to escape. Whoever tries to reduce the collage novel to a singular meaning discovers instead a network of references, which are mutually alienating and only held together by the book itself. They are present as material traces, yet the fullness of their meaning has not yet been completely exhausted. The collage novel also contains no unambiguous political messages. Art, according to Ernst, cannot replace political struggle.[99] The unwieldiness of the material is an expression of a world that has become foreign to those who insist on utilization. It is clear that *Une semaine de bonté* is nothing but a Dadaist machine in the form of a book: it would never work.

Translated by Anthony Enns

Notes

1 Max Ernst, *Une semaine de bonté ou Les sept éléments capitaux* (Paris: Georges Duval, 1934). The title *Une semaine de bonté* alludes to the Christian story of creation as well as a French charity organization of the same name.

2 Werner Spies, *Max Ernst: Collagen, Inventar und Widerspruch* (Cologne: DuMont, 1974), 9f. Spies challenges an interpretation that considers the contents of the serialized novels that Ernst appropriated.

3 Theodor W. Adorno, *Noten zur Literatur* (Frankfurt am Main: Suhrkamp, 1981), 103.

4 André Breton, introduction to *La femme 100 têtes*, by Max Ernst (Berlin: Gerhardt, 1962), np. See also Michel Gillet, "Machines de romans-feuilletons," *Romantisme: Revue du dix-neuvième siècle* 13, no. 41 (1983): 79–90.

5 Anne-Marie Thiesse, *Le roman du quotidien: Lecteurs et lectures populaires à la Belle Époque* (Paris: Chemin vert, 1984), 83.

6 Gerd Bauer, "Max Ernsts Collageroman *Une Semaine de Bonté*," *Wallraff-Richartz-Jahrbuch: Westdeutsches Jahrbuch für Kunstgeschichte* 39 (1977): 237–57 (251).

7 Lise Queffélec, *Le roman-feuilleton français au XIXe siècle* (Paris: Presses universitaires de France, 1989), 89.

8 Éric Bonnet, "Rêves et figures emblématiques: *Une semaine de bonté ou Les sept éléments capitaux*," in *Max Ernst: L'imagier des poètes*, ed. Julia Drost, Ursula Moureau-Martini, and Nicolas Devigne (Paris: Presses de l'université Paris-Sorbonne, 2008), 117–28 (120).

9 For more on the circumstances surrounding the collage novel's publication, see Werner Spies, "Die Desaster des Jahrhunderts," in *Max Ernst: Une semaine de bonté*, ed. Werner Spies (Cologne: DuMont, 2008), 10–71.

10 Nora Atkinson, *Eugène Sue et le roman-feuilleton* (Nemours: André Lesot, 1929), 5.

11 Danielle Aubry, *Du roman-feuilleton à la série télévisuelle: Pour une rhétorique du genre et de la sérialité* (Bern: Peter Lang, 2006), 28.

12 Jürgen Habermas, *Strukturwandel der Öffentlichkeit: Untersuchungen zu einer Kategorie der bürgerlichen Gesellschaft* (Darmstadt: Luchterhand, 1979), 74.

13 Aubry, *Du roman-feuilleton à la série télévisuelle*, 17.

14 Atkinson, *Eugène Sue et le roman-feuilleton*, 7.

15 Many writers operated collaborative writing workshops in order to satisfy the tremendous demand for serials, and French literary critic Charles Sainte-Beuve was the first to discuss the concept of industrial literature in 1839. See Aubry, *Du roman-feuilleton à la série télévisuelle*, 1.

16 Queffélec, *Le roman-feuilleton français*, 5.

17 See Roger Chartier and Henri-Jean Martin, eds., *Histoire de l'édition française*, 4 vols. (Paris: Promodis, 1982–1986), 3: 469.

18 Eugène Sue's *Les mystères de Paris* (The Mysteries of Paris, 1842) influenced a whole series of mysteries, culminating in Victor Hugo's *Les misérables* (The Miserable Ones, 1862) and Émile Zola's *Les mystères de Marseille* (The Mysteries of Marseilles, 1867). See Helga Grubitzsch, ed., *Materialien zur Kritik des Feuilleton-Romans* (Wiesbaden: Akademische Verlagsgesellschaft Athenaion, 1977), 1f.

19 Umberto Eco, "Eugène Sue: Sozialismus und Trost," in *Apokalyptiker und Integrierte: Zur kritischen Kritik der Massenkultur*, trans. Max Looser (Frankfurt am Main: Fischer, 1989), 233–71.

20 Alexander Gall, "Authentizität, Dramatik und der Erfolg der populären zoologischen Illustration im 19. Jahrhundert: *Brehms Thierleben* und die *Gartenlaube*," in *Inszenierte*

Wissenschaft: Zur Popularisierung von Wissen im 19. Jahrhundert, ed. Stefanie Samida (Bielefeld: transcript, 2011), 103–26 (121).

21 Marjorie Elizabeth Warlick, "Max Ernst's Collage Novel *Une semaine de bonté*: Feuilleton Sources and Alchemical Interpretation," PhD diss. (University of Maryland, 1984), 72.

22 Stuart Sillars, *Visualisation in Popular Fiction 1860–1960: Graphic Narratives, Fictional Images* (London: Routledge, 1995), 33.

23 Walburga Hülk, *Als die Helden Opfer wurden: Grundlagen und Funktion gesellschaftlicher Ordnungsmodelle in den Feuilletonromanen* Les mystères de Paris *und* Le juif errant *von Eugène Sue* (Heidelberg: C. Winter Universitätsverlag, 1985), 58. See also Queffélec, *Le roman-feuilleton français*, 13.

24 Warlick, "Max Ernst's Collage Novel," 56. See also Thiesse, *Le roman du quotidien*, 107.

25 See Queffélec, *Le roman-feuilleton français*, 29. See also Warlick, "Max Ernst's Collage Novel," 56.

26 The precision of the woodcut was the reason why many newspapers still preferred to use engravings of photographic images at the end of the nineteenth century.

27 Atkinson, *Eugène Sue et le roman-feuilleton*, 5.

28 Hans-Jörg Neuschäfer, *Populärromane im 19. Jahrhundert: Von Dumas bis Zola* (Munich: Wilhelm Fink, 1976), 22.

29 Hans-Jörg Neuschäfer, Dorothee Fritz-El Ahmad, and Klaus-Peter Walter, *Der französische Feuilletonroman: Die Entstehung der Serienliteratur im Medium der Tageszeitung* (Darmstadt: Wissenschaftliche Buchgesellschaft, 1986), 12.

30 Queffélec, *Le roman-feuilleton français*, 30. See also Gillet, "Machines de romans-feuilletons," 79.

31 David H. Walker, *Outrage and Insight: Modern French Writers and the 'Fait Divers'* (Oxford: Berg, 1995), 19.

32 Michel Foucault, *Überwachen und Strafen: Die Geburt des Gefängnisses*, trans. Walter Seitter (Frankfurt am Main: Suhrkamp, 1977), 369.

33 Michel Foucault, *Les anormaux: Cours au Collège de France, 1974–1975*, ed. Valerio Marchett and Antonella Salomoni (Paris: Seuil/Gallimard, 1999), 57f.

34 Werner Spies, ed., *Max Ernst: Dream and Revolution* (Ostfildern: Hatje Cantz, 2008), 30.

35 See Umberto Eco, *Il superuomo di massa: Retorica e ideologia nel romanzo popolare* (Milan: Bompiani, 1990), 15.

36 Ibid., 53f., 68f.

37 See Warlick, "Max Ernst's Collage Novel," 49; Thiesse, *Le roman du quotidien*, 140; Eco, *Il superuomo di massa*, 11.

38 Gillet, "Machines de romans-feuilletons," 81. Helga Grubitzsch also noted that "[Eugène] Sue furnished the criminals with physical features that conveyed their natural inclination to commit crimes according to phrenology." Grubitzsch, *Materialien zur Kritik des Feuilleton-Romans*, 9.

39 Spies, *Max Ernst*, 179.

40 Foucault, *Überwachen und Strafen*, 369.

41 Neuschäfer, *Populärromane im 19. Jahrhundert*, 33. See also Aubry, *Du roman-feuilleton à la série télévisuelle*, 15.

42 Neuschäfer, Fritz-El Ahmad, and Walter, *Der französische Feuilletonroman*, 14.

43 Neuschäfer, *Populärromane im 19. Jahrhundert*, 33.

44 According to Ines Lindner, Ernst identified the degree to which serialized novel illustrations offered attractions to the voyeuristic gaze of (male) readers by presenting women's bodies in lascivious poses next to scenes of violence and misfortune.

Ernst consistently stripped women bare in order to make their function as objects of sexual desire explicit. He also caricatured the seemingly uninvolved detachment of the voyeur by showing explorers in the distance gazing down at sleeping women like visitors at a zoo, or he collapsed the distance by entangling the voyeur with the object. Lindner demonstrates this by comparing the fourth page of "Easter Island" with its template from French novelist Jules Mary's *Les damnées de Paris* (The Damned of Paris, 1884). In the original illustration a young woman embraces a soldier, but instead of looking at his face she turns and looks into the space over his shoulder in the direction of the viewer, thus baring her breasts to the gaze of the voyeur. In his collage Ernst places a statue-headed figure next to the soldier, and it grabs onto the neckline of the woman in order to "make the use of what it presents to the observer palpable." Ines Lindner, "Economie technique et effets surréels: Stratégies de montage dans *Une semaine de bonté*," in *Max Ernst: L'imagier des poètes*, ed. Julia Drost, Ursula Moureau-Martini, and Nicolas Devigne (Paris: Presses de l'université Paris-Sorbonne, 2008), 121–44 (131).

45 Max Ernst, *Une semaine de bonté oder Die weiße Woche: Ein Bilderbuch von Güte, Liebe und Menschlichkeit* (Berlin: Gerhardt, 1963), np.

46 Bauer, "Max Ernsts Collageroman," 242.

47 Spies, *Max Ernst*, 181.

48 According to Hans-Jörg Neuschäfer, one can be outraged by the disruption of "the bourgeois Edmond Dantès' need for harmony" and identify with him as a victim while also being amused by the excessive violence with which he takes revenge on his tormentors. See Neuschäfer, *Populärromane im 19. Jahrhundert*, 15. Hans-Jörg Neuschäfer, Dorothee Fritz-El Ahmad, and Klaus-Peter Walter also describe him as follows: "His similarity to a god is justified by a quasi-Christological transformation, and fate shows that he is right to proceed in the fight for what is good regardless of human law." Neuschäfer, Fritz-El Ahmad, and Walter, *Der französische Feuilletonroman*, 218.

49 Neuschäfer, *Populärromane im 19. Jahrhundert*, 35f.

50 Dieter Wyss, *Der Surrealismus: Eine Einführung und Deutung surrealistischer Literatur und Malerei* (Heidelberg: Lambert Schneider, 1950), 66.

51 Ibid., 72.

52 Ibid.

53 See Wolfgang Fritz Haug, *Einführung in Marxistisches Philosophieren* (Hamburg: Argument, 2006), 162.

54 Ibid., 37.

55 Gramsci can also be read as not denouncing Nietzsche's philosophy of the Übermensch but rather sounding a note of caution with respect to its supposed followers, for whom "it is appropriate to question [...] whether this concept [...] is of a purely Nietzschean origin [...] or whether it has a more modest origin, such as a connection with serial literature." Antonio Gramsci, *Marxismus und Literatur*, ed. and trans. Sabine Kebir (Hamburg: VSA, 1991), 222. Umberto Eco recognized that Gramsci was referring here to Italian fascist leader Benito Mussolini, who also wrote serialized novels. Eco, *Il superuomo di massa*, vi.

56 Ernst's collage novel was certainly a reaction to the National Socialists' rise to power in Germany, but it also dealt with impressions from the trip he took through fascist Italy. The collage novel emerged in the context of this trip at the Castello di Vigoleno, which was owned by Duchess Maria Ruspoli de Gramont. See Neuschäfer,

Populärromane im 19. Jahrhundert, 37; Neuschäfer, Fritz-El Ahmad, and Walter, *Der französische Feuilletonroman*, 128f.

57 German psychologist Dieter Wyss misunderstands this asymmetry as an opposition between the "superego (General)" and the "natural drives (lion)." Wyss, *Der Surrealismus*, 65.

58 See Eco, *Il superuomo di massa*, 13; Neuschäfer, Fritz-El Ahmad, and Walter, *Der französische Feuilletonroman*, 218.

59 See Eco, *Il superuomo di massa*, 75; Neuschäfer, Fritz-El Ahmad, and Walter, *Der französische Feuilletonroman*, 91f and 142.

60 Simon Baker, *Surrealism, History and Revolution* (Bern: Peter Lang, 2007), 58f.

61 Wyss, *Der Surrealismus*, 72.

62 Bauer, "Max Ernsts Collageroman," 242.

63 Qtd. in Spies, *Max Ernst*, 95.

64 Ibid.

65 Max Ernst, *Écritures* (Paris: Gallimard, 1970), 16.

66 See Max Ernst, "Some Data on the Youth of M.E.," in *Max Ernst: Beyond Painting and Other Writings by the Artist and His Friends*, ed. Robert Motherwell (New York: Wittenborn, Schultz, 1948), 26–123 (28).

67 André Breton, *Die Manifeste des Surrealismus*, trans. Ruth Henry (Reinbek bei Hamburg: Rowohlt, 1968), 14f.

68 Ernst, *Écritures*, 31.

69 Werner Spies, *Max Ernst, Loplop: Die Selbstdarstellung des Künstlers* (Munich: Prestel, 1982), 38. See also Elza Adamowicz, *Surrealist Collage in Text and Image: Dissecting the Exquisite Corpse* (Cambridge: Cambridge University Press, 1998), 43.

70 Spies, *Max Ernst*, 55.

71 Ernst, *Écritures*, 15.

72 Ibid.

73 Spies, *Max Ernst, Loplop*, 52f. This was the reason why Ernst repeatedly invited Spies "to touch the collages and decode them like Braille." Spies, "Die Desaster des Jahrhunderts," 22.

74 Max Ernst, *Die Nacktheit der Frau ist weiser als die Lehre des Philosophen: La nudité de la femme est plus sage que l'enseignement du philosophe* (Cologne: Galerie Der Spiegel, 1970), np.

75 Claude Lévi-Strauss, *Das wilde Denken*, trans. Hans Naumann (Frankfurt am Main: Suhrkamp, 1994), 30. He offered a less ample illumination of the principle of collage in his essay on Ernst and Surrealism. See Claude Lévi-Strauss, "Meditative Malerei," in *Der Blick aus der Ferne*, trans. Hans-Horst Henschen and Joseph Vogl (Frankfurt am Main: Suhrkamp, 2008), 355–60.

76 Ernst also compared this to the experience of a blind swimmer. See Ernst, *Écritures*, 244f.

77 Lévi-Strauss, *Das wilde Denken*, 30.

78 Ibid., 33.

79 Ibid., 31.

80 Ibid., 33ff.

81 Ernst, *Écritures*, 35.

82 Adorno, *Noten zur Literatur*, 102.

83 Werner Spies, "Nightmare and Deliverance," in *Max Ernst: A Retrospective*, ed. Werner Spies and Sabine Rewald (New York: Metropolitan Museum of Art, 2005), 21–35 (30).

84 See Sidra Stich, *Anxious Visions: Surrealist Art* (New York: Abbeville, 1990), 33.

85 Helmut Lethen, *Verhaltenslehren der Kälte: Lebensversuche zwischen den Kriegen* (Frankfurt am Main: Suhrkamp, 1994), 246.

86 Bauer, "Max Ernsts Collageroman," 253f.

87 Ernst, *Écritures*, 184.

88 Gilles Deleuze and Félix Guattari, *Anti-Ödipus*, trans. Bernd Schwibs (Frankfurt am Main: Suhrkamp, 1977), 8.

89 Spies, *Max Ernst*, 11. The Surrealist collages of Ernst's collage novels differ from his Dadaist collages insofar as they are "synthetic," as individual elements are joined to form new images, for which the full-page illustrations of serialized novels are particularly suitable. In contrast, his Dadaist collages are primarily "analytical," as they "come from *one* overriding and framework-forming context, which becomes a place where the encounter and interpenetration of disparate elements occurs" [emphasis in original]. Ibid., 105.

90 Herta Wescher, *Die Geschichte der Collage: Vom Kubismus bis zur Gegenwart* (Cologne: DuMont, 1974), 16.

91 Ernst, *Écritures*, 24f.

92 See Paul Eluard, "Beyond Painting," in *Max Ernst: Beyond Painting and Other Writings by the Artist and His Friends*, ed. Robert Motherwell (New York: Wittenborn, Schultz, 1948), 191.

93 Walter Benjamin, "Der Surrealismus: Die letzte Momentaufnahme der europäischen Intelligenz," in *Gesammelte Schriften, Band 2, Teil 1*, ed. Rolf Tiedemann and Hermann Schweppenhäuser (Frankfurt am Main: Suhrkamp, 1991), 295–310 (304).

94 Bauer, "Max Ernsts Collageroman," 243.

95 Robert Storr, "Past Imperfect, Present Conditional," in *Max Ernst: A Retrospective*, ed. Werner Spies and Sabine Rewald (New York: Metropolitan Museum of Art, 2005), 51–66 (53).

96 Gilles Deleuze and Félix Guattari, *Milles plateaux* (Paris: Éditions de Minuit, 1980), 10.

97 Rosalind E. Krauss, *The Optical Unconscious* (Cambridge, MA: MIT Press, 1993), 34.

98 Lethen, *Verhaltenslehren der Kälte*, 213.

99 Werner Spies, *Max Ernst: Die Rückkehr der Schönen Gärtnerin* (Cologne: DuMont, 2000), 20.

Chapter 8

FROM PENNY DREADFUL TO GRAPHIC NOVEL: ALAN MOORE AND KEVIN O'NEILL'S GENEALOGY OF COMICS IN *THE LEAGUE OF EXTRAORDINARY GENTLEMEN*

Jeff Thoss

In 1890, British media mogul Alfred Harmsworth launched the halfpenny comic magazine. By reducing the page size and opting for the cheapest paper and ink, Harmsworth was able to undersell his competitors' penny-priced output and created a publishing success that was widely imitated and ushered in the age of comics as a mass medium.[1] In 2002, DC Comics started its Absolute Edition series, which reprints popular titles that originally appeared as pamphlets in oversized hardcover books (complete with dust jacket, slipcase, and ribbon) that cost between $50 and $100. Evidently, something has changed in the way that comics are produced and marketed, and one may well surmise that this change of formats is linked to the change in the cultural status they have experienced in the past few decades. At the turn of the twentieth century, comics "came at or near the bottom […] in the pantheon of […] literature,"[2] a judgment of taste that finds its material equivalent in their disposable nature. At the beginning of the twenty-first century, comic books—especially deluxe editions like DC's Absolute series—are more likely to find themselves displayed in a bookcase than placed in the dustbin. And, with Art Spiegelman's *Maus* (1986/1991) winning a Pulitzer Prize in 1992 and Alan Moore and Dave Gibbons's *Watchmen* (1987) being included in *Time* magazine's 2005 list of the "All-TIME 100 Novels," their position in the pantheon has clearly been revised. Yet interestingly, *Maus* and *Watchmen* only received these accolades after they had been repackaged as graphic novels, both having previously been published in magazine or pamphlet format.

To tell the story of comics' establishment as a "legitimate" art form is, among other things, also to tell the story of their shifting publication formats.

In this chapter, I propose to look at the curious evolution of comics through the lens of a series that harks back to the late-Victorian media landscape that British comics emerged from and that simultaneously embodies and questions the current state of the medium. Alan Moore and Kevin O'Neill's *The League of Extraordinary Gentlemen* (1991-2019) relates the adventures of a superhero team made up of characters from nineteenth-century classics, such as Mina Murray from Bram Stoker's *Dracula* (1897) and Allan Quatermain from H. Rider Haggard's *King Solomon's Mines* (1885). In the first volume (1999) they face Sherlock Holmes's archenemy Professor Moriarty along with a "yellow peril" in London's East End. The second volume (2003) restages the Martian invasion from H. G. Wells's *The War of the Worlds* (1898), after which the series moves on to the twentieth century. These early parts squarely fit into what has come to be known as Neo-Victorian fiction[3] and offer the typical exploitation of popular character archetypes and narrative tropes along with a revision of nineteenth-century attitudes toward race, class, and gender.[4] In addition, Moore and O'Neill explore the material (pre)history of their own medium and, especially in the paratexts of their work, refer to Victorian print media, such as illustrated newspapers, novels, penny dreadfuls, boys' weeklies, and, of course, comics.[5] The result is a playful pastiche—understood here as a not overtly parodic imitation and collage—of nineteenth-century literature, a sort of game where readers are invited to spot the references, as well as a rewrite of comics history that highlights and perhaps also resurrects comics' affinities with a largely paraliterary tradition yet also strives to transcend any division between highbrow and lowbrow. In disrespecting the border between individual texts, *League* also disrespects the border between venerated classics and half-forgotten trash and invites its readers to imagine a genealogy of comics that encompasses James Malcolm Rymer's penny dreadful *Varney the Vampire* (1845–47) as easily as Aubrey Beardsley's illustrations to Oscar Wilde's *Salomé* (1894).

As good Neo-Victorians, Moore and O'Neill reinterpret the past mainly to negotiate the present. *League* was published after the watershed of *Maus* and *Watchmen*, and its forays into the nineteenth century can only be read against recent developments in comics. Its conception of a tradition that disregards distinctions between high and low can also be seen as a direct reaction against a contemporary historiography that all too readily describes how comics metamorphosed from disposable children's magazines into proper books and a mature art form at some point in the mid-1980s.[6] Yet, paradoxically, *League* might very well be the new type of comic Spiegelman and Moore himself seemingly paved the way for a decade earlier. With its numerous and often obscure allusions to nineteenth-century culture in both text and image as well as its sustained reflection on comics history, it is a textbook example of an ambitious and demanding comic, its extensive reworking of the historically popular becoming—once again, paradoxically—a hallmark of its sophistication. Occasionally, it appears that Moore and O'Neill's book is not so much a continuation of their earlier work in the superhero genre but rather in line with the literary trend of historiographic metafiction, as seen in Neo-Victorian novels like John Fowles' *The French Lieutenant's Woman* (1969) and A. S. Byatt's *Possession* (1990). In any case, *League* ennobles the medium of comics via strategies such as self-reflexivity, intertextuality, and the creation of a tradition at the same time that it problematizes this ennoblement. And of course *League* has been repackaged from its original pamphlets and published as a graphic novel (both in hardcover and paperback) and even been given the deluxe treatment of an Absolute Edition by DC. In this last version, the first two volumes of Moore and O'Neill's work retail for $75 each. In the following paragraphs, I will explore the workings and implications of this $150 comic that takes us back to the age when comic papers and related print forms proudly advertised "1d" or even "1/2d" on their front pages.

One of the main features of nineteenth-century print media that Moore and O'Neill quote and imitate is the front covers of illustrated newspapers—a format initiated by the *Illustrated London News*, which became notorious for its coverage of the Ripper murders. The cover to volume 1, issue 1, for instance, is modeled after an illustrated newspaper,[7] and Jess Nevins, who has compiled companion books containing detailed annotations to *League* and upon whose invaluable work I will draw more than once in this chapter, specifically lists the *Illustrated Police News*, which became notorious for their coverage of the Ripper murders, as an influence (see Figure 8.1).[8] In any case, these covers, with their lurid headlines and drawings of half-clad women, generally recall the sensationalism associated with this type of publication. In keeping with the spirit, *League* does not announce itself as a comic but as a "grand new picture paper." As a matter of fact, Moore and O'Neill go to great lengths to prevent the term "comic" (as well as "graphic novel") from appearing anywhere. In the authors' biographical notes on the back cover of the first volume, Moore is introduced as a writer of chapbooks and penny dreadfuls ("produced with the younger reader in mind"), while O'Neill is presented as a pictorial satirist and illustrator, famed for producing such works as the "Queen Victoria and Emily Pankhurst Girl-on-Girl Novelty Flipbook." Elsewhere, one finds expressions such as "picture-periodical" or "comical narrative,"[9] and an advertisement for volume 1 at the end of volume 2 highlights its "coloured cover and plates,"[10] as if it were an illustrated Victorian novel or penny dreadful.

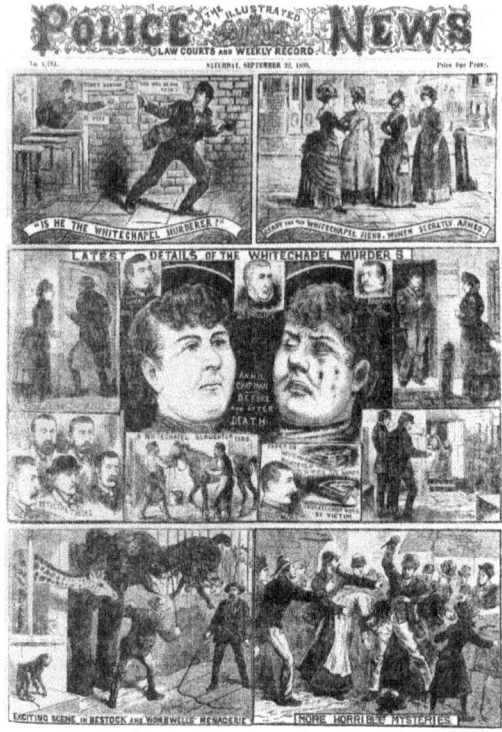

Figure 8.1 Front page of *Illustrated Police News*, September 22, 1888.

According to Kevin Carpenter, the term "comics" came into regular use around 1890,[11] so its use would not have been anachronistic. Still, it may have had too modern connotations to go well with Moore and O'Neill's project of fashioning themselves as Victorian artists. What is more important, though, is that the terms that are used in its stead neatly allow the creators to link comics to, and locate them within, a field of other media that combine text and image or use pictures to tell stories. Despite an often ironic undertone, *League*'s historiography does not present penny dreadfuls, illustrated newspapers, and flipbooks as historical curiosities or embarrassments, as Victorian ephemera that were thankfully displaced by the arrival of the proper format of comics; rather, they are made out to have been an integral part of the formation of comics and are thus accorded their place in the medium's tradition. Moore and O'Neill are actually in line with noted comics historians here: Roger Sabin sees the origin of British comics in illustrated newspapers, penny dreadfuls, boys' weeklies (on which more later), and cartoon magazines[12]—a perspective also adopted by the British Library's 2014 exhibition "Comics Unmasked: Art and Anarchy in the UK."[13] David Kunzle's two-volume

History of the Comic Strip even goes back as far as late-medieval broadsheets. Yet *League* not only emphasizes the continuity between Victorian comics and earlier media, as the terminological anxiety displayed by Moore and O'Neill is also reminiscent of that surrounding "graphic novel" nowadays, and one can detect numerous contemporary resonances in the authors' dealings with the nineteenth century. To modern readers, *League* indirectly seems to plead that the term "graphic novel" will not displace "comics" and that the however questionable emergence of mature and sophisticated comics will not silence a long history of childish, sleazy, and cheap comics.

The issue covers of *League*, volume 1, continue to masquerade as Victorian printed matter. For instance, the second one features cigarette cards of the series' protagonists, the cigarette brand being "Blue Dwarf," the name of a popular penny dreadful character. On the cover to issue 4, the title is printed in thick black letters on an orange background, below which is reproduced a sketch of a majestic Mr. Hyde raising his fist against a group of stereotypical Chinese villains. According to Kevin O'Neill, this reflects the look of "early Arsène Lupin publications,"[14] but its pulp magazine quality is evident even beyond this specific source. Issue 5 is done, again in the artist's own words, "[i]n the style of [a] late Victorian book cover, the sort that had [an] image printed on [a] cloth bound cover and an inset full colour image pasted on."[15] This cover is of note since the authors mostly quote the material features of decidedly lowbrow publications targeted at the working classes and here introduce respectable, middle-class culture. Yet this only serves the series' aim of questioning these categories, of imagining an alternative history in which these distinctions never existed, in which comics could as easily be accepted as descendants of the penny dreadful as they could be seen in a novelistic, book-focused storytelling tradition. It is with the cover to volume 1's closing issue that *League* finally imitates its most recognizable antecedent: the comic paper. Flaunting a large title banner at the top followed by a grid of six rectangular panels with cartoonish drawings and narration underneath, this layout is based upon the front page of comics like *Illustrated Chips* (see Figure 8.2) or *Comic Cuts* (Harmsworth's revolutionary halfpenny publications).[16] There is even a period-appropriate advertisement (for cigarettes) in the page header.

In all these cases, there is an obvious discrepancy between what readers are actually holding in their hands and what the cover design suggests or announces that they are holding. Even issue 6's cover does not constitute comics as we know them; the lack of speech bubbles in late-Victorian comics is immediately palpable. As Christine Ferguson notes, Moore and O'Neill here "perform what we might term a Brechtian move, forcing readers to confront the political implication of the genre's form instead of allowing them simply

Figure 8.2 Front Page of *Illustrated Chips*, September 9, 1899.

to immerse themselves in plot."[17] Whereas comic book covers generally function as straightforward gateways into the storyworld, *League*'s covers first seem
to ask its audience "What does this have to do with comics?" And, in a way,
the answer is always "This also is comics." Each issue requires that readers establish a connection and see the similarities and mutual interactions
between what is now known as comics and whatever medium the cover has
disguised itself as, be it a trashy tabloid or a clothbound classic.

This strategy of cross-linking and merging supposedly distinct cultural
forms is also what characterizes Moore and O'Neill's pastiche narrative. The
main characters and plot elements are almost exclusively lifted from familiar
classics by the likes of Wells, Stevenson, Verne, or Conan Doyle, but this
may be more of a pragmatic rather than an aesthetic choice. After all, most
characters or storylines from Victorian paraliterature have been forgotten;
arguably, even Sweeney Todd's fame is based upon a musical and its film
adaptation rather than a penny dreadful. However, in the realm of supporting or minor characters, one can find such people as Rosa Coote, a staple
of Victorian pornography; Broad Arrow Jack, from the eponymous penny

dreadful; or Ally Sloper, the "first true British comic strip hero."[18] The series' creators are also not afraid to reference works that have not nearly had the impact on contemporary popular culture as the abovementioned authors, which is shown by the inclusion of Anthony Trollope's Plantagenet Palliser as prime minister.

If *League*'s cover design continually reminds readers to draw connections between different publication formats, then its handling of characters invites them to disregard such distinctions altogether. And, of course, unless one reads Nevins's companion books or looks up names on the internet, one is unlikely to spot all the allusions and detect, for instance, that there is something fishy in Broad Arrow Jack serving aboard Captain Nemo's Nautilus. Still, one always knows that the whole narrative has been cobbled together from already existing narratives, even if one cannot pinpoint the exact sources, and this combination of a lingering general awareness and a blissful ignorance of the details might contribute to the pleasure of reading *League*. One may even view Moore and O'Neill's practice of borrowing everything as a kind of covert homage to the rampant "borrowing" that went on in the comics of the 1890s. As Kunzle observes, "The whole phenomenon of cheap comic papers in England depended from their inception on the availability of foreign sources which could be plagiarized at will and without fear of legal repercussions."[19] In any case, *League* fantasizes about a world in which a character's origin in this or that publication format, whether it be a respectable novel or an erotica magazine, has lost all relevance and anything can be combined.[20] As Alan Moore himself describes the aim of the series, it is about "having fun by pulling down the barriers between High Literature and pulp literature and pornography and low literary forms like that."[21]

Perhaps *League*'s most ingenious mix of literary forms and most intriguing material feature is the existence of an illustrated prose narrative that is appended to the first volume. Its title is "Allan and the Sundered Veil," and it purports to be the first issue of a boys' weekly called *The "Boys' First-Rate Pocket Library" of Complete Tales*, which sells for the regular one penny.[22] All of this information can be gleaned from its cover, which naturally looks very much like a boys' magazine cover (see Figure 8.3).[23]

The publisher is listed as "Aldine Publishing Company," and the next page features an advertisement for *The Rival*, another Aldine title. Nevins's research shows that the advertisement is authentic and that the publisher and magazine, which reprinted American dime novels, did indeed exist.[24] It looks as if form and content finally matched, as if Moore and O'Neill had come full circle and included a pseudo-facsimile of the kind of publication that served as *League*'s inspiration. Appearances are once again deceiving, however, as "Allan and the Sundered Veil," which functions as a prequel to the events of

Figure 8.3 Cover of *Boys' First-Rate Pocket Library* No. 190, ca. 1890s.

volume 1, is by no means a straightforward pulp affair. While the narrative does draw upon pulp stalwarts Edgar Rice Burroughs and H. P. Lovecraft, it also incorporates material from the more respectable Haggard and Wells. Still, what is most striking is that the story is written in a "rococo, lush, and over-ripe style"[25] that is especially fond of describing the decay of luxurious objects (e.g. "magnificent Axminster carpets annexed long since by the creep of moss and slug and fungus").[26] As Nevins points out, this is a "deliberate recreation of the style of *fin-de-siècle*, Yellow Nineties Decadent writers [...] , as if one of them had written a boys' magazine story."[27]

Basically, then, "Allan and the Sundered Veil" fuses *The Boys' First-Rate Pocket Library* and *The Yellow Book*, creating a strange matrimony between two publication formats that could not be further apart: on the one hand, the penny-priced boys' weekly that does not even contain original material and, on the other hand, the five-shilling literary quarterly that features contributions by avant-garde artists and writers. Moore and O'Neill thus take what one might see as the end points of the lowbrow-highbrow scale and tie a knot between them, inciting their readers to reflect on the merit of this dichotomy at the same time as they provide an example of a text that seems to have already surpassed it. This technique is succinctly summed up in an item that also finds itself at the back of volume 1: a "painting-by-numbers" version of Basil Hallward's portrait of Dorian Gray, "produced," as the instructions inform us, "with children or the amateur painter in mind."[28] Here, the aesthete and the amateur meet, and the icon of late-Victorian Decadence is turned into lowbrow kitsch, art for those who have neither the necessary skill nor taste to engage with art, just as the unique, auratic artwork is transformed into a mass-produced commodity. Yet note that the painting-by-numbers portrait is not presented as some defacement or travesty of the actual painting by ignorant brutes but as Hallward's own invention. It is he who "envisions" this "innovative painting-made-simple concept"[29] and thus comes to represent the union of high and low Moore and O'Neill aim for, the fictional artist of the *fin de siècle* becoming a model for the real artists of today. Finally, the hybrid material composition of volume 1, which contains a "regular" comic book, an illustrated prose story, and miscellaneous visual material such as the portrait, also indicates that the comics tradition the authors have in mind encompasses more than what a standard definition of the medium might allow for.

Yet, for all its attempts to level distinctions between popular and elite culture and rewrite the history of comics as inclusive, as spanning a wide range of pictorial and narrative traditions as well as publication formats, *League* is, of course, still affected by the way mainstream comics are produced, distributed, and consumed nowadays. As with any successful series, its single issues are collected into graphic novels encompassing a single story arc, and, as already mentioned, it also takes part in the recent trend of releasing comics in formats that have more in common with expensive art books than flimsy magazines. In order to fully characterize the vantage point from which Moore and O'Neill look back to the nineteenth century, I would like to return briefly to that crucial period of the mid-1980s, when the decision to repackage comics as graphic novels apparently flicked a switch in the general public's perception of them.

Longer comics published in book format have existed at least since the 1970s, and continental Europe has a long tradition of reprinting stories from magazines or newspapers in albums, yet in the English-speaking world it was only when the "Big Three"—*Maus*, *Watchmen*, and Frank Miller's *Batman: The Dark Knight Returns* (1986)—appeared that the status of comics was revised in any significant way. Suddenly, comics reached a larger audience since they were sold no longer mainly in specialist fan shops but also in high street bookstores, they were bought by public libraries, they were reviewed in the mainstream press, and mainstream book publishers took interest in them.[30] (To this, one could add that it was only with *Maus* that comics regularly found their way into schools and universities.) The sea change that took place is pithily demonstrated by Sabin's quote from a fan shop owner who claimed that "in the old days" he occasionally "had to put comics in brown paper bags like pornography," whereas "the new book format seemed to short-circuit that psychological barrier."[31]

It must be stressed that none of the "Big Three" were originally conceived as graphic novels, and while Art Spiegelman actively sought to reprint the *Maus* stories from *RAW* magazine in book format, it seems unlikely that DC, the publisher of the other two and a company that is notorious for its disdain of creators' rights, gave Moore or Miller much say in the way that their comics were marketed and distributed. Nevertheless, the simple fact that one could suddenly read exactly the same story in a traditional book that one could previously read only in pamphlets seemingly made all the difference. While there was a backlash against the graphic novel hype, this period nonetheless marked "the transition of part of the comics industry from a 'comics culture' to a 'book culture'" and "rema[d]e comics in prose literature's image."[32] Sabin made this statement in 1993, and in the intervening years this transition can only be said to have accelerated and taken in larger parts of the industry (even though the emergence of webcomics and digital comics obviously also shifted part of the attention onto this sector).

Moore and O'Neill's obsession with the ephemera of yesteryear is clearly a reaction against this process, in which comics have lost their disposable nature. However, theirs is not a nostalgic look back to an age of innocence, simple stories, and crude pictures. To those critics who describe the mid-1980s as the *annus mirabilis* that saw the birth of comics as a true art form, the *League* series replies that this can only have been the result of their myopic perspective and that comics have always had more to offer than they were given credit for. And yet, one cannot look past the fact that *League* is evidently a comic that has to a considerable extent remade itself in the image of prose literature, which comes, if one so desires, in an expensive, prestigious, and collectible format, and which demands quite a lot from its readers if they are to be fully let in on the game being played. There are times when it appears that Moore and O'Neill's work is in some ways a rather highbrow enterprise that caters to an exclusive readership in its very attempt to be as inclusive as possible.

According to Nevins,

> The series sold surprisingly well, with higher sales than a number of industry mainstays. In trade paperback form *League*'s sales are very high, and the comic has been translated into several languages and is sold in 30 countries. Beyond mere sales, however, the series has proven to be popular with audiences beyond

ordinary buyers of comic books. A significant number of fans of *League* are men and women who don't buy other comic books, including authors, editors, literature students and literature professors.[33]

There are two things of interest here: one is *League*'s success as a graphic novel—Moore himself concurs that "in bookshops it is probably the best-selling graphic novel"[34]—and the other is its popularity with the audience Nevins describes. Although Nevins does not explicitly state this, one might be tempted to see a correlation between the two and assume it to be more likely that this larger readership buys the *League* graphic novels in bookshops rather than hunting down single issues in specialist fan shops. Of course, there is nothing wrong with a comic attracting a wider audience that prefers to buy books. Yet one may suspect that Moore and O'Neill's creation appeals precisely to the authors, editors, literature students, and professors Nevins so conspicuously singles out because these people possess an education that greatly facilitates the appreciation of *League*, so they get the most out of it. I have mentioned earlier that, for its most significant characters and themes, the series draws upon literary classics that have become part of popular culture. One may not have read *Dracula*, *King Solomon's Mines*, the Sherlock Holmes stories, *The War of the Worlds*, or *Vingt mille lieues sous les mers* (20,000 Leagues Under the Sea, 1870), yet these texts are still familiar through their countless adaptations. In many other cases, one may notice that some text is being alluded to without knowing precisely which text it is. *League* thus ensures that a basic degree of recognizability always exists, which allows its readers to more or less pass over the allusions they do not get. In fact, one could doubt whether the comic would have had the kind of success Nevins and Moore describe if this were not so.

Nevertheless, in a comic that consists of nothing but references to other texts, spotting these references is an integral part of the reading experience, and there are moments when Moore and O'Neill's "reference mania" appears bent on causing frustration, when it seems as if the comic will not let us in on a joke because our knowledge of nineteenth-century (para)literature is simply not vast enough. How many readers are familiar enough with Victorian illustrated newspapers to actually identify them as the source for the cover to issue 1 or realize that the representation of Mars at the beginning of volume 2 conflates Edgar Rice Burroughs's *Barsoom* stories, Edwin Lester Arnold's *Lieutenant Gullivar Jones: His Vacation* (1905), C. S. Lewis's *Out of the Silent Planet* (1938), and Wells's *The War of the Worlds*? Evidently, *League* is catering to a small coterie of readers for whom the identification of such allusions provides an additional (or even the main) gratification. At first sight, this might not appear very different from similar practices within mainstream comics, as when superhero titles appeal to their readers' detailed knowledge of continuity (the shared history of a particular publisher's characters and fictional universe); however, what sets Moore and O'Neill's enterprise apart is its obvious tryst with literary history. Sebastian Domsch has noted that *League*'s boundless intertextuality in this regard may represent a disturbing, even "monstrous and unnatural," element to a comics audience that regards literature as "alien,"[35] while Moore himself has described *League* as "this complex literary joke that is probably about a lot of books that [comic readers] haven't read and would never be interested in reading."[36] Should one construe this to mean that the series was indeed meant to bypass a core comics readership and explicitly target authors, editors, literature students, and professors? If Moore and O'Neill created their comics genealogy for the sole benefit of an audience that ordinarily does not buy comics and were not interested in whether traditional comic readers would like to know more about the texts they used to construct this genealogy, then wouldn't *League* defeat its own purpose?

Luckily, for those not in the know, there are Nevins's companion books, in which one can always look up the origin of some particular element, though the existence of these guides is in itself worthy to be commented upon. Phillip E. Wegner, in an essay on the "modernism of the graphic novel," associates Nevins's books with the guides to James Joyce's *Ulysses* (1922) or Thomas Pynchon's *Gravity's Rainbow* (1973), "some of [*League*'s] most important modernist and postmodernist print predecessors."[37] I am not sure to what extent this is a compliment and to what extent it surreptitiously places *League* in a tradition of notoriously "difficult" books that are so evidently in need of explanation that regular recourse to a guidebook seems necessary. Similarly, the "modernism of the graphic novel" might in this case conjure up a rather negative image of modernism as hermetic and elitist by suggesting that it consciously shuns and spurns the accessibility and immediate gratification of popular culture.

If all of this does not seem to apply to *League*, then a discussion of the end of volume 2 may redress this situation. So far, I have not drawn upon the second volume as much as the first one because it largely follows its example and is not quite as heavily invested in historical print culture and materiality as the first book; however, there is one feature that stands out: a mock-Victorian tour guide titled "The New Traveler's Almanac," which is appended to the main story much like "Allan and the Sundered Veil." This guide essentially describes a world in which the endless amount of fictional places authors have dreamt up in the course of literary history are real and coexist on the same planet. As to the number of literary references Moore and O'Neill make in it, suffice it to say that there are 127 pages worth of annotations for this guide in Nevins's companion book. Recognizing and identifying these allusions appear to be the main draw of this section of *League*, as it provides a matter-of-fact survey with little in the way of plot, characters, dialogue, and so on. One could see this guide as a kind of supplement, an additional offer for the abovementioned coterie that others may simply skip, yet the authors also hid a crucial plot element within it: Allan Quatermain and Mina Murray, by now the series' protagonists, become immortal—a fact that is continuously alluded to but never explicitly explained in subsequent volumes, which trace their adventures up to the early twenty-first century.

"The New Traveler's Almanac" definitely constitutes a virtuoso display of intertextuality that would shame any modernist or postmodernist writer, as it is a grandiose attempt to create a storyworld that contains all other storyworlds (including that of Jorge Luis Borges's "El Aleph" ["The Aleph," 1945]), yet it will surely also strike some as a self-indulgent and perhaps random canni-balization of all the texts of the past, to paraphrase Fredric Jameson's famous critique of postmodernism.[38] Here, Moore and O'Neill heap references upon references without integrating them into the kind of accessible and riveting narrative they cared for elsewhere. The plot point about Allan and Mina gaining immortality constitutes something akin to the ultimate reward for those who have followed the authors' lead to the end, but few beyond the most diehard fans of intertextuality, who approach the *League* equipped with Nevins's guidebook or an internet connection close by, may have actually been willing to do so. Labeling *League* as difficult, elitist, or inaccessible may, in these sections, no longer seem to be entirely unjustified, and one may argue that the comic here overshoots its mark in its attempts to ennoble the medium, expediting rather than questioning the division between the new, sophisticated graphic novels and the old, humble comics.

League has been described as "a kind of recycling plant, turning elements of old popular fiction into new popular fiction,"[39] but in view of what I have just said, one may perhaps also view it as turning old popular culture into new high culture. In reflecting on the history of comics and the various publica-tion forms that have shaped it, in reworking Victorian (para)literature into highly self-conscious narratives, Moore and O'Neill are producing a work that shows all the marks of high culture and attracts an audience that is famil-iar with historiographic metafiction, Neo-Victorianism, or other varieties of postmodernist fiction. One can hardly blame the creators for the existence of graphic novel and deluxe editions of their work; this is a standard industry practice. Moore, in fact, has in the past been quite vocal about his opposition to the term "graphic novel," denouncing it as a mere marketing ploy that "just came to mean 'expensive comic book'" and, through its inflationary use, "tended to destroy any progress that comics might have made in the mid-'80s."[40] Still, the graphic novel seems to be a format that is perfectly suited to the new kind of audience *League* addresses, which would not otherwise buy comics. And it is clearly most rewarding to readers who come equipped with a decent knowledge of nineteenth-century literature and who are willing to invest in the companion books (early versions of which can be accessed online) or read up on characters, texts, and Victorian print media they were unaware of elsewhere.

And yet, *League* is not something akin to the "Waste Land" of comics. It is also about a team of superheroes (even if they are unusual superheroes), it participates in mainstream comics' long tradition of crossovers between fictional universes, and it belongs to the popular genre of steampunk as much as it belongs to the perhaps more literary phenomenon of Neo-Victorianism. The series may be most gratifying to a coterie, yet this coterie may be composed of Victorianists willing to tackle what appear to be modern children's magazines, comic readers unafraid of forays into literature, or those who have always been in-between. Moore and O'Neill continuously straddle the line between lowbrow and highbrow, and while their work may occasionally appear too complex for its own sake, they always know what is currently at stake in comics. If the graphic novel is not to become detached from the rest of comics' history, if it is not to be perceived as the legitimate and respectable counterpart to the trashy and trivial comic pamphlets, then its connection to that history must be emphasized and partly excavated. It is impossible to avoid the paradox of producing an expensive, clothbound book that praises cheap magazines printed on paper so brittle that the magazines would disintegrate even if they were not thrown away, but this paradox can be explored and discussed within the book itself. If the various pictorial and storytelling traditions that have existed since Victorian times are to be kept alive, then the best method of doing this might just be to engage in a balancing act and write a sophisticated graphic novel that demonstrates how even in the most sophisticated graphic novel there is a trace of the penny dreadful—and vice versa.

Notes

1 Roger Sabin, *Adult Comics: An Introduction* (London: Routledge, 1993), 21.
2 Ibid.
3 See Ann Heilmann and Mark Llewellyn, *Neo-Victorianism: The Victorians in the Twenty-First Century, 1999–2009* (Basingstoke: Palgrave Macmillan, 2010); Dianne F. Sadoff and John Kucich, "Introduction: Histories of the Present," in *Victorian Afterlife: Postmodern Culture Rewrites the Nineteenth Century*, ed. John Kucich and Dianne F. Sadoff (Minneapolis: University of Minneapolis Press, 2000), ix–xxx.
4 For a reading of *The League of Extraordinary Gentlemen* that focuses heavily on these aspects, see Sebastian Domsch, "Monsters against Empire: The Poetics and Politics

of Neo-Victorian Metafiction in *The League of Extraordinary Gentlemen*," in *Neo-Victorian Gothic: Horror, Violence and Degeneration in the Re-Imagined Nineteenth Century,* ed. Marie-Luise Kohlke and Christian Gutleben (Amsterdam: Rodopi, 2012), 97–121.

5 For a lengthy discussion of Neo-Victorianism's engagement with material culture, see Nadine Boehm-Schnitker and Susanne Gruss, "Introduction: Spectacles and Things—Visual and Material Culture and/in Neo-Victorianism," *Neo-Victorian Studies* 4, no. 2 (2011): 1–23.

6 Roger Sabin writes that "[o]vernight, it was claimed, comics had developed from cheap throwaway children's fare to expensive album-form 'novels' for adults to keep on bookshelves." Sabin, *Adult Comics,* 235.

7 See Alan Moore and Kevin O'Neill, *The League of Extraordinary Gentlemen,* 2 vols. (La Jolla: DC Comics/Wildstorm, 1999–2003), 1: 178. In my discussion of *League,* I will be referring to the trade paperback edition, which is the most widely available version. While it regrettably omits some of the original pamphlets' paratexts, such as mock-Victorian tables of contents, advertisements, and letter pages, it also introduces some new material that is of use to my argument. Originally, both volumes are unpaginated; page references follow the pagination established by Nevins.

8 Jess Nevins, *Heroes & Monsters: The Unofficial Companion to* The League of Extraordinary Gentlemen (Austin: MonkeyBrain, 2003), 110.

9 Moore and O'Neill, *League,* 1: 5, 4.

10 Ibid., 2: 224.

11 Kevin Carpenter, *Vom Penny Dreadful zum Comic: Englische Jugendzeitschriften, Heftchen und Comics von 1855 bis zur Gegenwart* (Oldenburg: Bibliotheks- und Informationssystem der Universität Oldenburg, 1981), 61.

12 Roger Sabin, *Comics, Comix & Graphic Novels: A History of Comic Art* (London: Phaidon, 1996), 12–14.

13 Paul Gravett and John Harris Dunning, *Comics Unmasked: Art and Anarchy in the UK* (London: British Library, 2014).

14 Qtd. in Nevins, *Heroes & Monsters,* 118.

15 Ibid., 118–19.

16 See Moore and O'Neill, *League,* 1: 184.

17 Christine Ferguson, "Steam Punk and the Visualization of the Victorian: Teaching Alan Moore's *The League of Extraordinary Gentlemen* and *From Hell*," in *Teaching the Graphic Novel,* ed. Stephen E. Tabachnick (New York: MLA, 2009), 202.

18 Denis Gifford, *Victorian Comics* (London: Allen & Unwin, 1976), 7.

19 David Kunzle, *History of the Comic Strip,* 2 vols. (Berkeley: University of California Press, 1973–1990), 2: 333.

20 This has taken on a new significance in some of the later installments that take place in the twentieth century. The existence of international copyright laws, which one cannot simply ignore as one could in late-Victorian times, has here led the creators to mask the identity of characters they have, for example, borrowed from the *James Bond* or *Harry Potter* franchise.

21 Jess Nevins, *A Blazing World: The Unofficial Companion to* The League of Extraordinary Gentlemen, Volume Two (Austin: MonkeyBrain, 2004), 254.

22 Boys' weeklies were supposed to offer a "'wholesome' alternative" to the dreadfuls' sensationalism and questionable morality. In practice, though, there was considerable overlap between the two, so "Allan and the Sundered Veil" may just as well be read in the context of the penny dreadful. The association of comics with the dreadfuls

is perhaps stronger because both were massively campaigned against for being an alleged threat to youth, which in the case of comics led to a ban on certain genres and subject matter from the 1950s to the 1980s. See Sabin, *Comics, Comix & Graphic Novels*, 14; Carpenter, *Vom Penny Dreadful zum Comic*, 13–14; Martin Barker, *Comics, Ideology, Power and the Critics* (Manchester: Manchester University Press, 1989), 99.

23 Moore and O'Neill, *League*, 1: 153.

24 Nevins, *Heroes & Monsters*, 98–99.

25 Ibid.

26 Moore and O'Neill, *League*, 1: 155.

27 Nevins, *Heroes & Monsters*, 99.

28 Moore and O'Neill, *League*, 1: 186.

29 Ibid.

30 Sabin, *Comics, Comix & Graphic Novels*, 165.

31 Sabin, *Adult Comics*, 94.

32 Ibid., 247.

33 Nevins, *Heroes & Monsters*, 15–16.

34 Qtd. in Nevins, *A Blazing World*, 271.

35 Domsch, "Monsters against Empire," 103.

36 Qtd. in Nevins, *A Blazing World*, 259.

37 Phillip E. Wegner, "Alan Moore, 'Secondary Literacy,' and the Modernism of the Graphic Novel," *ImageTexT* 5, no. 3 (2010), http://imagetext.english.ufl.edu/archives/v5_3/wegner.

38 Fredric Jameson, "Postmodernism, or the Cultural Logic of Late Capitalism," *New Left Review* 146 (1984): 53–92 (65–66).

39 Maciej Sulmicki, "The Author as Antiquarian: Selling Victorian Culture to Readers of Neo-Victorian Novels and Steampunk Comics," *Otherness: Essays and Studies* 2, no. 1 (2011), https://www.otherness.dk/fileadmin/www.othernessandthearts.org/Publications/Journal_Otherness/Otherness__Essays_and_Studies_2.1/6.MaciejSulmicki.pdf.

40 Barry Kavanagh, "The Alan Moore Interview," *Blather*, October 17, 2000, http://www.blather.net/projects/alan-moore-interview.

Chapter 9

COMIC BOOKS VERSUS GRAPHIC NOVELS: COMMODITY FORMS AND CULTURAL PRESTIGE

Anthony Enns

Apart from *The Oxford Companion to the Book* (2010), there are few works on book history that even mention the history of comic books. This is perhaps due to the fact that comic books are generally dismissed by critics as a para- or subliterary field that is far removed from the realm of mainstream publishing. As Jan Baetens points out, comic books are perceived as a form of mass media entertainment not only because of their lowbrow content but also because of their industrial mode of production: "The internal excesses of the genre [...] and [...] the external constraints of the comics industry, which imposed a crudely capitalistic, fully Taylorized production system, are both responsible for a lowbrow image that still prevails in many well-educated circles."[1] In the late twentieth century, comic books were also eclipsed by the rise of the "graphic novel"—a new publishing format that was often praised for transforming graphic narratives into a legitimate literary genre. Stephen Tabachnick argues, for example, that "the graphic novel has little in common with traditional comic books" because it is "much more like full-length prose novels."[2] The term "graphic novel" thus conveys a sense of cultural prestige that was often seen as lacking in comic books, and this newfound prestige was inextricably linked to its material form, as "graphic novels are as thick as regular prose books, and they are printed on better paper and with better ink than usual comic books."[3]

There are several problems with this distinction, however, as the graphic novel format has proven to be difficult to define. For example, Roger Sabin defines graphic novels as "lengthy comics in book form,"[4] and Tabachnick describes this format as "an extended comic book"[5]—definitions that appear to be based on length, although extended narratives are common in comic books, and many of them have the same number of pages. In contrast, Edward T. Sullivan emphasizes the brevity of graphic novels by noting that they often contain "a single story"[6]—a definition that would also apply to comic books featuring self-contained narratives. Jan Baetens and Hugo Frey similarly argue that graphic novels reject the logic of serialization, which "functions as a symptom of a craving for prestige that aimed at definitively cutting through the possible ties to comics,"[7] yet this definition ignores the countless graphic novels that are published in character-based series. Charles Hatfield also notes that "a graphic novel can be almost anything: a novel, a collection of interrelated or thematically similar stories, a memoir, a travelogue or journal, a history, a series of vignettes or lyrical observations, an episode from a longer work—you name it."[8] There are thus no inherent genre differences between comic books and graphic novels, and it is not uncommon for the same material to be published in both formats, as even the most prestigious graphic novels are often initially serialized in comic books. This problem is exacerbated by Stephen Weiner's definition of the graphic novel as "a story told in comic book format"[9]—a definition that seems to acknowledge the impossibility of distinguishing between these formats. *Publishers Weekly* accurately described the sense of confusion surrounding this format by noting that "not even the people who write and/or publish them can agree on just what they are."[10]

While the graphic novel has enhanced the cultural prestige of graphic narratives, it appears that the distinction between comic books and graphic novels has little to do with their content; rather, it is based primarily on their commodity forms, including their packaging, promotion, distribution, and consumption. For example, the fears of cultural decline associated with comic books were directly attributed to their material qualities, which made them appear to be nothing more than standardized, mass-produced, and disposable commodities, and graphic novels were often differentiated from comic books through their paper and binding, which made them appear to be durable works of literature that were worthy of being sold in bookstores and preserved in archives. Graphic novels also tended to include paratextual elements, such as introductions, annotations, and appendices, which served to elevate their status by emphasizing their cultural importance and exceptionalism. The distinction between comic books and graphic novels thus remains ambiguous because it is largely based on material and paratextual cues.

The significance of these material and paratextual cues reinforces Pierre Bourdieu's argument that works categorized as serious literature reject economic profit in favor of symbolic capital, which supposedly reflects the superior taste of the literary elite, whereas works categorized as popular fiction reject literary prestige in favor of economic capital, which supposedly reflects the inferior taste of the mass reading public.[11] Graphic novels can similarly be understood as a bid for symbolic capital, as Christina Meyer points out, because they "helped to bring a fresh view into the field of comics" by "freeing them from the demonized status they had been given" and elevating them "to a 'higher,' more literary, or novelistic, level."[12] In other ways, however, graphic novels also challenged these cultural distinctions by allowing publishers to maximize profits through the creation of new revenue streams for content that had previously been perceived as lowbrow. This was made possible because the work of cultural recuperation that they performed was exclusively dependent on their materiality rather than their content. The tension between these competing commodity forms thus "tells us something about the discursive formation of the label through its repetitive use by diverse agents ranging from critics and fans to publishers."[13]

The following chapter will examine the history of the graphic novel as a "discursive formation" by exploring how this new format simultaneously resisted and reinforced traditional distinctions of taste. It will also show how the stigma associated with comic books was inherently linked to their material form and how the material form of the graphic novel was used to evade this stigma by allowing publishers to appeal to critics, librarians, educators, and readers who would not normally be interested in comic book material. The primary examples will be Frank Miller's *Batman: The Dark Knight Returns* and Art Spiegelman's *Maus: A Survivor's Tale*, which were both published in 1986. Although these two works have virtually nothing in common—the former features a middle-aged Batman who comes out of retirement to defeat his archenemies, while the latter is a nonfictional account of the experiences of the artist's parents during the Holocaust—they were among the earliest comic books to be republished as graphic novels, and they played a key role in establishing the commercial viability of this format. They also received similar levels of critical attention, and the frequent comparisons between them clearly show how their cultural status was dependent on their materiality rather than their content.

As historians often point out, the comic book was first introduced in the United States during the Great Depression—a time when publishers sought to improve declining sales by repackaging previously published material. The earliest comic books consisted of comic strips that had previously appeared in newspaper supplements, but in the mid-1930s some publishers began to feature new material, and many of them adopted the production methods used in the pulp magazine industry by introducing character-based serial narratives. This gradually led to the introduction of superheroes, and by 1940 superhero comic books were the best-selling products on the market. The "Golden Age" of comic books was thus made possible through the industrial logic of mass production, which reinforced the perception of comic books as lowbrow.

In 1940, for example, an editorial written by Sterling North, literary critic at the *Chicago Daily News*, argued that comic books placed "a strain on young eyes and young nervous systems" because they were "badly drawn, badly written, and badly printed," and he added that the "antidote to the 'comic' magazine poison can be found in any library or good bookstore."[14] North thus claimed that the potential dangers posed by this commodity form were due to their mode of production and that children were better off reading "real" books because of their material properties.

One of the most vocal opponents of comic books was psychiatrist Fredric Wertham, who claimed that comic books were a leading cause of juvenile delinquency. He first presented this theory at a symposium on "The Psychopathology of Comic Books" organized by the Association for the Advancement of Psychotherapy in New York in 1948, and the *Saturday Review of Literature* subsequently published a condensed version of his presentation, in which he described the crusade against comic books as a battle between concerned parents and greedy capitalists.[15] While he initially focused on the representation of race, sexuality, and violence, he gradually expanded the scope of his critique by arguing that comic books were a leading cause of "reading disorders" due to their material properties:

> Print is easy to read when the paper background is light and the printing a good contrasting black. Yet most comics are smudgily printed on pulp paper. The printing is crowded in balloons with irregular lines. Any adult can check on the eyestrain involved by reading a few comics himself. We can produce the most beautifully printed books. [...] Yet to our children we give the crudest and most ill-designed products.[16]

Like North, therefore, Wertham concluded that the material form of the comic book was physically unhealthy, and the only cure for these physical symptoms was for children to read "beautifully printed books".

Librarians and educators expressed similar concerns. For example, an editorial in the *Wilson Library Bulletin* emphasized "the basic crudeness of the medium," which was described as "a monument to bad taste in color and design."[17] An article in *Elementary English Review* similarly argued that the only cure for "comicitis" (a term that referred to the illnesses caused by comic books) was to bring children into the library, where proper "treatment" could be administered.[18] An article in the *New Mexico Library Bulletin* similarly emphasized that comic books were a leading cause of "eyestrain and headaches" due to the fact that they were "badly drawn and poorly printed."[19] Like North and Wertham, therefore, librarians and educators similarly argued that the material form of comic books was physically unhealthy—particularly for younger readers. As Allen Ellis and Doug Highsmith point out, librarians "found fault with the physical aspects of comic books, such as cheap paper, small print, and what they saw as unpleasant and lurid colors,"[20] and "the fact that comics were published in an ephemeral, intrinsically difficult-to-preserve format made it just that much easier to decide that they [...] had no place in library collections."[21]

Paul Lopes has shown how these arguments produced a social stigma that was directly associated with the commodity form of the comic book and how comic book readers responded to this stigma by creating a subculture that celebrated alternative forms of "fan knowledge": "Fans' simple possession of 'expert knowledge' of a cultural form sets a popular aesthetic that works against the power of elite critics."[22] Jeffrey Brown also notes that the interpretive practices of fans often mirror those of the literary elite, as they similarly involve the comparison and evaluation of comic books in order to identify a "canon" of great works and great artists. Instead of promoting the accumulation of "symbolic capital," however, fans seek to accumulate "subcultural capital," which elevates their status within the subculture: "Comic fandom allows its participants to achieve the social prestige and self-esteem that accompanies cultural capital without surrendering to the hegemonic rules of Official culture."[23] This strategy serves to reinforce the distinction between low and high art by allowing fans to celebrate rather than challenge their outsider status. Another way of resisting this stigma was to seek mainstream recognition. Beginning in the 1950s, for example, there were several attempts to publish comic book material in book form, beginning with Arnold Drake and Leslie Waller's *It Rhymes with Lust* (1950)—a 128-page digest-size "picture novel" that was designed to target an adult readership. As Drake explained, they "wanted this to be a link between a comic book and a *book* book," and it was published in black and white "so the reading public would recognize it as being closer to '*lit*-er-a-*ture*'" [emphasis in original].[24] Despite their desire for mainstream recognition, however, they were still afraid to reveal their names on the cover: "We weren't about to ruin our prospects in the literary establishment, where comic books were looked upon as garbage."[25] These comments reflect the tremendous importance placed on the material properties of the book, which ultimately failed to transcend the stigma associated with comic books, as bookstores refused to carry it.

The term "graphic novel" did not emerge until the 1970s. In 1971, for example, Gil Kane and Archie Goodwin published *Blackmark*—a 119-page mass-market paperback that contained a full-length adventure story. The book was also published in black and white, the writing was typeset rather than hand-lettered, and the page layouts were extremely irregular, which helped to distance this work from comic books by evoking the tradition of illustrated novels. Like Drake and Waller's earlier experiment, *Blackmark* was also aimed at nontraditional comics readers, and the publisher included an introduction that described the book as a "new fusion of images and words in an action book—the next step forward in pictorial fiction."[26] In 1976 the term "graphic novel" was also used to describe Jim Steranko's *Chandler: Red Tide* (a digest-sized paperback that used the term "visual novel" on its cover and "graphic novel" in its introduction), George Metzger's *Beyond Time and Again* (a 48-page hardcover book that was subtitled "a graphic novel" on the title page), and Richard Corben's *Bloodstar* (a book that was published simultaneously in softcover and hardcover editions and that used the term "graphic novel" on its dust jacket). *Bloodstar* was initially serialized in color, but the book edition was published in black and white, and it also featured an introductory essay that described it as "a new, revolutionary concept—a graphic novel, which combines all the imagination and visual power of comics strip art with the richness of the traditional novel."[27] Like *Blackmark*, *Bloodstar* also featured typeset prose, which more closely resembled the format of a printed book.[28] These features were thus designed to enhance the cultural prestige of the work by presenting it as an illustrated novel rather than a comic book.

Three additional graphic novels were published in 1978: Jack Katz's *The First Kingdom* (a collection that reprinted the first six issues of the comic book series of the same name), Don McGregor and Paul Gulacy's *Sabre* (a 38-page science fiction story that was described as a "comic novel" on the credits page), and Will Eisner's *A Contract with God and Other Tenement Stories* (a 192-page book that was published simultaneously in softcover and hardcover editions and that used the term "graphic novel" on its cover). While *The First Kingdom* and *Sabre* featured rather conventional action-adventure narratives, Eisner's work was clearly different, as it focused on working-class Jewish life in New York during the Great Depression. As Eisner explained in an interview, "I sat down and tried to do a book that would physically look like a 'legitimate' book and at the same time write about a subject matter that would never have been addressed in comic form, which is man's relationship with God."[29] Eisner thus described this work as "a departure from the standard [...] comic book format" not only in terms of its content but also in terms of its physical appearance, which was designed to make it seem "legitimate." He also confessed that his desire for cultural prestige was motivated by his embarrassment at being a comic book artist: "Comic book artists then were regarded both socially and in the profession as what the Germans called an *Untermensch*, a subhuman. It was not uncommon for those of us who were doing comic books not to say we were doing comic books; when we were at a cocktail party, we'd say we did illustrations."[30] While *A Contract with God* was not the first work to be marketed as a graphic novel, and Eisner was not the first artist who sought to use this term to evade the stigma associated with comic books, Dan Mazur and Alexander Danner note that his "literary ambition and drive to bring serious comics […] into the broader mainstream did much to popularize the term and to jump-start the re-branding of comics as an art form for grown-ups."[31]

Comic book publishers soon took advantage of this new format and its ability to attract the interest of mainstream distributors and retailers. Between 1974 and 1980, for example, Fireside (the trade paperback division of Simon & Schuster) published a series of books containing reprinted material from Marvel and DC, and in 1978 Simon & Schuster published Stan Lee and Jack Kirby's *The Silver Surfer*, which featured an original book-length story written specifically as a graphic novel.[32] In 1982 Marvel also introduced a series of oversized trade paperbacks featuring original superhero narratives, and DC created its own graphic novel line the following year. While these graphic novels were primarily sold in specialist comic book stores, they were unlike comic books in that they were published on glossy paper, they did not contain fan letters or internal advertising, and their cover prices were much higher ($5.95 or $6.95 instead of 60¢). By the early 1980s, therefore, the market was already saturated with graphic novels featuring superhero narratives, which were primarily aimed at comic book collectors, who were willing to pay higher prices for higher quality publications. This shift was clearly due to the rise of direct market sales, which allowed retailers to bypass distributors, but it also seemed to threaten Eisner's bid for cultural prestige, as Hatfield points out:

> Eisner's aim was to break into bookstores, not comic shops. Yet, ironically, Eisner's term would eventually serve to legitimize a new, costlier way of selling comics to the initiated direct market fan. […] That audience was increasingly self-conscious, relatively affluent, and eager for belated recognition of the comic book as "art," a hunger that made the upscale format of the graphic novel doubly attractive. For all that the graphic novel provided a new platform for alternative comics, it also became a kind of wish-fulfilling totem for mainstream comics.[33]

In other words, graphic novels did not initially feature new kinds of content, and they were not always released by mainstream publishers and sold in mainstream bookstores; rather, they mostly consisted of superhero narratives that were aimed at existing comic book readers.

The first major change in this marketing strategy was signaled by Frank Miller's *Batman: The Dark Knight Returns*—a four-issue limited comic book series that was published in "prestige format," which included square binding, glossy paper, and cardstock covers. Despite the fact that each issue cost $2.95, it sold remarkably well and went through several printings before it was collected as a graphic novel later that year. Three editions of the graphic novel were released simultaneously, as Warner Books published softcover and hardcover editions and Graphitti Designs published a limited hardcover edition that included additional pages of sketches and artwork. While the limited series and the limited hardcover edition were aimed at comic book collectors, which was consistent with DC's direct-market approach, Warner's editions were sold in mainstream bookstores and marketed to a broader readership. Warner's softcover edition even became a featured selection of the Quality Paperback Book Club—a mail-order service that offered low-cost paperbacks covering a wide range of literary genres and interests. As Eileen Meehan points out, publishers "tapped different systems of distribution, placing the *Dark Knight* in different kinds of retail outlets, tapping the markets of fandom and general readers to determine if the grim version of Batman could gain acceptance from both specialized and generalized consumers."[34] This strategy was so successful that it not only created an audience for the first Batman film franchise (1989–1997) but also transformed the way comic books were produced and distributed, as Douglas Wolk explains:

> [B]y the mid-'90s, every comics publisher of any importance was publishing squarebound book collections of its comics and keeping them in print. As it turned out, that was where the money was, and within a few years the economic engine of the industry had made a major conversion: instead of trade paperbacks being a way to capitalize further on successful comics, periodical comics became a way to amortize the cost of producing the books of which they were components.[35]

William Uricchio and Roberta Pearson similarly note that this publishing strategy "gains the industry an unaccustomed measure of respectability" by using different formats to appeal to different audiences, and they describe *Batman: The Dark Knight Returns* as the "opening salvo in the Batman's high-end marketing offensive."[36] In other words, this publishing strategy served to expand the market for superhero narratives by dispelling the stigma associated with comic books, and it was so successful that *Batman: The Dark Knight Returns* became one of the most profitable graphic novels ever produced.

Newspapers and magazines helped to promote this graphic novel by proclaiming that comic books were now appropriate for adult readers. For example, a profile of Frank Miller in *Rolling Stone* described him as "the single most exciting figure to come along in comics for the last generation or more," and his work was described as raising "new hopes within the industry for the maturation of a long-devalued art form."[37] *The St. Petersburg Times* similarly noted that *Batman: The Dark Knight Returns* was "as far away from standard pow-biff-sock comics as *Masterpiece Theatre* is from *Gilligan's Island*."[38] *Newsday* also emphasized that it "looks very little like a comic book" due to its 200-page length, its $12.95 cover price, and the fact that it "is lushly printed and bound on heavy stock."[39] Reviewers thus repeatedly emphasized the importance of its material form, and Miller was also quoted as saying, "I wanted to do something you wouldn't be ashamed to take on an airplane with you,"[40] as its material form demanded more serious attention:

> Comic books began as collections of newspaper strips, and the newspaper mentality toward production has persisted, especially as cheap pulp paper gave way to cheaper, and metal plates gave way to plastic, making the books so fuzzy it takes the dedication of a child to read them. But now, very suddenly, as a direct consequence of the increased power of the talent, the ante has been raised, comics are being published in formats that demand the level of attention from production that slick magazines and fine art books do.[41]

What had changed, in other words, was not the content of comic books but rather their modes of production, distribution, and reception, as new publishing formats appealed to different readers who interpreted them in different ways.

Reviewers also frequently compared *Batman: The Dark Knight Returns* to *Maus* due to similarities in their length, paper quality, cover price, and sales figures. For example, *The Los Angeles Times* noted that these two graphic novels had together "provoked the first aesthetically serious discussions of the comic book as an art form in America."[42] Unlike Miller, however, Spiegelman was not involved in the mainstream comic book industry. Instead, he got his start in the underground comix movement, and the earliest version of *Maus* was a three-page story published in the underground comix anthology *Funny Aminals* (1972).[43] Spiegelman also cofounded the avant-garde comic magazine *RAW*, in which his revised version of *Maus* was first serialized. As Wolk points out, "*RAW* was considerably fancier than the other independent comics of its day" because it was "printed on better paper, larger than standard comic or even magazine size, [and] more expensive."[44] Spiegelman thus sought to take advantage of new publishing formats in order to endow his work with a greater sense of cultural prestige. In 1986 the first six chapters of *Maus* were also collected in a softcover graphic novel by Pantheon Books (a subsidiary of Random House), which was known for publishing serious works of literature.[45] It was a remarkable achievement to have a graphic novel featured in the Pantheon catalogue at this time, and Spiegelman reported that the book had been rejected by several publishers before it was finally accepted (Pantheon even rejected the book the first time it was submitted for consideration). Michael Barson, the publicity manager at Pantheon, also noted that "comics have had a kind of stigma here in the U.S." and that "when you're 11 you're supposed to put them away."[46] Barson thus saw the graphic novel as a way to dispel the stigma associated with comic books by making it possible for Spiegelman's work to be sold in mainstream bookstores rather than specialist comic book stores, and it also became a featured selection of the Quality Paperback Book Club. While these graphic novels bore no resemblance to one another in terms of their content, they were both produced and promoted in ways that elevated their cultural status. As Robert Hutton explains, "It was the social capital and means of distribution that Pantheon provided which allowed *Maus* to find its way into the hands of the literati."[47]

Maus first gathered mainstream attention with a positive notice in the *New York Times Book Review*, which claimed that Spiegelman's "goal is to expand the very notion of what a comic strip can do, to make intelligent readers reconsider—and reject—the widespread notion of, in Mr. Spiegelman's phrase, 'comics-as-kid-culture.'"[48] The reviewer for the *Chicago Tribune* similarly argued that "the bulk of what is being printed still features what many among the industry's more progressive element deride as 'underwear heroes' [...] and is still bought primarily by members and not-yet-members of the Clearasil Generation," but "the comic that could awaken the most people to the format's potential is Spiegelman's 'Maus,' because it is getting attention and stretching traditional genre boundaries."[49] Spiegelman used similar arguments to distance his work from mainstream graphic novels by arguing that most of them "are simply superhero tales 'printed on better paper' but still geared toward males 'with arrested development.'"[50] He also described the potential danger that could result from conflating *Maus* with mainstream works like *Batman: The Dark Knight Returns*:

> In 1986, Frank Miller's *Batman: The Dark Knight Returns* [...] and my own *Maus: A Survivor's Tale* [...] each met with commercial success in bookstores. They were dubbed graphic novels in a bid for social acceptability. [...] What has followed is a spate of well-dressed comic books finding their way into legitimate bookshops. Sadly, a number of them are no more than pedestrian comic books in glossy wrappings, and the whole genre, good and bad, may find itself once again banished to the specialty shops before serious artists and serious readers can find each other.[51]

These two works were thus conflated because they employed the same publishing format and marketing strategy,[52] which allowed them to expand the market for comic book material. However, their similarities remained limited to their commodity forms, and Spiegelman worried that the little prestige his work had accrued might be lost if the graphic novels produced by comic book publishers failed to reinforce the cultural distinctions that this new format was supposed to embody.[53]

The entry of graphic novels into the trade book market was soon followed by their entry into libraries. While librarians had been among the most vocal opponents of comic books in the 1940s, they gradually became avid proponents of graphic novels as a format capable of enticing young people to read books. Michael Lavin notes, for example, that the main concerns of librarians were that "the physical format of comic books is too fragile; comics won't stand up to heavy use; they'll be stolen from the library; the subject matter is inappropriate for younger readers; [and] they're too difficult to acquire and catalog."[54] Graphic novels seemed to resolve most (if not all) of these problems, and "even librarians who might strongly resist the notion of establishing a comic book collection find purchasing graphic novels to be an acceptable practice."[55] This shift began as early as 1988, when an article in *Voice of Youth Advocates* asserted that graphic novels fit the standard definition of "books" and should thus be "something for libraries to consider."[56] In 1990, *Library Journal* and *Publishers Weekly* also featured several articles that described which graphic novels were most appropriate for bookstores and libraries.[57] In the mid-1990s, two bibliographies—D. Aviva Rothschild's *Graphic Novels* (1995) and Steve Weiner's *100 Graphic Novels for Public Libraries* (1996)—also provided key resources for librarians seeking to develop graphic novel collections.[58] Allen Ellis and Doug Highsmith thus conclude that "the rise of the graphic novel [...] is certainly the single most important such change insofar as enhancing the status of comic books as appropriate for inclusion in library collections, by making them appear to be more like 'real' books."[59] Amy Nyberg similarly argues that the graphic novel was essential to the inclusion of comics in libraries, as librarians were "willing to grant them a legitimacy that comic books never achieved."[60]

Nyberg also notes that this shift in policy was a direct result of the attention paid to graphic novels at academic conferences, which similarly sought to legitimize these texts and promote their cultural significance.[61] One of the first academic conferences devoted to graphic narratives was The Graphic Novel: A Twentieth Anniversary Conference, which was held at the University of Massachusetts in 1998. Comics studies has since become an established discipline that supports four annual conferences in the United States alone, and the longest-running is the "Comic Art and Comics" area at the annual Popular Culture Association Conference. The University of Florida Conference on Comics and Graphic Novels was also launched in 2002, and it continues to be held annually in Gainesville. These conferences fueled the production of scholarship in this field, which led to the creation of several academic journals, including *ImageTexT* (2004–), *The Comics Grid: Journal of Comics Scholarship*

(2009–), *Journal of Graphic Novels and Comics* (2010–), *Studies in Comics* (2010–), and *Inks: The Journal of the Comics Studies Society* (2017–). The expansion of this field has also encouraged numerous educators to explore the potential use of graphic novels in the classroom.[62]

Graphic novels thus conveyed a sense of cultural prestige, as they could make people expect the sort of format, serious intent, and weighty heft of traditional literature."[63] However, the equation of graphic novels and literature still remains controversial. For example, Hatfield warns that "a too-exclusive embrace of the term *graphic novel* risks eliding much of what is interesting in comics history, mystifying the economic relations on which the art form depends, and cheating us of an appreciation for those great comics that do not look at all like novels."[64] Daniel Raeburn similarly rejects the use of the term "because a 'graphic novel' is in fact the very thing it is ashamed to admit: a comic book, rather than a comic pamphlet or comic magazine."[65] Catherine Labio similarly argues that the use of this term "reinforces the ongoing ghettoization of works deemed unworthy of critical attention" and that "much would be lost if scholars were to jettison the comparative study of the complex sociolinguistic and cultural codes associated with comics in favor of a monocultural, one-note 'graphic novel' in a sad search for respectability."[66] Bart Beaty similarly argues that the emphasis on this format within the field of comics studies has reinforced rather than dispelled the stigma associated with comic books: "The rise of comics scholarship has been largely abetted by the social construction of the 'graphic novel' as a discrete category that obscures the commercial origins of comic books [... and reduces] the range of texts that are appropriate subjects for study in a desire to align the field with the better-established and more powerful field of literary studies."[67] These critics thus conclude that graphic novels enhanced the cultural prestige of graphic narratives at the cost of reinforcing the stigma associated with comic books and that the attempt to preserve this cultural distinction is inherently artificial, as their only real difference lies in their commodity forms.

While critics often challenge the inherent elitism implied by the term "graphic novel," artists more often reject the term because it is used by marketers to elevate the status of inferior work, as Alan Moore explains: "The problem is that 'graphic novel' just came to mean 'expensive comic book' and so what you'd get is people like DC Comics or Marvel Comics—because 'graphic novels' were getting some attention, they'd stick six issues of whatever worthless piece of crap they happened to be publishing lately under a glossy cover."[68] Eddie Campbell's "Graphic Novel Manifesto" similarly argues that graphic novelists are "forging a whole new art" and that the term "'graphic novel' signifies a movement rather than a form." He also asserts that the "goal of the graphic novelist is to take the form of the comic book, which has become an embarrassment, and raise it to a more ambitious and meaningful level."[69] In other words, Campbell argues that the graphic novel is valuable because it implies a level of sophistication that is seen as lacking in comic books, which is limited by the superhero genre, and the material form of the graphic novel thus becomes the embodiment of a particular kind of intention or ambition that exceeds the commercial limitations of the comic book industry. Campbell later expanded on this idea in interviews, in which he reiterated the importance of the intention behind these works rather than their commodity form: "The graphic novel doesn't exist. 'Graphic Novel' is an abstract idea. It's a sensibility[;] it's an advanced attitude toward comics." Campbell also called for the "graphic novel movement" to distance itself from "comic-book culture" as much as possible: "The comic book is a genre. [...] It's gone too far to reverse it. What we have to do is establish another camp, over here away from that one, where we somehow avoid association with it."[70] Like the earliest proponents of this new format, therefore, Campbell conceived of comic books and graphic novels as two distinct genres, and he argued that their cultural status was inherently linked to their material properties.

The tensions between critics and artists clearly reflect the ambiguity of this new publishing format. While the graphic novel helped to promote the acceptance of graphic narratives as a legitimate art form by providing an easy way to distinguish between "good" and "bad" comics, this distinction was somewhat paradoxical, as most graphic novels did not possess the kinds of formal and aesthetic qualities that artists, publishers, reviewers, librarians, and educators associated with the term, and their publication did not necessarily represent a rejection of the commercial imperatives of the comic book industry. For example, graphic novels like *Batman: The Dark Knight Returns* consist of material that was originally serialized in comic books and then collected in book form, which allowed it to be sold in bookstores, reviewed in magazines, collected in libraries, and included on course syllabi, regardless of the fact that its content did not represent a significant departure from that of most mainstream comic books. The graphic novel format also encouraged reviewers to conflate this work with *Maus*, regardless of their obvious differences in content, as they shared the same commodity form and marketing strategy. Their frequent conflation in the popular press thus reflects an attempt to identify the graphic novel as a new literary genre despite the fact that there were no inherent differences between comic books and graphic novels at the level of content; rather, they only differed in terms of their material properties, marketing strategies, and target audiences. In other words, the critical reception of these works shows how the function of the graphic novel as a publishing category was assumed by its commodity form, which was used to introduce a cultural distinction that could not be sustained at the level of content. And the commodity form was able to supplant genre as a differentiating criterion and thereby establish the cultural legitimacy of graphic narratives precisely because its modes of production and distribution allowed it to circumvent the stigma associated with comic books.

This chapter has explored the complex and contentious history of the graphic novel in order to demonstrate how commodity forms often influence the reception of texts by shaping the expectations and interpretations of readers.[71] While it may seem impossible to establish, justify, or sustain cultural distinctions based solely on a work's material properties, these distinctions are often crucial for publishers seeking to target different readerships, librarians seeking to determine which works are worth preserving in their collections, educators seeking to engage students and maintain cultural standards, and artists seeking to balance their appreciation for comics and their desire to transcend both the low cultural status of comic books and the economic constraints of the comic book industry. Despite the difficulty of defining the graphic novel or differentiating it from the comic book, this format still serves an essential function within the realms of commerce, art, and academia by signifying distinctions of taste, and this function is largely dependent on its material properties.

Notes

1 Jan Baetens, "Graphic Novels," in *The Cambridge History of the American Novel*, ed. Leonard Cassuto, Clare Virginia Eby, and Benjamin Reiss (Cambridge: Cambridge University Press, 2011), 1137–53 (1140).

2 Stephen E. Tabachnick, "From Comics to the Graphic Novel: William Hogarth to Will Eisner," in *The Cambridge Companion to the Graphic Novel*, ed. Stephen E. Tabachnick (Cambridge: Cambridge University Press, 2017), 26–40 (26).

3 Ibid.

4 Roger Sabin, *Comics, Comix and Graphic Novels* (London: Phaidon Press, 1996), 165.

5 Stephen E. Tabachnick, "The Graphic Novel and the Age of Transition: A Survey and Analysis," *English Literature in Transition* 53, no. 1 (2010): 3–28 (3).

6 Edward T. Sullivan, *Reaching Reluctant Young Adult Readers: A Practical Handbook for Librarians and Teachers* (Lanham, MD: Scarecrow Press, 2002), 52.

7 Jan Baetens and Hugo Frey, *The Graphic Novel: An Introduction* (Cambridge: Cambridge University Press, 2015), 14.

8 Charles Hatfield, *Alternative Comics: An Emerging Literature* (Jackson, MS: University of Mississippi Press, 2005), 5.

9 Stephen Weiner, *The 101 Best Graphic Novels* (New York: NBM Publishing, 2004), 5.

10 Beth Levine, "Graphic Novels: The Latest Word in Illustrated Books," *Publishers Weekly*, May 22, 1987: 45–47 (45).

11 Pierre Bourdieu, *The Rules of Art: Genesis and Structure of the Literary Field*, trans. Susan Emanuel (Stanford: Stanford University Press, 1995), 142.

12 Christina Meyer, "Un/Taming the Beast, or Graphic Novels (Re)Considered," in *From Comic Strips to Graphic Novels: Contributions to the Theory and History of Graphic Narrative*, ed. Daniel Stein and Jan-Noël Thon (Berlin: De Gruyter, 2013), 271–99 (276).

13 Ibid.

14 Sterling North, "A National Disgrace and a Challenge to American Parents," *Childhood Education* 17, no. 2 (1940): 56.

15 Fredric Wertham, "The Comics … Very Funny!" *Saturday Review of Literature*, May 29, 1948: 6–7, 27–29.

16 Fredric Wertham, *Seduction of the Innocent* (New York: Rinehart, 1954), 139.

17 Stanley J. Kunitz, "Libraries, to Arms!" *Wilson Library Bulletin* 15, no. 8 (1941): 670–71 (670).

18 Franklyn M. Branley, "The Plague of the Comics," *Elementary English Review* 19, no. 5 (1942): 181–82.

19 Elizabeth S. Margulis, "The Comics Dilemma," *New Mexico Library Bulletin* 18 (1949): 3–5 (4).

20 Allen Ellis and Doug Highsmith, "About Face: Comic Books in Library Literature," *Serials Review* 26, no. 2 (2000): 21–43 (26).

21 Ibid., 39.

22 Paul Lopes, "Culture and Stigma: Popular Culture and the Case of Comic Books," *Sociological Forum* 21, no. 3 (2006): 387–414 (397).

23 Jeffrey A. Brown, "Comic Book Fandom and Cultural Capital," *Journal of Popular Culture* 30, no. 4 (1997): 13–31 (29).

24 Qtd. in David Hajdu, *The Ten-Cent Plague: The Great Comic-Book Scare and How It Changed America* (New York: Picador, 2008), 167.

25 Ibid., 168.

26 Gil Kane, *Blackmark* (New York: Bantam Books, 1971), interior cover.

27 Richard Corben, *Bloodstar* (Leawood, KS: Morning Star Press, 1976), 5.

28 The 1979 reprint featured hand-lettered text that more closely resembled a comic book.

29 Andrew D. Arnold, "The Graphic Novel Silver Anniversary," *Time*, November 14, 2003: content.time.com/time/arts/article/0,8599,542579,00.html.

30 Gary Groth and Robert Fiore, *The New Comics: Interviews from the Pages of the Comics Journal* (New York: Berkeley, 1988), 16.

31 Dan Mazur and Alexander Danner, *Comics: A Global History, 1968 to the Present* (London: Thames & Hudson, 2014), 181.

32 This book was clearly meant to convey a sense of cultural prestige, as Stan Lee noted in the preface that the character has "a special significance, which goes beyond the normal fascination for a bigger-than-life cosmic-powered character," and that he was frequently compared to Ulysses, Gandhi, and "early religious martyrs." Stan Lee and Jack Kirby, *The Silver Surfer* (New York: Simon & Schuster, 1978), 10.

33 Hatfield, *Alternative Comics*, 29.

34 Eileen R. Meehan, "'Holy Commodity Fetish, Batman!': The Political Economy of a Commercial Intertext," in *The Many Lives of the Batman: Critical Approaches to a Superhero and His Media*, ed. Roberta E. Pearson and William Uricchio (New York: Routledge, 1991), 47–65 (53).

35 Douglas Wolk, *Reading Comics: How Graphic Novels Work and What They Mean* (Cambridge, MA: Da Capo Press, 2007), 46.

36 William Uricchio and Roberta E. Pearson, "I'm Not Fooled By that Cheap Disguise," in *The Many Lives of the Batman: Critical Approaches to a Superhero and His Media*, ed. Roberta E. Pearson and William Uricchio (New York: Routledge, 1991), 182–213 (190 and 209).

37 Mikal Gilmore, "Comic Genius," *Rolling Stone* 470 (March 27, 1986): 56–58 (58).

38 "Novel Comics: The American Comic Book Is Growing Up," *St. Petersburg Times*, January 7, 1987: 3D.

39 David Firestone, "Holy Nightmare, Batman! A Crime-and-Corruption Infested Gotham City Has Turned Millionaire Bruce Wayne into a Brutal Vigilante," *Newsday*, January 20, 1987: 4.

40 Andra Varin, "Comic Books of Yore Now Graphic Novels," *Sun Sentinel*, March 1, 1987: 8F. The desire to dispel the stigma associated with comic books is also reflected within the story, as the public outrage against Batman reiterates many of the accusations made against comic books in the 1940s. At one point, for example, journalists report that "the Council of Mothers [...] petitioned the mayor to issue a warrant for the immediate arrest of the Batman, citing him as a harmful influence on the children of Gotham." The lead spokesman in this crusade is a psychologist, who claims that Batman is directly responsible for the rise in juvenile delinquency: "Every anti-social act can be traced to irresponsible media input. Given this, the presence of such an aberrant, violent force in the media can only lead to anti-social programming." Just as comic book reading was historically described as a disease (often referred to as "comicitis"), so too are the representations of Batman in the media described by these characters as a "social disease"—an attitude that the graphic novel clearly challenges by presenting Batman in a sympathetic light. Frank Miller, *Batman: The Dark Knight Returns* (New York: DC Comics, 1996), 59 and 66.

41 Kim Thompson, "Frank Miller: Return of the Dark Knight," *Comics Journal* 101 (1985): 58–79 (74).

42 Charles Solomon, "The Comic Book Grows Up," *Los Angeles Times*, April 16, 1989: 6.

43 This story was reprinted in Don Donahue and Susan Goodrick, eds., *The Apex Treasury of Underground Comics* (New York: Links Books, 1974); *Comix Book* #2 (New York: Marvel, 1975); and Art Spiegelman, *Breakdowns: From Maus to Now, An Anthology of Strips* (New York: Nostalgia Press, 1977).

44 Wolk, *Reading Comics*, 42.

45 Following the publication of the second volume of *Maus* in 1991, the first volume was republished in both softcover and hardcover editions.

46 Thaddeus Rutkowski, "Comic Books for Grown-Ups," *Adweek*, November 7, 1988: HP12.

47 Robert Hutton, "A Mouse in the Bookstore: *Maus* and the Publishing Industry," *South Central Review* 32, no. 3 (2015): 30–44 (34–35).

48 Ken Tucker, "Cats, Mice and History—The Avant-Garde of the Comic Strip," *New York Times*, May 26, 1985: BR3.

49 Steve Johnson, "Are Comic Books Growing Up?," *Chicago Tribune*, August 28, 1986: www.chicagotribune.com/news/ct-xpm-1986-08-28-8603040486-story.html.

50 Deirdre Donahue, "Comic Books Grow Up into Graphic Novels," *USA Today*, November 25, 1987: 1D.

51 Art Spiegelman, "Commix: An Idiosyncratic Historical and Aesthetic Overview," *Print* 42, no. 6 (1988): 61–73, 195–96 (196).

52 Hatfield notes, for example, that "together they established a beachhead for 'graphic novels' in the book trade." Hatfield, *Alternative Comics*, 30.

53 These concerns were also reflected in a *New York Times* review of the second col-
    lected volume of *Maus*, which began with the somewhat bizarre assertion that "Art
    Spiegelman doesn't draw comics." A *Village Voice* review similarly emphasized that
    "*Maus* is not exactly a comic book" because "comics are for kids." Joseph Witek cor-
    rectly points out that these "guardians of elite taste" were attempting to reinforce "the
    crucial ideological distinction between high and low art," yet he overlooks the fact
    that the classification of Spiegelman's work as "high" art was only made possible by
    the emergence of the graphic novel format, which explains why critics largely ignored
    his earlier work. Lawrence L. Langer, "A Fable of the Holocaust," *New York Times Book
    Review*, November 3, 1991, 1; Elizabeth Hess, "Meet the Spiegelmans," *Village Voice*,
    January 14, 1992, 87; Joseph Witek, "Imagetext, or, Why Art Spiegelman Doesn't
    Draw Comics," *ImageTexT: Interdisciplinary Comics Studies* 1, no. 1 (2004), http://www
    .engl.../witek/index.shtml.
54 Michael R. Lavin, "Comic Books and Graphic Novels for Libraries: What to Buy,"
    Serials Review 24, no. 2 (1998): 31–45 (32).
55 Ibid., 33.
56 Patrick Jones, "Getting Serious about Comics," *Voice of Youth Advocates* 11 (1988):
    15–16.
57 Keith R. A. DeCandido, "Picture This: Graphic Novels in Libraries," *Library Journal*,
    March 15, 1990: 50–55; Calvin Reid, "Picture This," *Publishers Weekly*, October 12,
    1990: 17–19, 22–23.
58 D. Aviva Rothschild, *Graphic Novels: A Bibliographic Guide to Book-Length Comics*
    (Westport, CT: Libraries Unlimited, 1995); Steve Weiner, *100 Graphic Novels for Public
    Libraries* (Northampton, MA: Kitchen Sink Press, 1996).
59 Ellis and Highsmith, "About Face," 40.
60 Amy Kiste Nyberg, "How Librarians Learned to Love the Graphic Novel," in *Graphic
    Novels and Comics in Libraries and Archives: Essays on Readers, Research, History and Cataloging*,
    ed. Robert G. Weiner (Jefferson, NC: McFarland, 2010), 26–40 (37).
61 Ibid., 38.
62 See, for example, Rocco Versaci, "How Comic Books Can Change the Way our
    Students See Literature: One Teacher's Perspective," *English Journal* 91, no. 2 (2001):
    61–67; Gretchen Schwarz, "Graphic Novels for Multiple Literacies," *Journal of
    Adolescent & Adult Literacy* 46 (2002): 262–65; Don Gallo and Stephen Weiner, "Bold
    Books for Innovative Teaching: Show, Don't Tell: Graphic Novels in the Classroom,"
    English Journal 94, no. 2 (2004): 114–17; Michael Cromer and Penney Clark, "Getting
    Graphic with the Past: Graphic Novels and the Teaching of History," *Theory and
    Research in Social Education* 35, no. 4 (2007): 574–91; J. B. Carter, ed., *Building Literacy
    Connections with Graphic Novels: Page by Page, Panel by Panel* (Urbana, IL: National Council
    of Teachers of English, 2007); Nancy E. Frey and Douglas B. Fisher, eds., *Teaching
    Visual Literacy: Using Comic Books, Graphic Novels, Anime, Cartoons, and More to Develop
    Comprehension and Thinking Skills* (Thousand Oaks, CA: Sage, 2008); and Stephen E.
    Tabachnick, *Teaching the Graphic Novel* (New York: Modern Language Association,
    2009).
63 Paul Gravett, *Graphic Novels: Everything You Need to Know* (New York: HarperCollins,
    2005), 8.
64 Hatfield, *Alternative Comics*, 162.
65 Daniel Raeburn, *Chris Ware* (New Haven: Yale University Press, 2004), 110.
66 Catherine Labio, "What's in a Name? The Academic Study of Comics and the
    'Graphic Novel,'" *Cinema Journal* 50, no. 3 (2011): 123–26 (126).

67 Bart Beaty, "Some Classics," in *The Cambridge Companion to the Graphic Novel*, ed. Stephen E. Tabachnick (Cambridge: Cambridge University Press, 2017), 175–91 (176).

68 Barry Kavanaugh, "The Alan Moore Interview," *Blather*, October 17, 2000: www .blather.net/projects/alan-moore-interview.

69 Eddie Campbell, "Graphic Novel Manifesto," *Comics Journal Message Board* (2005): lucaflect.com/handouts/eddie_campbell_manifesto.pdf.

70 Dirk Deppey, "The Eddie Campbell Interview," *Comics Journal* 273 (2006): 66–114 (83).

71 Critics like Hillary Chute attempted to resolve this terminological problem by adopting the generic term "graphic narrative," which was defined as "a book-length work in the medium of comics"—a definition that once again relies on commodity forms to establish a cultural distinction. Daniel Stein and Jan-Noël Thon thus conclude that "the development of graphic narrative has been, and continues to be, intricately tied to the physical media through which individual forms of graphic storytelling have emerged as prominent cultural artifacts and practices." Hillary Chute, "Comics as Literature? Reading Graphic Narrative," *PMLA* 123, no. 2 (2008): 452–65 (453); Daniel Stein and Jan-Noël Thon, "Introduction: From Comic Strips to Graphic Novels," in *From Comic Strips to Graphic Novels: Contributions to the Theory and History of Graphic Narrative*, ed. Daniel Stein and Jan-Noël Thon (Berlin: De Gruyter, 2013), 1–23 (7).

Section Four

ELECTRONIC PUBLISHING AND READING PRACTICES

Chapter 10

THE BOOK AND THE E-BOOK: FOOTNOTES, MARGINS, AND TYPOGRAPHY IN *THE BRIEF WONDROUS LIFE OF OSCAR WAO*

Bernhard Metz

What books essentially are is still an intriguing question, especially due to the rise of e-books, e-texts, and e-readers.[1] Electronic reading devices—like the Kindle and the iPad, computer monitors and screens, and the displays of handheld tablets and mobile phones—have redefined not only what reading is but also what books are and can be, as texts are increasingly written, distributed, and read on electronic media. What are the intersections, interactions, and reciprocal influences between both the analogue and the digital, between conventional and electronic writing, printing/publishing, and reading? How are books changed by this development, and how can "bookishness" be seen as combining both traditional print and electronic books?[2] To what extent is "bookishness" related to the materiality of written or printed books, to the form and format of books, to printed books as material things and tactile/sensual objects?[3] On what does their cultural and social status depend if e-books become more and more common? Do e-books still represent the end of the book as printed matter and material object, or do printed books still possess some degree of resistance and inalienability? Are electronic media the end or the future of reading?[4]

So far, these new electronic devices and reading practices have not fundamentally altered what could be considered to be a book. On the contrary, they also seem to support the old-fashioned attributes and values related to printed books and their specific distribution and reception.[5] It still seems to be a question not of printed versus electronic books but rather of how books and e-books are produced, distributed, and used: incautiously and carelessly or meticulously and carefully, paying tribute to the centuries-old traditions of fine print and typographic standards. It might be the case that typography, as a more or less ideal combination of an easy and comfortable-to-read layout that arranges graphic signs in a certain size and format (including the interplay between margin and text or between black and white), is essential for any symbol-carrying device and any printing/publishing process.[6] If so, then the most important reading instrument would be the page and likely also the double page as a display or synoptic carrier of typographic signs that constitute—in a series of pages—the written or printed book in the codex format.[7] This is again related to the material form of the book and its cultural and social status.

The question remains whether and how these qualities of bookishness can be transferred to digital formats. The typographic restrictions of e-readers, like unfortunate line and page breaks, the lack of color, the limited number and adjustability of typefaces, and the still poor resolution, clearly influence the way they can be used for reading, which also influences their cultural prestige, as the meticulous line breaks, page breaks, and the entire dual page display of the printed book cannot easily be transferred to e-readers—or at least not to electronic standards like Kindle's MOBI file format or other current e-book formats. New digital reading devices thus change texts by reducing them aesthetically, and they install and establish new reading habits and possibilities that are different from the codex book format, as they often depend instead on an infinite scroll that, in turn, might also influence the way printed books are used.[8] On the other hand, e-books in their various types and versions as "enriched e-books" might also be considered realizations of concepts and ideas that were less effectively applied in the printed book, such as books that use links or reference systems to jump between notes and textual expansions.

This chapter describes and analyzes the questions posed earlier in relation to the theme of popular culture and the mixture of highbrow and lowbrow elements in Junot Díaz's novel *The Brief Wondrous Life of Oscar Wao* (from now on abbreviated as *Wao*). It particularly focuses on the question of what books are and whether and how the cultural status of e-books is related to their typographic realization and the absence of the material properties of printed books. It seems that "bookishness" cannot be obtained without the more or less conventional and traditional material aspects of printed books. It also seems that the cultural status and prestige of printed books cannot completely be transferred to e-books and the digital realm, or at least not now. This is likely related to the material form of printed books, such as their typographic realization, including the double-page display in codex formats as well as aspects like printing quality, resolution, immobility, and weight. There also remains the question of whether literary works like *Wao*, which was written in

English and translated into many languages, need the medium of the printed book to be conceived as globally read world literature.[9] It seems that international or global literary success is correlated with the publication of a title in print or only as an e-book, as critical and economic success are connected more likely to printed books than to electronic formats.[10]

Wao was published in 2007 by Riverhead, a Penguin USA imprint, which is currently the world's largest publisher of literary books. The novel was designed by Stephanie Huntwork, currently the art director at Clarkson Potter (Penguin Random House), using Adobe Caslon as a body typeface and ITC Biblon and Gotham Rounded for titles and display typography. On the title page and between the three main parts of the novel black-and-white or grayish graphic elements refer to comic book superheroes, popular culture, and science fiction. But Diáz's novel also contains 34 footnotes, which are central to the narrative and provide a scientific or at least learned undertone, which makes *Wao* part of the important literary tradition of the footnote novel. Most of these material properties, including the typographic design of the printed edition of *Wao*, are almost completely lost in the officially available e-book versions, resulting in the impossibility of understanding the novel as it was originally published, including its different narrative layers and voices. Nevertheless, these e-books are more widely sold and presumably also more widely read than the printed book, at least in its first hardcover edition (there are several softcover editions but so far no illustrated "deluxe edition" or something comparable).

That the e-book versions differ so extremely from the original printed version marks a historic change. Amazon's Kindle was introduced in 2007, and the e-book of *Wao* came out in 2009, two years after the publication of the hardcover book and therefore also after the softcover book and other book licenses. This is not much of a surprise, as footnote novels—defined as annotated fiction that includes footnotes (endnotes and marginal notes are different)—often lose their notes in reprints and reeditions. The careless transition from print to e-book is nevertheless of importance, particularly since Díaz's one and only novel (so far) is largely considered to be among the most important novels of the early twenty-first century.[11]

The novel narrates the life of Hypatía Belicia Cabral-de León, mother of two children, Lola and Oscar, who lives and suffers under Rafael Trujillo's dictatorship in the Dominican Republic before emigrating to New Jersey. However, it mainly focuses on the story of Oscar, or rather that of his *fukú* (curse), which is connected to Trujillo and his violence. This *fukú* eventually leads to Oscar's execution in a sugarcane field, as had long been common practice in the disappearance of opposition members under Trujillo. It also weighs heavily on Oscar's family, as his mother Belicia is nearly beaten to death and later dies painfully of cancer; his grandfather Abelard Cabral is tortured to death; and his sister Lola lives unhappily. However, this *fukú* refers not only to the fate of an individual or a family but also to the past and future of colonial and postcolonial oppression. The novel thus begins as follows: "They say it came first from Africa, carried in the screams of the enslaved. [...] *Fukú americanus*, or more colloquially, fukú—generally a curse or a doom of some kind; specifically the Curse and the Doom of the New World."[12] An apotropaic effect is also attributed to the narration, which is described as a remedy or counter-magic to banish the *fukú*: "Even now as I write these words I wonder if this book ain't a zafa of sorts. My very own counterspell."[13]

The first-person narrator is Yunior de Las Casas, a sexually hyperactive, handsome college student, who shares a room to Oscar's sister for some time and becomes engaged to his sister Lola, who also narrates chapter I, 2.[14] Yunior is the author of 34 footnotes, but he is also an unreliable narrator, which he admits at times.[15] In addition, he often cannot tell and explain everything. He tries hard to investigate the truth, and his footnotes are stuffed with historical details, but in the end this mission is impossible due to the fact that much of the Dominican Republic's violent history can no longer be reconstructed, since documents and records were destroyed and only blank pages and silence remain.[16] The novel is therefore about giving voice and memory back to the disappeared and nameless, as exemplified by Oscar's family as well as many others. And one of the main purposes of the footnotes is this investigation into truth, which attempts to provide historical and memorial justice for the marginalized and oppressed victims.[17]

This goal explains Yunior's diverse narrative approaches and interruptions, as he illuminates the history of Oscar's family and that of his country of origin from different perspectives and positions. Some of the footnotes try to fill in gaps and supply nonofficial aspects in order to not let anything be forgotten.[18] In the end, however, Yunior is aware that his story (or counterstory) cannot clear up and explain everything. Indeed, he must engage the reader to fill in the gaps. Thus, he only partly explains the reasons that might have turned Trujillo against Oscar's grandfather and in the end led to the persecution and curse-laden destruction of the entire family, which even extended beyond the Dominican Republic and into the grandchildren's generation. The reader is asked to cooperate with this effort:

> So which was it? you ask. An accident, a conspiracy, or a fukú? The only answer I can give you is the least satisfying: you'll have to decide for yourself. What's certain is that nothing's certain. We are trawling in silences here. Trujillo and Company didn't leave a paper trail—they didn't share their German contemporaries' lust for documentation. And it's not like the fukú itself would leave

a memoir or anything. The remaining Cabrals ain't much help, either; on all matters related to Abelard's imprisonment and to the subsequent destruction of the clan there is within the family a silence that stands monument to the generations, that sphinxes all attempts at narrative reconstruction. A whisper here and there but nothing more. Which is to say if you're looking for a full story, I don't have it. Oscar searched for it too, in his last days, and it's not certain whether he found it either.[19]

While Yunior cannot provide the full story, he suggests that other intra-fictional readers and figures might still get to see and comment on the manuscript before it goes to print.[20] He is also a faithful editor, as he has Oscar's notebooks at his disposal[21] and does not change the family history that was retold to him out of respect for this oral tradition,[22] as in footnote 22: "There are other beginnings certainly, better ones, to be sure—if you ask me I would have started when the Spaniards 'discovered' the New World—or when the U.S. invaded Santo Domingo in 1916—but if this was the opening that the de Leóns chose for themselves, then who am I to question their historiography?"[23] Díaz thus succeeds in writing a new history of the Dominican Republic, the Caribbean, the Dominican diaspora in the United States, and the intersections of these cultures based on a fragmentary description of a single family's fate.

Oscar has a weakness for anime, comics, and fantasy. The epigraph is correctly identified as coming from the Marvel comic book series *Fantastic Four*: "Of what import are brief, nameless lives to … **Galactus**??"[24] Galactus does not seem to play a significant role for Oscar, but this is the only occurrence of bold type in the novel, and he is also mentioned in a footnote that links the character to the relationship between dictators and writers:

> What is it with Dictators and Writers, anyway? Since before the infamous Caesar–Ovid war they've had beef. Like the Fantastic Four and Galactus, like the X-Men and the Brotherhood of Evil Mutants, like the Teen Titans and Deathstroke, Foreman and Ali, Morrison and Crouch, Sammy and Sergio, they seemed destined to be eternally linked in the Halls of Battle. Rushdie claims that tyrants and scribblers are natural antagonists, but I think that's too simple; it lets writers off pretty easy. Dictators, in my opinion, just know competition when they see it. Same with writers. *Like, after all, recognizes like.*[25]

Many of the annotations reflect the editor's personal bias in this manner, and one could thus say that both the epigraph and the Galactus allusion are editorial ingredients; accordingly, the last footnote of the novel is also a commentary on the means of the comic book, as Oscar's farewell to his mother, his sister, and all the women he has ever loved is annotated via messages: "'No matter how far you travel ... to whatever reaches of this limitless universe ... you will never be ... ALONE!' (The Watcher, *Fantastic Four* #13 May 1963)."[26]

While one side of the cultural frame of reference encompasses lowbrow culture, the footnotes retain their learned or scientific connotation and thus occupy the place of reliable knowledge. But this is just another way of writing serious, valid, and academically situated scholarship in order to fill it with content that is rarely found there, such as when Trujillo is compared to Sauron from J. R. R. Tolkien's *The Lord of the Rings* (1954–1955) or to a character from *The Twilight Zone* (1959–1964).[27] This ends in an amalgamation of pop culture references (to fantasy, science fiction, comics, kung fu movies, and TV series) and the modes of expression of scholarly and scientific writing. The way Oscar Wilde functions as the name of the main character and the title of the novel provides another example for this mixture and hybridity, as Oscar's nickname, Oscar Wao, results from his friends mistaking his Doctor Who costume at Halloween for an Oscar Wilde costume.

The comparison between Trujillo and comic book supervillains, as seen in footnote 11, becomes a deliberate transgression of boundaries or an ahistorical and unacademic form of connection and comparison.[28] Díaz commented on this, among other aspects, in an interview:

> I think there was sort of this constant poetic in the book where I was trying to imprint the real with the crazy, or contaminate the real with all this nerdy narrative, and then the same way just doing the exact reverse—contaminating the nerdy with the painfully real. There's nothing that historians and serious academics dislike more than someone drawing a flip analogy with a figure from popular culture, but by the same token what's fascinating is how much fanboys and consumers of what we'll call "nerd culture" resist any infection by the real. [...] In some ways I'm equally committed to both cultures, but I'm an artist, so try to avoid being too much of a partisan.[29]

But highbrow culture is also present in the novel, as the page following the Galactus epigraph includes an extended passage from Nobel Prize–winner Derek Walcott's "The Schooner Flight" (1979). Likewise, many of the footnotes, even if they sometimes use coarse language,[30] are stuffed with erudition and objectively referenced historic and cultural knowledge, which is associated with notes and annotations. It is ultimately also that of the author, who reportedly read or reread a considerable amount of historical specialist literature as well as pop-cultural material in preparation for writing the novel.[31]

Concerning its materiality, the book can be described as follows: the book block measures 209 × 137 × 23 millimeters, is relatively compact, and weighs 490 grams with the dust jacket (470 g without), which is rather light for a 340-page hardcover, as the paper is comparatively thin and not very opaque. The color white is conspicuously predominant everywhere, including the dust jacket, the cover, and the spine. The dust jacket of the original edition has little to do with the design of the contents or the cover, and it is the only place where any indication of the genre of the book is found, since it specifies that it is "a novel."[32] It also uses Gotham Rounded in 66/90pt for the title and intertitles and Helvetica in 11/17pt for the blurbs, short synopsis, and author's biography.[33] As already mentioned, the book uses Adobe Caslon in 9/10pt for the main text and the footnotes, which allows for a maximum of 45 lines per page, with no page consisting only of notes.[34] Initials and inter-titles or chapter headings were set in ITC Biblon in 14/20pt, but also gray and not black, thus with lower contrast. In addition, there are four graphic elements, also in gray, on the title page and before the intermediate chapters. These graphic elements thematize Oscar's nerdiness, such as his preference for lowbrow culture, but they normally do not appear in descriptions of the novel and in the critical literature.[35] If mentioned, they are merely considered ornamental.[36] There is italicization for emphasis in the text but also the use of capital letters. The binding is also white, with silver as a decorative color evoking the impression of purity and integrity. The endpaper is white as well, although any other color would have been possible. In contrast to this, there is on the main page of the dust jacket, and on the front inside flap, the cutout of a head with curly hair, which can well be imagined as a representation of Oscar de León. The red color might be associated with blood, as his life ends by being shot in a sugarcane field, and the color spray of this silhouette drips down from the back of the head, indicating the exit of a bullet or the wing of a bird or angel. The novel thus carries the death of the title character already on its dust jacket.[37]

The typographic layout of *Wao* is something the e-book versions simply cannot display, or at least not in the currently available editions and formats. The typographic design of the Kindle version, offered by Riverhead/Penguin, is totally insufficient and does not contain any of the footnotes; instead, they have simply been placed after the main text as endnotes. The only other offi-cially available e-book version by Faber & Faber does not contain footnotes either, but it did at least transform them into endnotes that are included at the end of each chapter. The artwork is also missing from these versions, and the nuances of the different typefaces are lost. Using other forms of display, such as the Kindle for Mac, one has at least a two-page view on a computer or tablet, but there is still no satisfying representation of the footnotes. None of the current e-readers have problems with displaying PDFs, but the pages and fonts are so small that one cannot read them easily.

Regarding the initial reflections concerning the relationship of the e-book and the printed book, it is time to discuss three ways in which e-books alter the material properties and, therefore, also the cultural status of literary texts. The first is seriously problematic, the second less so, and the third should be resolved in the next few years.

1: *Literary texts lose their typographic elements, layout, and specific look when they are read on e-readers, as the typography cannot be experienced as in the printed book (as we are used to it and as it is needed for easy and comfortable reading).* This is particularly significant with regard to footnote literature, as there is currently no e-book that contains footnotes or marginal notes. This is possible when PDF files are displayed, and there are other alternatives, such as fixed-layout e-books based on Apple's iBooks Author or the app studios offered by QuarkXPress and Adobe's Digital Publishing Suite; however, this is not the norm with popular publishers and a relatively recent phenomenon in specialist academic literature. The original PDF preprint file of Díaz's novel never entered into the book trade.

If they are not completely omitted, notes in the e-book are normally realized as endnotes, but this makes them lose their specific simultaneity in reading. An electronic endnote is easier to find (and easier to leave out), but footnotes and marginal notes realize a special structure between main text and note text, which is precisely not one of linear sequence. Realizing footnotes or marginal notes as pop-up notes doesn't solve the problem either. What e-books normally do not contain are font size differences between both; these, too, are constitutive of foot and marginal note systems, as the hierarchy between note text and main text is usually made clear through indentation, if at all, or through special markings, such as italics. In all these cases, footnote and marginal note text in particular (whether in literary texts or not) are impossible to transpose into the currently popular e-book formats.[38]

Another problem, which is particularly noticeable in footnote literature, is that e-books are normally not designed with two fonts. This means that it is difficult to incorporate notational systems that distinguish between main text and notes not only through different font sizes but also through different fonts. In addition, there is always the restriction to only one or a few fonts. For example, the Kindle 1 only had one font, while the Kindle 3 had three— or rather it had one font in three styles (Caecilia, Caecilia Condensed, and Caecilia Sans Serif). In contrast, the most widely used e-reader on the market when Díaz's novel was published, the Sony-PRS-T1, had seven internal fonts

(Original, Amasis, Frutiger, Palatino, Really No 2, Univers, and Verdana; older Sony e-readers had only one internal serif font). Technically, it is possible to install OpenType (OTF) or TrueType (TTF) fonts or to replace the existing ones, but e-books with Digital Rights Management (DRM) can then normally no longer be displayed. With regard to Díaz's novel, there is currently no e-book reader or other mobile device that would have the original Adobe Caslon font.

2: *Literary texts lose their proportions when they are read on e-readers, as they cannot be experienced as they are displayed in the printed book (as we are used to it and as it is needed for easy and comfortable reading).* There are no such great differences here; indeed, it has to be admitted that even the proportions of printed books sometimes get properly confused by footnotes and marginal notes or do not align themselves with what is required. *Wao* is also an example of this. However, certain e-readers have different margins from the outset, in conjunction with pockets and transport systems too. It also makes a difference how large a device is and whether its physical margins are already white (as with the Kindle 1, some iPads, or many Sony readers) or a different color.

Equal margins certainly reduce the ability to conceive of e-book publications as unique and as a specific typographic interpretation—a unity of content and form—of a given text. The Sony PRS-T1 offered the possibility to adjust the bars on the screen individually; however, due to the small screen it was then no longer possible to recognize much and to read easily. This was also not possible with the early Kindle readers. With the iPad, the PDF display is not stable but is oriented toward image content in order to display the image as large as possible (as a result, each page has a different size, the margins disappear completely, and the graphics are displayed incorrectly).

The format remains problematic. Even the largest tablets cannot display a double-page spread easily. However, literature—and footnote literature in particular—needs the contrast between central and marginal text elements, between center and periphery, as it strongly depends on the margins of the text. This is where 6-inch readers almost inevitably fail, no matter how high their resolution may be (even in the future). So far even the largest iPads or tablet computers offer less than a 13-inch display (12.9 inches). In 2017 Sony introduced the DPT-RP1, which is currently the lightest and slimmest e-reader on the market (weighing 349 g and measuring only 5.9 mm) as well as the one with the largest display (13.3 inches or 1,650 × 2,200 pixels), but in 2020 it was announced that this e-reader would be discontinued, and it's unlikely that there will be a successor.

3: *Literary texts lose their specific colors and high-resolution contrasts when they are read on e-readers, as they cannot be experienced as in the printed book (as we are used to it and as it is needed for easy and comfortable reading).* Here it makes a difference which e-reader one uses. The Kindle 3 had a resolution of less than 170 ppi with 6 inches (600 × 800 pixels with 167 ppi), and the 6-inch Amazon Kindle Paperwhite, available since 2012, already offered a resolution of 212 ppi. Current Kindle e-readers, like the Voyage, Paperwhite, or Oasis, offer a 6-inch display and 1,072 × 1,448 pixel resolution (300 ppi), 16-level grayscale, and LED frontlighting (the Kindle Oasis also comes with a 7-inch display and 1,680 × 1,264 pixels). But e-Ink devices cannot currently display color. The color displays of computers and tablets have quite high resolutions with the introduction of the Apple Retina Display with approximately 220 ppi, the Amazon Kindle Fire 8.9 inch with approximately 254 ppi, or even more the Google Nexus 10-inch tablet with approximately 300 ppi. However, there are still limitations when reading outdoors or with glare from bright sunlight through glass surfaces. The problem of having to accept limitations in either color or contrast could in theory be solved, but it is particularly significant for footnote literature, as smaller font sizes require higher resolutions for ease in reading.

In sum, one might say that literature with notes push e-books to their limits and show their restrictions more than anything else. These technological constraints force the text into a narrative linearity that the former printed book editions left far behind. This is, however, primarily a format problem, both in terms of technical storage formats and output display sizes. Apart from that, the switch to electronic reading can still be conceived as a loss because even with sufficiently large text carriers and good resolutions there is still an optical, olfactory, and haptic sameness that takes away the special character and appearance of each individual book, since every e-book feels and reads the same on the same e-reader. It always smells the same and, depending on the typographic setting, has more or less the same format, font, and margins.[39]

   There are also gains, and they consist not only in quick findability, comfort, or convenience. When footnotes are organized electronically, as any (dynamic) link shows, they are often easier and safer to find than by manual searching. What is lost is a visible hierarchy and relationship that presents the main text and the notes at a glance; instead, there is linear rather than simultaneous reading, which obscures any oversight of the text as a whole. In the case of *Wao*, like most works of footnote literature, this clearly does not work, as the dual page display and the synoptic interplay between the main text and the note text is essential to the reading experience. It is therefore evident that many of the criteria central to bookishness are difficult to realize with current electronic reading devices,[40] and the advent of new devices needs to be investigated against the background of the history of the book and printing. Rather than putting traditional printed books and new electronic media such as e-readers, tablets, and smartphones in opposition to one another, one should ask instead about their similarities. Thus far mobility and/or immobility have not been examined in relation to the printed book in its historical breadth from 1450 to the present. By examining the function of (im)mobility in print and electronic culture, ongoing debates about the bookishness of e-books are possible.[41] Until now electronic reading devices that left behind the characteristic double page of the codex and presented content only in one never-ending column were based on elements developed over centuries in the printed book.[42] From this perspective, printed books and e-books are not antagonists but rather have much in common.

While the rise of e-books has clearly changed how books are read and perceived, current e-books are still adapting the printed book instead of doing something completely new. Sometimes they simply consist of images of books printed long ago, such as the e-books offered by Google Books in "the world's largest e-bookstore," as they call it, which are mostly PDF files of already existing printed books. The technological possibilities of today's e-readers with their enormous computing capacities—at least compared to the typesetting devices used a couple of years ago—led to the assumption that this is only a question of time.[43] There will be better layouts and different reading experiences. There will be better types of enhanced e-books that offer narrative possibilities the printed book never contained. It is therefore intriguing to question not only what books are but also how they will develop in the future, although the physical object to remain—the material object loaded with social status and prestige—is likely to be the printed book.

Notes

1 Proclamations about the end of reading or the end of the book (in the way we have known it since Gutenberg) can be traced back at least to the late nineteenth century. See, for example, Octave Uzanne, "La fin des livres," in *Contes pour les bibliophiles* (Paris: May & Motteroz, 1895), 123–45.

2 For more of the notion of "bookishness," see George Steiner, "The End of Bookishness?," *Times Literary Supplement*, July 8, 1988: 754; Jessica Pressman, "The Aesthetic of Bookishness in Twenty-First-Century Literature," *Michigan Quarterly Review* 48, no. 4 (2009): 465–82; Kiene Brillenburg Wurth, Kári Driscoll, and Jessica Pressman, eds., *Book Presence in a Digital Age* (London: Bloomsbury, 2018); Christoph Benjamin Schulz, "Digital Bookishness and Digitally Enhanced Publications Against the Backdrop of Apologies of the Book during the Advent of Digital Media," in *Refresh the Book: On the Hybrid Nature of the Book in the Age of Electronic Publishing*, ed. Viola

Hildebrand-Schat, Katarzyna Bazarnik, and Christoph Benjamin Schulz (Leiden: Brill, 2021), 133–61; Bernhard Metz, "Bookishness and the Body of the Book/the Body of the Reader: On the Usages of Books," in *Refresh the Book: On the Hybrid Nature of the Book in the Age of Electronic Publishing*, ed. Viola Hildebrand-Schat, Katarzyna Bazarnik, and Christoph Benjamin Schulz (Leiden: Brill, 2021), 288–307.

3 Günter Karl Bose expands upon the future of the book, referring to "senseware" and the materiality, immobility, and specific weight of printed books. See Günter Karl Bose, *Das Ende einer Last: Die Befreiung von den Büchern* (Göttingen: Wallstein, 2013), 53–55.

4 Cf. some of the modern classics in media studies, for example Marshall McLuhan, *The Gutenberg Galaxy: The Making of Typographic Man* (Toronto: University of Toronto Press, 1962); Norbert Bolz, *Am Ende der Gutenberg Galaxis: Die neuen Kommunikationsverhältnisse* (Munich: Fink, 1993); Sven Birkerts, *The Gutenberg Elegies: The Fate of Reading in an Electronic Age* (Boston: Faber & Faber, 1994); Jeff Gomez, *Print Is Dead: Books in Our Digital Age* (Basingstoke: Palgrave Macmillan, 2007).

5 As Johanna Drucker points out, "Books of the future depend very much on how we meet the challenge to understand what a book is and has been." Johanna Drucker, "The Virtual Codex from Page Space to E-space," in *A Companion to Digital Literary Studies*, ed. Susan Schreibman and Ray Siemens (Oxford: Blackwell, 2007), 216–32 (231).

6 Calligrapher and typographer Robert Bringhurst emphasizes the importance of margins: "Perhaps fifty per cent of the character and integrity of a printed page lies in its letterforms. Much of the other fifty per cent resides in its margins." This is clearly something every typographer would claim. Robert Bringhurst, *The Elements of Typographic Style, Version 2.5* (Point Roberts, WA: Hartley & Marks, 2002), 165.

7 So far only one of the most expensive mobile phones on the market, Samsung's high-resolution double screen Galaxy Fold (2019), might give the impression of a codex book that the reader is able to hold and use like a printed book. The double-page display of the printed book (at least in most of the historic and normally practiced typographic layouts) as ensemble of two mirroring columns of text is described by Bringhurst as an "interlocking relationship of symmetry and asymmetry, and of balanced and contrasted shape and size": "The lefthand page is a mirror image of the right, but no mirror image runs the other way. The two-page spread is symmetrical horizontally—the direction in which the pages turn, either backward of forward, as the reader consults the book—but it is asymmetrical vertically—the direction in which the page stays put while the reader's eye repeatedly works its way in one direction: down." Bringhurst, *Elements*, 164.

8 This implies a switch back to the scroll format, as Christian Vandendorpe suggests: "Ironically then, the foreseeable future of the book could well be in an electronic recreation of the original scroll format, a development that would make digital reading as 'natural' as reading a codex is today." This can also be seen to be problematic as a sign of less status attributed to text typeset in long columns, as Bringhurst points out: "The very long and very narrow columns of newspapers and magazines [...] have come to suggest disposable prose and quick, unthoughtful reading. A little more width not only gives the text more presence; it implies that it might be worth savoring, quoting and reading again." Christian Vandendorpe, "Reading on Screen: The New Media Sphere," in *A Companion to Digital Literary Studies*, ed. Susan Schreibman and Ray Siemens (Oxford: Blackwell, 2007), 203–15 (214); Bringhurst, *Elements*, 163.

9 Rebecca Walkowitz makes this point with regard to Díaz's second story collection as a combined experience of reading world literature in printed books, claiming that "works such as Junot Díaz's *This Is How You Lose Her*, Paul Kingsnorth's *The Wake*, and Ali Smith's *How to Be Both* emphasize not only the experience of pages but also the experience of world languages on those pages: their font, shape, arrangement, spelling, punctuation; their absence; their presence; their appearance next to images; and their appearance as images produced through the arrangement of letters. These works utilize the resources of paper to reflect on the history and future of world literature." This "world literature" is nevertheless written in English and mainly published by major American or British editors. Rebecca Walkowitz, "The Persistence of Books," *World Literature Today*, May 2016: 26–9 (27).

10 E. L. James's *Fifty Shades of Grey* (2011) was a global book phenomenon, but it started as fan fiction based on Stephenie Meyer's *Twilight* (2005), and it was initially published as an e-book and print-on-demand publication on the internet. It only became internationally noticed and successful after it was published as a printed book by a major publisher. See Peter Osnos, "How 'Fifty Shades of Grey' Dominated Publishing," *The Atlantic*, August 28, 2012, https://www.theatlantic.com/entertainment/archive/2012/08/how-fifty-shades-of-grey-dominated-publishing/261653.

11 *Wao* was awarded the Pulitzer Prize for Fiction, the National Book Critics Circle Award for Best Novel, and many other prestigious awards. It was also hailed by *Time* and *New York Magazine* as the best novel of 2007 and was selected by U.S. critics in a poll organized by the BBC "as the best novel of the 21st century to date." See Alison Flood, "*The Brief Wondrous Life of Oscar Wao* Declared 21st Century's Best Novel So Far," *The Guardian*, January 20, 2015, https://www.theguardian.com/books/2015/jan/20/brief-wondrous-life-of-oscar-wao-novel-21st-century-best-junot-Díaz.

12 Junot Díaz, *The Brief Wondrous Life of Oscar Wao* (New York: Riverhead, 2007), 1.

13 Ibid., 7.

14 Ibid., 51–75. Yunior also narrates most of the stories in Junot Díaz's collections *Drown* (New York: Riverhead, 1996) and *This Is How You Lose Her* (New York: Riverhead, 2012).

15 See, for example, Ibid., 132n17.

16 See, for example, Ibid., 97n11. See also Christopher González, *Reading Junot Díaz* (Pittsburgh: Pittsburgh University Press, 2015), 64–65.

17 It also indicates the failure of memory and of the remembrance of all the victims, as Morán González argues: "Even as the main narrative strives to restore the stories and memories of lives lost due to state violence, the footnotes of *Oscar Wao* underscore the limits of such projects when they too are informed by the cultural legacies of state violence. Underscoring the problem of narrative authority in diasporic fiction's reconstructive historical projects, particularly those seeking to address the enduring impact of dictatorial regimes upon diasporic communities, the footnotes of *The Brief Wondrous Life of Oscar Wao* indicate not only the highly provisional nature of fictional recreations of shattered communal histories, but also how the archival impulse behind such reconstructive efforts itself generates its own *páginas en blanco*, or epistemological voids created by the coloniality of power still operational throughout the Americas." Morán González, "Páginas en blanco, Footnotes, and the Authority of the Archive in Junot Díaz's *The Brief Wondrous Life of Oscar Wao*," *Symbolism: An International Annual of Critical Aesthetics* 15 (2015): 57–72 (58).

18 This echoes another novel, Patrick Chamoiseau's *Texaco* (1992), which Andréas Pfersmann has discussed as an example of a historical footnote novel of *contre-histoire* (counterhistory). According to Monica Hanna, *Texaco* played an important role concerning the use of footnotes in *Wao*: "Díaz has acknowledged his use of Chamoiseau's *Texaco* as a model for his footnotes, including during the question-and-answer period following a talk at the Hammer Museum in Los Angeles in March 2008." Andréas Pfersmann, *Séditions infrapaginales: Poétique historique de l'annotation littéraire (XVIIe-XXIe siècles)* (Geneva: Droz, 2011), 429–68; Monica Hanna, "'Reassembling the Fragments': Battling Historiographies, Caribbean Discourse, and Nerd Genres in Junot Díaz's *The Brief Wondrous Life of Oscar Wao*," *Callalo* 33, no. 2 (2010): 498–520 (517).

19 Díaz, *Wao*, 243.

20 This is suggested in an annotation to Club El Hollywood: "A favorite hangout of Trujillo's, my mother tells me when the manuscript is almost complete." Ibid., 114n15.

21 This is revealed in the last chapter: "You'll understand when you read my conclusions. (It's the cure to what ails us, he scribbled in the margins. The Cosmo DNA.)" Ibid., 333.

22 Jennifer Harford Vargas combines the footnotes with oral history storytelling:

> As marginalia, the footnotes appear below the main narrative, visually resembling forms of undercover storytelling. That is, the footnotes structurally mimic the ways subaltern agents navigate repressive power by communicating information indirectly, secretly, and below the radar of the repressive regime's gaze. The spatiality of the notational apparatus in *The Brief Wondrous Life of Oscar Wao* reproduces the asides and interruptions that constitute oral narrative, for oral narratives do not strictly follow one single line of thought, often veering into associative connections and tangential narratives that build an interrelated network of details and sub-stories around the primary story.

> Jennifer Harford Vargas, "Dictating a Zafa: The Power of Narrative Form in Junot Díaz's *The Brief Wondrous Life of Oscar Wao*," *MELUS* 39, no. 3 (2014): 8–30 (20).

23 Díaz, *Wao*, 211.

24 Ibid., ix. The source is cited as "*Fantastic Four* Stan Lee and Jack Kirby (Vol. 1, No. 49, April 1966)."

25 Ibid., 97n11.

26 Ibid., 321n34. Here it is again a supervillain who speaks, although this time it is not Galactus but rather The Watcher, who fails to prevent the Silver Surfer from bringing the world-devourer Galactus to Earth.

27 Ibid., 2n1, 5n3, 23, 156, 173, 192, 217, 269.

28 As Monica Hanna explains,

> "Genre," in the minds of Oscar and eventually Yunior, is a more flexible narrative form than traditional historical narrative. It allows for the exploration of alternative worlds that don't comply with traditional realism. In this way, it is uniquely capable of addressing the reality of the diasporic subject. The text consistently asserts that "authoritative" history is not an adequate explanation. The heart of the text lies, rather, in the sections that employ fantasy. During a talk at the Hammer Museum in Los Angeles in March 2008, Junot Díaz noted the relationship between the immigrant experience and the act of reading science fiction;

he said that both require the learning of new codes. In this sense, the text's form requires the reader to enter into the position of the immigrant or outsider.

Hanna, "Reassembling the Fragments," 515.

29 Díaz also mentions popular culture as a condition for being able to write about certain phenomena:

> The book makes it clear that the Galactus figure, the Darkseid figure, and the Sauron figure are interchangeably dictatorships and also even the mindset found in the United States. I think that in some ways it's asking a question of the reader more than anything, because in some ways, depending on how you answer that question, it really decides whether you're Galactus or not. In some ways I think there are plenty of people who are members of the kind of brief and nameless lives, and yet they don't give a shit about other nameless lives. Some people are incredibly powerful and still think that. And so what's interesting about this is that the person that that's being asked in the comic book is the very character whom the narrator, Yunior, takes on as his narrative alter-ego, his nom de plume. Galactus is actually asking the question in the Fantastic Four comic book to the Watcher, to the person that's telling stories. So I always think that that's a question to the reader but also a question to writers in general. This was the only way that the book could begin. I was like, Yeah, I like that. Okay."

John Zuarino, "An Interview with Junot Díaz," *Bookslut*, September 2007, http://www.bookslut.com/features/2007_09_011634.php

30 See footnote 9: "Although not essential to our tale, per se, Balaguer is essential to the Dominican one, so therefore we must mention him, even though I'd rather piss in his face." Díaz, *Wao*, 90.

31 As Díaz stated in an interview,

> Obviously, a lot of research went into this. Where did you start? Is it from memory or did you have to do some footwork in Santo Domingo and Patterson? I've heard it said from other writers before that research is more fun than the actual writing. But I'm kind of this crazy history person—I basically knew all the texts that I needed to read for this book, so what ended up happening was I would just find myself going, "Hey that reminds me of something on page 70 of this one monograph I have, so let me go dig through and find the reference." And so it was kind of like, I had this enormous amount of historical knowledge in my head and nothing to do with it. It was more like reverse engineering. The book sort of gave me the map work and the instructions of what to cherry pick. Most of the research that I did was on a lot of the nerdy stuff. I had mostly packed that, more than any of the history, into my head pretty tight. But there was a bunch of nerdy stuff I had to go back into. I had to actually watch some of the movies that the narrator and the protagonist were obsessed with, so I found myself watching a lot of crazy movies.

Zuarino, "An Interview with Junot Díaz."

32 The genre indication "novel" is not printed anywhere else inside the book, although the imprint page includes the usual disclaimer: "This is a work of fiction. Names, characters, places, and incidents either are the product of the author's imagination

or are used fictitiously, and any resemblance to actual persons, living or dead, businesses, companies, events, or locales is entirely coincidental." Díaz, *Wao*, vi.

33 Gotham Rounded was a new typeface in 2007, the year *Wao* was published.

34 For the minimum number of lines, see pages 22, 97, and 155.

35 In her study on meta-testimonial narratives in *Wao*, Lauren Jean Gantz refers to an email conversation she had with Stephanie Huntwork regarding Díaz's involvement in the graphic design of the novel:

> [T]he artwork from the original 2007 Riverhead edition of *Oscar Wao* [...] has to date received minimal attention from scholars. Along with the cover art, this edition features a frontispiece (a rocket ship or missile) and three plates (an atom, a clenched fist, and a biohazard symbol), which divide the novel's sections. Through correspondence with Stephanie Huntwork, the book designer for this edition, I discovered that the frontispiece and plates were not part of the original book design—instead, "Junot specifically requested that imagery." While *Oscar Wao*'s investment in comic book culture is reason enough to scrutinize the novel's artwork, Díaz's deliberate selection of these images indicates that they should be read along with the written narrative. These four images recall Oscar's meticulously collected archive of comic books, stored in Yunior's basement refrigerators. In reading these images, we should therefore approach them as we would any graphic narrative.

Lauren Jean Gantz, "'Nothing Ever Ends': Archives of Written and Graphic Testimony in *The Brief Wondrous Life of Oscar Wao*," *ariel: A Review of International English Literature* 46, no. 4 (2015): 123–53 (136–37).

36 What they are, too, of course. To my knowledge, Bradley Reina is the only critic so far who has interpreted these elements as a subtext to otherwise not explicitly stated or easily overread aspects of the book:

> As a particularly good example of the direction of digital print, *The Brief Wondrous Life of Oscar Wao* also shows how graphic elements have come to be used by book designers and sometimes authors to augment the meaning of a book. *Oscar Wao*'s large title page and section-title graphics draw the reader's attention to a historical context and significance that may otherwise fall behind in this reference-rich text—the overwhelming fear of nuclear annihilation that characterized Cold War life in the United States. At many points during this text, Oscar notes his fears of apocalypse, or his complementary fantasies of post-apocalyptic romantic heroics. Many of Oscar's science fiction points of reference are either symbolically or directly related to nuclear war, such as *Akira* and *Watchmen*. Yet, when considered among the other major themes and characteristics of the novel (say, the Dominican American slang and the science fiction/genre references, the detailed and personal histories of the Dominican dictatorship and US involvement in that history) Díaz's artful deployment of atomic apocalypse and the historical use of US atomic weaponry can get lost. As simple symbols, the image of a bomb on the title page (though no bombing occurs in the plot), of an atom for the first part title, and a biohazard symbol for the third and final part all work to hint at this point of historical reference. [...] Furthermore, the large circular images of the atom and the biohazard symbol also call to mind the clock that begins each chapter of *Watchmen*, which counted down to nuclear apocalypse. The atomic fears that

permeate *Watchmen* are part of the semantic weight of the graphic novel in *The Brief Wondrous Life of Oscar Wao*, but this point of reference is made more accessible by the echoes between graphic symbols and textual meanings. The presence of these symbols serves to cement the importance of this otherwise less apparent context. Atomic symbolism and imagery are conspicuously prevalent at the more significant points in the Cabral family's tragic history.

Bradley Reina, "Digital Print in the Material World: Paratext in Service of Narrative," *Word & Image* 35, no. 1 (2019): 76–88 (84).

37 The dust cover was designed by Rodrigo Corral, who worked this way: "For the cover of *The Brief Wondrous Life of Oscar Wao*, he built off of author Junot Diaz's descriptions of Oscar, his obsessions with comic books, and incredible imagination, as well as the violence portrayed in the book. In order to avoid something more morbid that might keep readers away, Corral chose the now infamous paint-splattered side-silhouette of Oscar—a fanciful but unsettling depiction, because of its eerie synonymy with blood." Lauren Jean Gantz also associates the cover artwork with the comic book superhero Thor:

> Oscar is profiled in a deep crimson silhouette. The image's lines are spattered and runny, evoking graffiti or blood. Coming out of Oscar's head, the shape of a wing emerges, mimicking the trajectory of the bullet that ultimately kills him. It also suggests the winged helmet of Mercury—the Roman god of travelers and messengers, a trickster figure that guides souls to the land of the dead. Such an association is fitting for Oscar given his status as transnational diasporic subject, his voluminous writings, and his efforts to unearth long-buried family secrets. Likewise, it could reference Icarus' wax wings, foreshadowing Oscar's romantic over-reachings and untimely demise. However, Corral's commentary on the image indicates that, like the frontispiece and plates, it can be read as a reference to comic books. [...] I contend that this image might be a reference to the Marvel superhero Thor, created by Stan Lee and Jack Kirby in 1962. Aside from his mythical hammer Mjolnir, Thor's trademark is his winged helmet.

"The Brief and Wondrous Career of Rodrigo Corral," *Ooligan Press*, August 10, 2010, https://ooliganpress.pdx.edu/the-brief-and-wondrous-career-of-rodrigo-corral; Gantz, "'Nothing Ever Ends,'" 142–43.

38 Alexandra Horowitz has asked whether the e-book will kill the footnote, and as far as current formats are concerned, it seems so—or rather, even more so than with graphics, which e-books are generally good at incorporating, notes are something that currently don't work at all. It is not always clear why. It would be possible to include them at least as image files. Alexandra Horowitz, "De-Noted," *The New York Times*, October 9, 2011, BR39.

39 This is, of course, comparable to serial publications, which give all content the same typographical setting, layout, format, and so on.

40 Bringhurst expresses this typographic or bibliographic point of view: "A book is a flexible mirror of the mind and the body. Its overall size and proportions, the color and texture of the paper, the sound it makes as the pages turn, and the smell of the paper, adhesive and ink, all blend with the size and form and placement of the type

to reveal a little about the world in which it was made. If the book appears to be only a paper machine, produced at their own convenience by other machines, only machines will want to read it." Not to mention any electronic machine. Bringhurst, *Elements*, 143.

41 The outline for this approach can be found in Metz, "Bookishness and the Body of the Book," 296–304.

42 Drucker has described how e-books often simulate printed books:

> [M]ost of what is understood by a "book" in the design of "electronic books" is fairly literal simulation. For instance, a kitsch-y imitation of page drape from a central gutter is one of the striking signs of book-ness. This serves absolutely no purpose, like preserving a coachman's seat on a motorized vehicle. Icons that imitate paper clips or book marks allow the reader to place milestones within a large electronic document. As in paper formats, these serve not only for navigational purposes, but also to call attention to sections within a larger argument. The substitution of pages and volume with a slider that indicates the depth or place within the whole reinforces our necessity to understand information in a gestalt, rather than piecemeal. Finally, the reader's urge to annotate, to write into the text with responsive immediacy, has also been accommodated in electronic book designs as note taking capabilities for producing e-marginalia have been introduced. The many "drawbacks" of traditional books are, therefore, supposedly to be overcome by introducing into electronic ones features like a progress gauge, bookmarks, spaces for annotation, search capabilities, navigation, and comments by the author. Such a list is easily ridiculed, since every feature described is already fully present in a traditional codex and, in fact, the very difficulty resides in simulating in another medium the efficient functionalities that exist in the traditional form. [...] But other features of electronic space do add functionality—live links and real-time or frequent refresh of information. These are materially unique in digital media; even if linking merely extends the traditional reference function of bibliography or footnotes, it does so in a manner that is radically distinct in electronic space by the immediacy with which a surrogate can be called. Links either retrieve material or take the reader to that material, they don't just indicate a reference route. And the idea of rapid refresh materially changes the encoded information that constitutes a text in any state. Date stamping and annotating the history of editions will be increasingly important aspects of the information electronic documents bear with them. The capacity to materially alter electronic surrogates, customizing actual artifacts, or, at the very least, specifying particular relations among them, presents compelling and unique opportunities.

Drucker, "Virtual Codex," 219.

43 See Priya Ganapati, "Why E-books Look So Ugly," *Wired*, May 18, 2009, http://www.wired.com/gadgetlab/2009/05/e-book-design.

Chapter 11

E-BOOK COLLECTIONS AS AN OPPORTUNITY TO RECOVER UNPUBLISHED OR FORGOTTEN TEXTS

Laura Hatry

A decade ago e-book publishing was expected to completely reshape the book market, but the apocalypse for printed books that had been predicted did not occur; in fact, I will argue that there is a niche function in which e-books tend to foster rather than to harm the book market as a whole. This chapter aims at demonstrating that, if used judiciously, the e-book can be of great help to scholars and that it offers advantages to publishing houses in disseminating classic texts in e-book format. In particular, I will focus on the unprecedented opportunity to recover unpublished texts or those that were last published decades ago and that have since been set aside because publication was not economically feasible. Given that the cost for editions in e-book format is exceptionally low compared to their physical counterpart, publishers now have the unique opportunity to make decisions driven only by cultural and literary considerations. An example of this new approach is Clásicos Hispánicos, an e-book publishing venture created by a university scholar and a group of students in Madrid, of which I was a member, who undertook the project after realizing that there were no serious digital publishers for classical works of Hispanic literature in comprehensive scholarly editions.

As a result of this project, it was suddenly possible to recover material that had been neglected or even forgotten for cultural, political, or economic reasons. Another important aspect of such editions is that they are produced under the aegis of recognized academics, who annotate the texts with footnotes that explain them in historical, literary, and linguistic terms. Such an approach may help to undo the cultural stigma currently attached to electronic collections, which are widely considered ipso facto to be of poor quality and without scholarly rigor. It shows, on the contrary, that the era of digital editions need not imply a loss of quality but can even constitute an improvement for scholars and devotees of literature alike, who also benefit from a lower price structure. After reviewing a few general issues related to the e-book as a basis for discussion of the rivalry between e-books and print books, I will return to Clásicos Hispánicos and lay out some different examples of relevant texts and explain their utility. The aforementioned stigma might initially seem paradoxical, as why should they have a lower cultural status if they are simply digitized versions of printed books? I will explain how their status is related to the digital format by discussing the significance of editorial scholarship as well as their visual aspects, such as layout, choice of typography, and cover art, which are all reduced to the configuration of the e-reader. As Mark Simonson argues, "The variations in typeface influence the personality of the book," and "[s]ticking to one font is much like having the same actor play all the different parts."[1] And it is not just the text but also its container where variation and character are, in a way, suppressed and limited to a trite, plastic regularity. I believe this tendency, especially as far as the insides of the e-book are concerned, is likely to change as the market matures, much like what we saw with the internet when we compare the design of web pages in its early years to today.

Despite the fact that in 2010 "the book world was seized by collective panic over the uncertain future of print,"[2] we have witnessed a surprising reluctance to shift from the print to the electronic book market, even though it seems as if, in all other aspects, people tend to embrace the newer technology more enthusiastically. A *New York Times* article from September 2015 sums up this reluctance of the book-buying public:

> As readers migrated to new digital devices, e-book sales soared, up 1,260 percent between 2008 and 2010, alarming booksellers that watched consumers use their stores to find titles they would later buy online. Print sales dwindled, bookstores struggled to stay open, and publishers and authors feared that cheaper e-books would cannibalize their business. But the digital apocalypse never arrived, or at least not on schedule. While analysts once predicted that e-books would overtake print by 2015, digital sales have instead slowed sharply, [and even decreased] by 10 percent in the first five months of 2015, according to the Association of American Publishers.[3]

This tendency has only continued since 2015. In 2016, a survey "attributed the increase in print sales to children's fiction and to younger generations preferring physical books to e-readers,"[4] and in 2018, "e-book sales have slipped by 3.9 percent so far this year, according to data from the Association of American Publishers, while hardback and paperback book sales grew by 6.2 percent and 2.2 percent, respectively. During the first nine months of 2018, hardback and paperback sales generated nearly $4 billion combined; comparatively, e-books only raked in $770.9 million."[5] Some of the first e-book users have returned to print, and many have turned into what is known as hybrid readers—that is, readers who use both print and electronic editions. There are various reasons that could account for this reluctance, some of which I will discuss later, but one can easily imagine that, as a general matter, many of us—myself included—understand this special feeling when it comes to books and technology because we cherish the smell, the touch, and the toning of its pages with age, and we think that a text presented on some kind of electronic device is just not the same. Another development worth mentioning is that e-books used to be cheaper, but there has been a shift in the market, and physical copies of books are now often less expensive than their electronic counterpart "thanks to changes in Amazon's deal with publishers."[6]

When the e-book emerged, a change was before us that many likened to the transition from illuminated manuscripts that were made "copy-by-copy by monks, took months to decades to produce, and were kept by the church and kings. [...] When printed books first appeared, far from being embraced as a technological and cultural breakthrough, they were viewed with suspicion and derision, seen as inferior or even dangerous, compared with illuminated manuscripts."[7] This raises an interesting question—namely, "What is a book?" Alexis Madrigal argues that the answer to this question seems "pretty obvious" in the Kindle era:

> There is an implicit argument in the act of digitizing a book and removing it from the shelf: a book *is* its text. A book is a unique string of words, as good as its bits. But printed books are also objects, manufactured objects, owned objects, objects that have been marked by pencils and time and coffee cups and the oils from our skin [emphasis in original].[8]

On the basis of this fragment, Barbara Bordalejo concludes that Madrigal is wrong for two reasons. First, he is the victim of what Kirschenbaum calls the haptic fallacy—that is, the belief that e-books (or any kind of electronic object) are immaterial simply because we cannot touch them. Bordalejo insists that an e-book is an object, as the "buttons or sections of the screen that allow for switching pages or alterations of font size are just as material as pages or traditional codex covers."[9] I have to disagree with her on this point because the "object" she identifies is in no way related to the specific text that it projects, whereas the book as an object is individually designed for each particular text or edition of a text, and Madrigal's definition of object is clearly linked to stability or to change with reference only to a particular incarnation of a text over the passage of time, change of ownership, and so on. Furthermore, the fact that an object can be lost, damaged, destroyed, given away as a gift, or sold distinguishes it from any otherwise similar example: in principle, it is up to its owner what happens with it. In the case of an object that merely renders a text readable, the object itself might indeed succumb to the same fate as a book, but there are multiple possibilities in which the text, which is undeniably the more important part of our discussion, may be corrupted or distorted by other people.

In particular, there have been cases in which books were deleted from their owners' tablets, or in which control of the comments that users make or which sections they underline has been commandeered by external forces, which might be seen as an infringement of personal freedom through a surveillance policy that reaches even into the very private act of reading a book. And even though one has purchased an e-book, copyright issues often prevent one from lending it, selling it, or even opening it on different devices. Another potentially problematic issue is that of automatic updates to a text. While it can be extremely useful regarding the correction of typos or updating antiquated textbooks, if it transpires without an option to approve or reject the update, one is always obliged to have the newest edition on one's device, which might interfere with various aspects of historical and textual research or even prevent readers of the same text from communicating accurately because they are using different incarnations of it.

Bordalejo's second argument against Madrigal contends that she is wrong about the reduction of the book to "the text," because if that were true, poetry would become a mere concatenation of words, without verses and stanzas. Here, she seems to forget that electronic devices are perfectly able to maintain these distinctions and configurations, and the statement that a text is a unique string of words does not imply that it cannot have any line breaks or page breaks.

Now, even though I don't consider the foregoing to be a sufficient counterargument on behalf of Madrigal's statement, it does raise a very important aspect of e-book editing, which finally brings us to Clásicos Hispánicos. As I mentioned at the beginning, this publishing venture was founded precisely to redress the lack of rigorous electronic publications of classical Hispanic texts. One of its main concerns was that these publications should never be the string of words Bordalejo imagines; rather, they should always maintain the structure of the original printed text. While this does not present any particular difficulties in the case of prose texts, the coding becomes much more complicated in the case of poetry and drama. As is well-known, e-books are electronic documents with some content, mostly textual, ordered in a sequential way that can be read using different kinds of devices, such as e-readers, tablets, smartphones, or computers. Its most significant format is called EPUB (short for "electronic publication"), and it is based on web technologies, mainly

HTML, CSS, and XML. All editions published by Clásicos Hispánicos take special care in making sure that all texts are correctly coded and that line breaks and relevant formatting are maintained from the original text. During the workflow regular expressions convert the structure from Word and plain text into XHTML, and since 2015 the master format of the text is XML-TEI (a very helpful markup language for corpora and editorial projects). The texts are then converted into EPUB and MOBI files with XSLT, allowing most of the public to read the e-books on any device. They are all published under Creative Commons Licenses without any digital rights management schemes, which are various access control technologies that are used to restrict the usage and copying of documents. This means that if someone buys an e-book, they can share it, use it, and create derived products from it as long as the source is properly cited, but they cannot resell the product or use it for commercial purposes.

The original idea to create the publishing house, apart from the aforementioned factors, arose when the director of the collection—Pablo Jauralde Pou—received a call in 2012 from one of the main Spanish publishers of classical texts, saying that several thousands of volumes of one of his editions were going to be destroyed because the storage costs were already exceeding potential profits. This wasn't an edition of some minor text; rather, it was Francisco de Quevedo's *El Buscón* (1626)—one of the most important texts by one of the three major authors of the Spanish Golden Age of Literature. This edition was recovered in the Clásicos Hispánicos catalog, and it led to the examination of what kinds of publishers there were in the panorama of Spanish digital publishing. It turned out that most of the e-books of Spanish classical literature found on the internet were done by two types of projects. First, there are the big players like *Project Gutenberg* and *Amazon Classics*, which are very well known and have published thousands of texts, mostly free of charge. The second are groups of readers who create them in an amateur way to serve perceived textual needs. They do not constitute a formal group (like a company, research project, foundation, etc.), and the contributors publish the texts anonymously (including texts whose copyrights have not yet expired). This situation might lead to the public perception that almost any classical text is already available as an e-book for free. Of a printed classical edition, one would expect a scholar to have taken into account the previous edition of record, modernized it (or explained why it hasn't been modernized), explained its provenance through history, corrected typos and other similar problems, and, finally, annotated it to clarify linguistic, historical, or literary issues that may be relevant to a reader. Such conscientious philological work is what is normally expected and what constitutes the quality of an edition. However, the two main publishers of classical e-books that I just mentioned do not include such textual apparatus, as they normally do not even work with qualified scholars, and when you read a specific edition, you won't find information regarding the editorial process of preparing the text. As far as Gutenberg is concerned, they actually don't prepare new editions as such but rather digitize already existing ones.

This emphasis on philological quality is one of the crucial differences between Clásicos Hispánicos and the other currently existing publishers. In particular, it means that each text is prepared by an expert scholar in the field and that each edition contains a brief introduction to the text, an exact description of the basis on which the edition was prepared, and the text itself, along with explanatory footnotes. When the publisher receives the text, it is scrutinized not only orthographically but also philologically in order to verify that the contributor has actually followed the steps he has described in preparing the edition. Since 2012 more than 80 titles have been published, from medieval classics to well-known works of the twentieth century, encompassing very different genres (poetry, theater, theater in verse, novels, short stories, dialogues, and essays), and many more are currently being prepared by scholars from around the world. As far as what is eligible for publication, copyright laws are, of course, always respected, which means that only works whose author has died 70 years ago or longer may be considered.

This brings us to the question of unpublished or forgotten texts that have been published in the collection and the different varieties of works that have been or could be published in general by any digital collection with a similar approach. "Unpublished" might seem like a word with an easy definition, but if you include such notions as "new" or "unknown," then it isn't that simple. It is nevertheless possible to identify some basic categories and guidelines, and what follows is a set of possible situations that I will pair with examples from the collection to show how the collection made it possible to discover or recover the texts in question[10]:

1) If we try to be completely rigorous, unpublished texts are only those that have never been published in any form. An example would be Francisco de Enciso's *Diálogo de las verdades* (Dialogue of Truths), a manuscript from the sixteenth century that was basically unknown until it was discovered in 2007 in the repositories of the Spanish National Library.

2) Another category of unpublished texts would be those that from the time of their composition or first publication have never again been edited or were transmitted only orally in one way or another. Among these, we include texts such as dramatic or comedic works that were performed on stage and subsequently forgotten, though they might have been published in the corresponding period. An example of such a text is *El arca*

de Noé o El mundo al revés (Noah's Ark or The World Upside-Down, 1606), a comedy that is very likely to be the work of Lope de Vega, but which, since there is no definitive proof of authorship, was published under the hypothesis rather than the assertion that he is its author. Here, again, there is only one textual source that has been preserved—a manuscript that was discovered in the Institute of Theatre in Barcelona. Whether or not Lope de Vega should prove to be its author, its similarity to his other works still constitutes a valuable contemporary resource for comparative scholarly research on his comedies, and it brings to light a document that would otherwise be fairly well hidden.

3) There is another interesting group of texts that we could consider unpublished because of the manner in which they were previously published, such as those published only as part of a larger edition, and these editions offer the opportunity to focus on a certain aspect of the work in question. For example, Antonio Enríquez Gómez's long poem *El pasajero* (The Passenger, 1642) had never been published independently but always within a larger group of poems or works. Separate publication opens up the possibility of a different approach to the work, somewhat similar to an academic research article but including the entire text and scholarly apparatus, which in turn may lead to even more exhaustive study and/or easier access for the general public or nonspecialist academics. And there is also the reverse option—that is, restoring a work that was published separately without the other works in whose company it originally appeared, thereby recovering the totality of the work. An example is *Las obras de Boscán y Garcilaso trasladadas en materias cristianas y religiosas* (The Works of Boscán and Garcilaso Related to Christian and Religious Matters, 1575), which was originally published in four volumes, although Garcilaso's contribution was later extracted and circulated more widely. This edition thus reassembles and combines the four volumes in the way they were originally conceived for publication.

4) Another type of unpublished work is one that collects works previously published separately to form a new text, such as *Tres utopías ilustradas* (Three Illustrated Utopias), which consists of three eighteenth-century short stories that were published in installments in three different periodicals over a period of three years. By uniting all of the installments of each story and publishing them together, the reader is presented with a text that would be almost impossible to access given that they would have to find and possibly even purchase the various issues of each periodical. The Clásicos Hispánicos edition also offers the advantage of a preliminary study that relates these works with one another and gives a historical overview of the periodicals in which they originally appeared.

5) The designation "unpublished" is also used to describe old texts that were published during the period of their composition but have never been published since and are therefore accessible only in those antique editions. For example, Juan de Robles's *Diálogo entre sacerdotes* (Dialogue between Priests, 1642) was only published once until it was republished by Clásicos Hispánicos based on an edition held at the Library of the University of Sevilla.

6) A final group of texts includes those that, rather than being unpublished, were forgotten or set aside, which can happen for multiple reasons. Here I would like to mention two different examples. First, Peruvian feminist Mercedes Cabello de Carbonera's *La novela moderna: Estudio filosófico* (The Modern Novel: A Philosophical Study, 1882) was republished twice in 1948, about 50 years after its original composition, and again in 1975, after which it was inexplicably forgotten until 2002, when it was republished in Peru by Cavia Cobaya Editores. This might sound like an example of a book that was published not such a long time ago and is therefore not especially difficult to acquire, but for an average reader (i.e., somebody with no strong connections to the antiquarian book trade, where somebody might know somebody who knows somebody who has a copy), finding a copy was virtually impossible before the new edition by Clásicos Hispánicos was issued. As a second example, let me mention Lope de Vega's *Huerto deshecho* (Wasted Garden, 1653), which used to be unnecessarily difficult to obtain, especially in view of the fact that, unlike the putative Lope de Vega title mentioned earlier, this is one of the most interesting works by the Spanish playwright and therefore in regular demand among both scholars and ordinary readers.

All of these examples show how electronic publishing has the potential to rescue texts that have been cast into oblivion due to economic considerations that have nothing to do with their literary or even historical importance, as the commercial imperatives of the publishing industry have simply rendered them unpublishable. The fact that e-publishing implies a far lower monetary investment in its products, given that there are no fixed costs or that these costs are significantly lower, reopens the question of what it means for a book to *deserve* to be published. Apart from providing access to books that were either unobtainable or very difficult or costly to obtain, they are also significantly cheaper than normal editions. To put it in numeric terms, until 2020 around 80 percent of the e-books in the Clásicos Hispánicos catalog cost €4.49. The remaining e-books, including very long texts, medieval texts, and, especially, difficult editions, were offered at a slightly higher price of €6.49. This price level was unlikely to be an obstacle for almost any reader, and it still represented in aggregate a fair compensation for the work of the various people involved in their production. As of 2020, however, all of these editions are completely free of charge and available to be downloaded from the Clásicos Hispánicos' website.

One might be of the opinion that literature should be above the capitalistic dictates of the market, but of course we know that publishers often have no realistic option in the matter when it comes down to a choice between serving the humanistic values to which they have devoted their lives and the very real possibility of bankruptcy should their principles result in choices that fail to be ratified by their clientele. That is why I think that we, as literary academics, should embrace the opportunity that e-publishing provides as an option within the general ecosystem of literary, historical, and scholarly publishing, especially during a time of crisis in the humanities.[11]

Even if one were to take into account only their economic potential, however, the republication of out-of-print texts in e-book format could be exploited to generate meaningful returns. According to a 2012 study, for example, researchers calculated the

> total estimate of the consumer and producer surplus that could be created by digitizing all the world's 2.7 million out-of-print titles and making them available as eBooks by multiplying the 2.7 million and then scaling these estimates to account for the fact that 41.3% of our titles (40.8% to 41.8% with a 25% confidence interval) have propensity scores above 0.2, the cutoff point for obtaining reliable estimates in our data. After doing this, we find that bringing the world's 2.7 million out-of-print titles back into print as eBooks could create $740 million in revenue in the first year after publication, $460 million of which would accrue to the publishers and authors. In addition, we estimate that making these books available would create $860 million in consumer surplus in the first year after publication.[12]

Another strong potential of the e-book is in niches where books need to be updated so regularly or are so expensive that digitizing widens their reach, lowers their costs, and significantly reduces energy consumption and waste, such as with textbooks.[13] Pearson, the world's largest educational books publisher, announced in 2019 that "it would adopt a 'digital first' strategy" in the future, taking the e-book one step further in our age of subscriptions, where renting textbooks will become the default option.[14]

Ultimately, e-publishing represents not only an opportunity to salvage texts that would otherwise have fallen victim to the competitive market but also a way of democratizing access to material and knowledge, as these texts are no longer limited to sophisticated and wealthy aficionados, who can afford the rare and expensive volumes in which they are embodied, or to academics, whose privilege or special knowledge allows them to read the original manuscripts in national or university libraries; rather, they are now available to the general public, who can acquire them through open systems like the internet at a reasonable price. I would venture to suggest that this reduction of the gap between the privileged and those who are interested but could never previously afford the books in question is comparable to the historical moment when the industrialization of print that I mentioned at the outset first unlocked the vaults of knowledge and opened it up to the people.

Notes

1 Qtd. in Priya Ganapati, "Why E-Books Look So Ugly," *Wired*, May 18, 2009, https://www.wired.com/2009/05/e-book-design.

2 Alexandra Alter, "The Plot Twist: E-Book Sales Slip, and Print Is Far From Dead," *New York Times*, September 22, 2014, http://www.nytimes.com/2015/09/23/business/media/the-plot-twist-e-book-sales-slip-and-print-is-far-from-dead.html?_r=0.

3 Ibid.

4 Sian Cain, "Ebook Sales Continue to Fall as Younger Generations Drive Appetite for Print," *The Guardian*, March 14, 2017, https://www.theguardian.com/books/2017/mar/14/ebook-sales-continue-to-fall-nielsen-survey-uk-book-sales.

5 Joshua Fruhlinger, "Are E-Books Finally Over? The Publishing Industry Unexpectedly Tilts Back to Print," *The Observer*, March 11, 2018, https://observer.com/2018/11/ebook-sales-decline-independent-bookstores.

6 Zoe Wood, "Paperback Fighter: Sales of Physical Books Now Outperform Digital Titles," *The Guardian*, March 17, 2017, https://www.theguardian.com/books/2017/mar/17/paperback-books-sales-outperform-digital-titles-amazon-ebooks.

7 John W. Warren, "Innovation and the Future of e-Books," *The International Journal of the Book* 6, no. 1 (2009): 83–93 (83).

8 Alexis Madrigal, "What Is a Book?" *The Atlantic*, May 7, 2014, http://www.theatlantic.com/technology/archive/2014/05/what-is-a-book/361876.

9 Barbara Bordalejo, "Che cos' è un libro?," *Institutum Romanum Finlandiae*, March 25, 2015, https://core.ac.uk/display/251210109.

10 I would like to thank Pablo Jauralde Pou for his input on this classification for Clásicos Hispánicos, which has also been outlined briefly on his blog.

11 Another aspect of e-books that might benefit literary academics, mainly in digital humanities, is that they could provide a great way of reading our own corpora. For example, the research group for computational literary genre stylistics (CLiGS) at the University of Würzburg is already converting their texts into EPUBs in order to read the corpus.

12 Michael D. Smith, Rahul Telang, and Yi Zhang, "Analysis of the Potential Market for Out-of-Print eBooks," *Social Science Research Network*, August 4, 2012, https://ssrn.com/abstract=2141422.

13 E-books also have another valuable but rarely mentioned advantage over print books given that in conjunction with other innovations they can be made accessible to all, such as with TactoBook, "a computer-based system that translates fast

and automatically any eBook into Braille." See Ramiro Velázquez, Enrique Preza, and Hermes Hernández, "Making eBooks Accessible to Blind Braille Readers," *2008 IEEE International Workshop on Haptic Audio Visual Environments and Games Proceedings* (Piscataway, NJ: Institute of Electrical and Electronics Engineers, 2008), 25–29.

14 The downside to this new model might reside in the quality of the learning: "Digital text, digital work, is often engaged with at a lower level of attention. By moving everything online, it's going to become even more decontextualized. Overall, I think there's going to be less deeper learning going on." Brian Barrett, "The Radical Transformation of the Textbook," *Wired*, April 8, 2019, https://www.wired.com/story/digital-textbooks-radical-transformation.

Chapter 12

HOW MUCH DOES THE SYMBOLIC CAPITAL OF BOOKS COST? OPERATIONALIZING THE PRESTIGE OF BOOKS IN THE DIGITAL AGE

Pasqualina Sorrentino and Massimo Salgaro

In their introduction to this volume, Anthony Enns and Bernhard Metz seek to show how the material aspects of literary texts, such as the cover, binding, and typography, reflect or even determine their cultural status. Recent experimental research seems to confirm this hypothesis by showing that book covers play an important role in the first evaluation of a text.[1] As the history of the literary field shows, the prestige of books is the product of the tension between two competing capitals: symbolic and economic capital.[2] Their relation is inversely proportional, as symbolic capital increases the more economic capital decreases, and vice versa. When books are heavily promoted and consequently popular, for example, they are often perceived as trivial, whereas rare and complex books are more often perceived as serious and therefore prestigious. If, as the editors of the present volume seem to propose, the prestige of books changes depending on variations in book production, then the digital era should have a huge impact on this value.

The rise of the internet is only one aspect of the digital revolution—a technological transformation that has had, and continues to have, a profound impact on the publishing industry. The transformation that has affected the publishing industry at every level of the value chain is reflected by the growth of online retailers like Amazon as well as the much-publicized debates about digital books among literary critics. As Adriaan van der Weel puts it, thanks to digitality we are experiencing the third reading revolution of humanity, which is changing the "Order of the Book" that formed the basis of Western culture.[3] Van der Weel uses Walter Benjamin's concept of "aura" to describe the authority of the print book and the loss of the "aura" to describe the fate of the book in the digital age. This loss is precisely a loss of prestige, which is directly linked to the materiality of books. The digital text threatens the existence of the print book in several ways. First of all, digital copies of a text cannot be distinguished from the original.[4] Secondly, in a digital world, a literary text always runs the risk of "digital obsolescence" (i.e., the deterioration of its materiality).[5] Thirdly, for van der Weel, "all digital texts, regardless of provenance or quality, look identical," as they lack the typical paratextual qualities of print books given by typography, cover, size, color, and so on.[6] Following the inverse relationship between symbolic and economic capital, we can argue that in contemporary society the print book stands for symbolic capital and the e-book stands for economic capital. The prestige of books thus depends on their materiality, as the distinction between "highbrow" and "lowbrow" actually has less to do with their content than with their physical form.[7]

So far this is merely a stimulating sociocultural theory. We sought to test this theory using empirical research in order to assess whether, for actual readers, paperbound texts have more or less social prestige than digital texts. Based on van der Weel's assertion that digital texts lack an "aura," we hypothesized that contemporary readers would evaluate the social prestige of literary texts higher when they were presented in a print version compared to a digital version on an e-reader. To do this we needed to operationalize the concept of "social prestige," which involved creating a questionnaire to assess how readers perceive print books and e-books.

Operationalizing the Prestige of Books

To operationalize a concept means to translate it "from theoretical language to empirical language."[8] This is the definition we find in the *Dictionary of the Social Sciences*:

> The process of operationalization consists in transforming an abstract concept of theory into an empirical, testable subject of research. Proper operationalization is therefore crucial to obtaining relevant results and is especially at stake in the formulation of research methods. In sociological research based on surveys or interviews, for example, the construction of the line of questioning is essential.[9]

In other words, operationalization is the transformation of a concept into empirically observable properties. We start with a clear definition of this term, as we are conscious that quantitative approaches are not common in the humanities, where theoretical (qualitative) approaches prevail. There is also a gap between quantitative and qualitative approaches in the social sciences. For these scholars, the legitimization of quantitative or qualitative analysis depends upon the research object.[10]

"Operationalization" is not limited to the social sciences. Although "it must be the ugliest word"[11] he had ever used, it became fashionable in the humanities since its introduction by Franco Moretti. It has recently reached the field of literary theory as well thanks to Moretti's pithy definition:

> [Operationalization] describes the process whereby concepts are transformed into a series of operations—which, in turn, allow all manner of phenomena to be measured. Operationalizing means building a bridge from concept to measurement, and then to the world. In our case, [the bridge] is from the concepts of literary theory to some form of quantification and then to literary texts.[12]

Moretti is aware that "measurement is a challenge to literary theory,"[13] but he nevertheless sees the potentiality of this process in the current context of digital humanities and "distant reading":

> Digital humanities may not yet have changed the territory of the literary historian, or the reading of individual texts; but operationalizing has certainly changed, and radicalized, our relationship to concepts: it has raised our expectations, by turning concepts into magic spells that can call into being a whole world of empirical data; and it has sharpened our skepticism, because if the data revolt against the creator, then the concept is really in trouble. A theory-driven, data-rich research programme has become imaginable, bent on testing, and, when needed, falsifying the received knowledge of literary study. Of this enterprise, operationalization will be the central ingredient.[14]

What follows is a description of the operationalization of the concept of social prestige in the context not of digital humanities, as was done by Moretti, but of digital reading.

The Literary Evaluation Model: Moving from Theory to Practice

Social prestige refers to another crucial concept in literary studies—namely, literary evaluation—as it is the result of an evaluative process to which a subject or group submits a cultural object. We found the best definition for the attribution of literary value in the studies of two German scholars: Renate von Heydebrand and Simone Winko. According to von Heydebrand and Winko, the evaluation of a literary text has to take into account both social and individual aspects. The authors elaborated a model that helps to evaluate literature in a pluralistic way, since it includes social functions related to literature and abandons the notion of literary quality as an intrinsic characteristic of the text. The authors argued that the concept of value implies "a complex social act by which a subject attributes value to an object [e.g., a book], in a concrete situation and on the basis of a certain standard of value and certain categorizing assumptions."[15] In other words, von Heydebrand and Winko describe how a combination of numerous individual (micro-level) operations, which may have altogether different aims, results in the (macro-level) phenomenon of canon creation. The micro-level consists of a great diversity of actions, such as an author's choice of literary allusions, a reader's choice of one novel over another, an anthologist's inclusion or exclusion of a writer, a critic's comparison of several contemporary books, a professor's selection of works for a course syllabus, a student's choice of courses, and a journalist's memorial survey of an author. All of these actions involve value judgments regarding literary texts, although the judgments are made by individuals in a variety of roles and groups within the "system of literature." Following the thesis of von Heydebrand and Winko, a literary text is not intrinsically valuable; rather, it only acquires an attributive value in relation to standards of value. For cultivated readers, for example, a "good" book should be "complex" or "rhetorically elaborated" to meet their expectations, while for less sophisticated readers, a "good" book can be a "suspenseful" love story or detective novel. As von Heydebrand and Winko point out, "Literary evaluation is by no means limited by professional judgment on literary texts," as different groups of readers can employ different standards of value.[16]

The evaluative process might be elicited by aesthetic, educational, and economic factors, since the assessment of literary quality is regulated by norms that are influenced by both the economic sphere and the cultural sphere. While the former aims at maximizing profits according to the law of supply and demand, the latter regulates "the possible gains in terms of knowledge, action orientation, gratification, prestige."[17] Their model focuses on two distinct forms of literary evaluation: explicit verbal utterances and nonlinguistic acts of selection (e.g., buying one book instead of another). The standards of value are governed by four dimensions: formal values, content values, relational values, and reception values. While the first three take place on a social level, the fourth takes place on an individual level.

In our operationalization of the concept of social prestige, we focused on reception values, because the aim of our study was to test whether the genre of a literary text (prose vs. poetry) and the reading support through which it is presented (an antique book vs. an e-reader) might influence the attribution of literary quality among contemporary readers. Von Heydebrand

and Winko classified reception values in two areas: individual values and social values. The subdimension of individual values looks at the qualitative values of literary texts with regard to personal needs,[18] and it includes the following psychological assets: cognitive value (reflection and memorability), practical value (making sense and significance), and hedonistic value (pleasure and entertainment). The subdimension of social values considers the evaluation of literary texts in terms of economic value, which captures literary works as objects of the economic system, and prestige value, which represents symbolic capital and the boost in prestige among literature in general or within particular texts. We then reviewed the main studies investigating reading experiences in order to build a questionnaire that would fit our needs, and we adopted items from scales like the Poetry Reception Questionnaire,[19] the Experiencing Questionnaire,[20] the Foregrounding Questionnaire,[21] the Reading Experience Questionnaire,[22] and the Transportation Scale[23] to construct the three subscales to measure individual values. Those questionnaires have already been tested and validated in other studies, and items were chosen according to the definitions that von Heydebrand and Winko gave for each subscale. We did not find any models for measuring social values, so we designed our own items to operationalize them:

1) *Cognitive value*: This subscale recognizes the effects that a literary text might have on a reader in terms of the acquisition of knowledge.[24] This value includes cognitive engagement, which takes into account such phenomena as the ease of cognitive access and a strong cognitive focus. When individuals focus their cognitive resources on the narrative world, they experience a loss of time and a loss of self-awareness.[25] In order to operationalize this concept, we selected the following items from the abovementioned questionnaires:
   - "I think the text/poem introduces a new perspective."[26]
   - "The text/poem makes me look at things differently."[27]
   - "The text/poem makes me stop and think."[28]
   - "The subject of the text/poem concerns questions I have often thought about."[29]

2) *Practical value*: This subscale encompasses the scope of everyday actions, life, and ethics. A reader's absorption into a story or transportation into a narrative world may show the effects of the story on their real-world beliefs. We operationalized transportation into a narrative world as a distinct mental process—an integrative melding of attention, imagery, and feeling following the Reading Experience Questionnaire and the Transportation Scale. The following items were selected:

- "I felt that some aspects of the text/poem are important for my everyday life."[30]
- "This text/poem continued to influence my mood after I finished reading it."[31]
- "After reading this text/poem I felt refreshed, renewed, and revitalized."[32]
- "After reading this text/poem it was easy to concentrate again on other things."[33]

3) *Hedonistic value*: This subscale aims to measure the feelings or sensory perceptions triggered by literary language. Readers reflect on their reading experience to appreciate the beauty of a literary text and its emotional or intellectual impact. This subscale helps to explore the emotions that arise from an encounter with literary language. The following items were selected:
- "While reading the text/poem I noticed the language."[34]
- "The text/poem is fascinating."[35]
- "It is a worth reading this text/poem."[36]

4) *Economic value*: This subscale aims to measure the evaluation of the literary text as a product. The material format in which the text is presented plays a particularly important role in this subscale, such as when the text is a precious manuscript, an antique book, or an e-book. Since our focus was on the genre (prose vs. poetry) as well as the reading medium (antique book vs. e-book), we had to create one item that measured the economic value of prose and another that measured the economic value of poetry. Each of these items was presented with an answer scale of 1–5 (€200–€5,000):
- "A German book publisher paid 5,000 euros for the (printing/digital) rights to a Günter Grass anthology, while another publisher paid 200 euros for the rights to an Oswald Wiener anthology. How much did a German publisher pay for the rights to the anthology that contains the text you have just read?"
- "A German book publisher paid 5,000 euros for the (printing/digital) rights to an Erich Fried anthology, while another publisher paid 200 euros for the rights to a Friedrich Achleitner anthology. How much did a German publisher pay for the rights to the anthology that contains the poem you have just read?"

5) *Prestige value*: This subscale also reflects a text's capital, although in this case we are talking about symbolic rather than economic capital. More specifically, prestige value denotes the gain in prestige or social status that the handling of literature might bring to the actors (readers, editors, publishers, etc.). In a society in which literature is very

highly estimated, for example, the act of owning a book and the skill to talk about it competently might confer prestige to the owner.[37] To our knowledge, the prestige value of a literary text has never before been empirically investigated. Since no adequate questionnaire to measure it exists, we created a suitable one based on von Heydebrand and Winko's literary evaluation model. We then worked with Arthur Jacobs and Jana Lüdtke, two neuropsychologists at the Free University of Berlin, to translate this concept into an "operational" questionnaire to be submitted to readers.[38] Each item was presented with a five-point Likert scale ranging from –2 (completely disagree) to +2 (completely agree):

- "Do you think that this text/poem won a literary prize?"
- "Do you think that literary critics rated this text/poem as important?"
- "Do you think that this text/poem should be taught in school?"
- "Do you find this text/poem trivial?"

Table 12.1 Mean values and standard deviations for each subscale

	Independent Variables Genre *and* Medium			
	Story		*Poem*	
	Book	*E-Reader*	*Book*	*E-Reader*
Dependent Variables	Mean (SD)	Mean (SD)	Mean (SD)	Mean (SD)
Cognitive Value	2.89 (1.04)	2.74 (0.97)	2.59 (0.95)	2.56 (0.94)
Practical Value	3.10 (0.90)	3.25 (0.91)	3.50 (0.84)	3.51 (0.94)
Hedonistic Value	3.56 (0.89)	3.22 (1.07)	2.86 (1.03)	2.89 (1.05)
Economic Value	4.25 (1.52)	3.83 (1.68)	3.80 (1.67)	3.63 (1.54)
Prestige Value	3.12 (0.77)	3.04 (0.84)	2.63 (0.76)	2.97 (0.79)

The resulting questionnaire has already been successfully used in two experiments.[39] Each of our subjects (37 women and 22 men between the ages of 18 and 70) had to read 2 prose texts (1 on paper and 1 on screen) and 2 poems (also 1 on paper and 1 on screen) before completing the questionnaires we have just described. In each case, the order of the texts (including both the genres and the reading media) was randomized. Reliability analyses were then conducted to evaluate the subscales of the questionnaire, which were used to study the effects of both genre and medium. To do this, a 2 × 2 repeated measure ANOVA was carried out for each subscale, with genre (prose vs. poetry) and medium (book vs. e-reader) as the two independent variables. The mean values and standard deviations for the subscales from the questionnaire are reported in Table 12.1.

The results for cognitive value (story mean = 2.81; poem mean = 2.57), hedonistic value (story mean = 3.39; poem mean = 2.88), and prestige value (story mean = 3.08; poem mean = 2.82) indicated that the subjects rated the stories higher than the poems. On the practical value subscale, the subjects assigned higher values to the poems compared to the stories (story mean = 3.17; poem mean = 3.51). The economic value subscale revealed a significant effect for the medium alone, as the subjects assigned higher values to all texts presented in a book compared to those presented on an e-reader (book mean = 4.04; e-reader mean = 3.72). The prestige value subscale also revealed a significant interaction between genre and medium, as the subjects assigned higher values to stories presented in a book (book mean = 3.12; e-reader mean = 3.04) and to poems presented on an e-reader (book mean = 2.63; e-reader mean = 2.97).

Our experiment showed that economic value and prestige value are the most important indicators related to the literary value of a text in a paperbound or e-book format. The experiment thus explicitly operationalized the category of social prestige introduced by von Heydebrand and Winko. However, the results of these exploratory studies should not be overemphasized. Like other studies, they merely indicate that the print book still has an important position in our society and that e-books are not taking over.[40] The results of the last four years of research on the effects of digitization on reading behaviors conducted by the members of the Evolution of Reading in the Age of Digitisation (E-READ) research initiative have similarly shown that print continues to be the preferred reading medium for longer texts, especially when reading for deeper comprehension and memorization. The results of this research are summarized in the Stavanger Declaration Concerning the Future of Reading, which concludes that the transition from print to digital texts is not neutral and that there is reason for caution when introducing digital technologies to education.[41]

Notes

1 Arūnas Gudinavičius and Andrius Šuminas, "Choosing a Book by Its Cover: Analysis of a Reader's Choice," *Journal of Documentation* 74, no. 2 (2018): 430–46.
2 Pierre Bourdieu, *The Rules of Art: Genesis and Structure of the Literary Field*, trans. Susan Emanuel (Stanford: Stanford University Press, 1995).
3 Adriaan van der Weel, *Changing Our Textual Minds: Towards a Digital Order of Knowledge* (Manchester: Manchester University Press, 2011), 2.
4 Ibid., 181–82.
5 Ibid., 181.
6 Ibid., 186.
7 Ellen Gruber Garvey, "Ambivalent Advertising: Books, Prestige, and the Circulation of Publicity," in *A History of the Book in America*, ed. David D. Hall, 5 vols. (Chapel Hill: University of North Carolina Press, 2000–2010), 4: 171.

8 Piergiorgio Corbetta, *Metodologia e Tecniche della Ricerca Sociale* (Bologna: Il Mulino, 2014), 89.

9 "Operationalization," in *Dictionary of the Social Sciences*, ed. Craig Calhoun (Oxford: Oxford University Press, 2002), https://www.oxfordreference.com/view/10.1093/acref/9780195123715.001.0001/acref-9780195123715-e-1200?rskey=INdJ7W&result=1200.

10 Corbetta, *Metodologia*, 70.

11 Franco Moretti, "Operationalizing," *New Left Review* 84 (2013): 103–19 (103).

12 Franco Moretti, "'Operationalizing': Or, the Function of Measurement in Modern Literary Theory," *Pamphlet of the Stanford Literary Lab*, December 2013, https://litlab.stanford.edu/LiteraryLabPamphlet6.pdf.

13 Moretti, "Operationalizing," 113.

14 Ibid., 119.

15 Renate von Heydebrand and Simone Winko, "The Qualities of Literatures: A Concept of Literary Evaluation in Pluralistic Societies," in *The Quality of Literature: Linguistic Studies in Literary Evaluation*, ed. Willie van Peer (Amsterdam: John Benjamins, 2008), 223–39 (226).

16 Ibid., 225.

17 Ibid., 230.

18 Renate von Heydebrand and Simone Winko, *Einführung in die Wertung von Literatur* (Munich: Schöningh, 1996), 111–31.

19 Jana Lüdtke, Burkhard Meyer-Sickendieck, and Arthur M. Jacobs, "Immersing in the Stillness of an Early Morning: Testing the Mood Empathy Hypothesis of Poetry Reception," *Psychology of Aesthetics, Creativity, and the Arts* 8, no. 3 (2014): 363–77.

20 Don Kuiken, Paul Campbell, and Paul Sopčák, "The Experiencing Questionnaire: Locating Exceptional Reading Moments," *Scientific Study of Literature* 2, no. 2 (2012): 243–72.

21 Willie van Peer, Jèmeljan Hakemulder, and Sonia Zyngier, "Lines on Feeling: Foregrounding, Aesthetics and Meaning," *Language and Literature: International Journal of Stylistics* 16, no. 2 (2007): 197–213.

22 Markus Appel, Erik Koch, Margrit Schreier, and Norbert Groeben, "Aspekte des Leseerlebens: Skalenentwicklung," *Zeitschrift für Medienpsychologie* 14, no. 4 (2002): 149–54.

23 Melanie C. Green and Timothy C. Brock, "The Role of Transportation in the Persuasiveness of Public Narratives," *Journal of Personality and Social Psychology* 79, no. 5 (2000): 701–21.

24 Von Heydebrand and Winko, *Einführung in die Wertung von Literatur*, 125.

25 Rick Busselle and Helena Bilandzic, "Measuring Narrative Engagement," *Media Psychology* 12, no. 4 (2009): 321–47.

26 Van Peer, Hakemulder, and Zyngier, "Lines on Feeling," 213.

27 Ibid.

28 Ibid.

29 Appel et al., "Aspekte des Leseerlebens," 151.

30 Ibid.

31 Ibid.

32 Ibid.

33 Green and Brock, "The Role of Transportation," 704.

34 Appel et al., "Aspekte des Leseerlebens," 151.

35 Lüdtke, Meyer-Sickendieck, and Jacobs, "Immersing in the Stillness of an Early Morning," 368.

36 Ibid.

37 Von Heydebrand and Winko, *Einführung in die Wertung von Literatur*, 131.

38 The collaboration started in 2017 and lasted nearly a year. The experiment was funded by the European Cooperation in Science and Technology's Evolution of Reading in the Age of Digitisation (COST E-READ) research initiative, and the University of Verona financed the costs for the participants.

39 Massimo Salgaro, Pasqualina Sorrentino, Gerhard Lauer, Jana Lüdtke, and Arthur M. Jacobs, "How to Measure the Social Prestige of a Nobel Prize in Literature? Development of a Scale Assessing the Literary Value of a Text," *TXT* 4 (2018): 134–43.

40 Pablo Delgado, Cristina Vargas, Rakefet Ackerman, and Ladislao Salmerón, "Don't Throw Away Your Printed Books: A Meta-Analysis on the Effects of Reading Media on Reading Comprehension," *Educational Research Review* 25 (2018): 23–38.

41 "COST E-READ Stavanger Declaration Concerning the Future of Reading," January 2019, https://ereadcost.eu/wp-content/uploads/2019/01/StavangerDecla-ration.pdf. See also Massimo Salgaro, "Die Nebeneffekte des Lesens lehren," *Neue Züricher Zeitung*, November 20, 2019, https://www.nzz.ch/meinung/die-nebeneffekte-des-lesens-lehren-ld.1519703.

INDEX

Milton Keynes UK
Ingram Content Group UK Ltd.
UKHW021953050524
442194UK00001B/95